TEMPERED STEEL

Embers of Youth

Mandy Doré

Hodge Publishing

Published by Hodge Publishing 17165 Linda Lane

Conroe, Texas 77306 – www.HodgePublishing.com

ISBN: 978-0-578-77352-0

Edited by Tim Caw

Cover design by David James

DEDICATION

This book is dedicated to my Loving Husband Steven Dore, without your love and gentle nudging, I would have quit writing this book in the first Chapter. To my Amazing Children who sat patiently listening to my stories and understand that I am perfectly flawed. To my rock, my Mom, Kathleen for being my kindred spirit and believing in me.

CONTENTS

FOREWORD

As a caution, this foreword is for the Readers consideration with a warning for tender natures.

This book is an account of events that happened during the formative years of my life. No detail has been spared for content or consideration, aside from names. This Memoir is raw and indignant, but necessary in telling the story of situations and growing pains that made me who I am today.

These pages are filled with truths that I endured and survived.

If the reader is sensitive and repulsed by the realities and horrors that can and do happen during the journey of life, DO NOT READ this book.

Remember truth is stranger than fiction and often more depraved than one can bring to the imagination. Unfortunately, as humans, we are conditioned to look away or deny the realities of life. I, for one, have chosen to look and talk about it. I will no longer be held a prisoner in my own life for the actions of myself or others.

I am owning my life!

This book is filled with tragic, offensive and insulting moments. These pages are also filled with funny occurrences, strange and unusual events, and happy moments.

If the Reader chooses to indulge further, do so at will, but remember you were warned.

For those who are curious enough to continue, I invite you to indulge yourself in this intimate look into the journey of my life. As the reader will see, life is all encompassing as we witness and endure many things. Some would consider life a curse, other would consider it a blessing. Either way, I am grateful to have the opportunity to share my life with you.

This story is about love, survival and overcoming obstacles that beset so many of us.

This is my story.

UNCONVENTIONAL BEGINNINGS

WHERE DO I BEGIN NOW? I ponder this question as I peer out my kitchen door to gaze upon my neglected swimming pool. I haven't done anything with it since Hurricane Barry blew through last summer. I am utterly disappointed in my poor custodial management of the pool.

In my neglect, nature has taken over and new life has sprung from the transition. The water is now a keen shade of viridian green from the leaves and grass that have fallen over into it.

The tadpoles are plentiful, and I find watching them break the surface to eat during a rainy afternoon very therapeutic. I continue to observe them as they bobble up and down, one after another, almost in a musical pattern that mesmerizes me.

I know I will have to get started on the cleaning soon, and I do ache at the thought of what demise lies ahead for all those little creatures.

I guess there is no rush…I am stuck at home on furlough from my job, due to the Coronavirus, also known as COVID-19.

The whole world has been quarantined from each other.

Meaning, job shutdowns across the board that eventually led to job losses. No more eating out on Friday nights with our Besties. No more bar hopping for the wicked. No more tattoos for the ink addicted. Everything is shut down and the roads are bare.

Weekends are usually bustling with noise and activities down Main St in New Iberia. Now it is akin to an eerie ghost town.

Funny, I never thought I would miss the noise…

Everyone was hoping the quarantine would be lifted soon, so we can all get back to life as it were. I had a feeling it would last longer than what the initial two-week period first outlined.

I was correct…

he quarantine has been extended twice since the beginning, which caused me to fear the inevitable. Initially, I was considered an "Essential Employee", however, my "essentialness" ran its course when the businesses I delivered first aid and safety supplies to, began shutting their doors.

I received a text from my boss, on a meeting for "Business Updates", which struck me as odd and left an unsettling feeling in my gut. I sent a group text to my fellow Service Sales Reps to see if any of them had received the same text.

We discovered that text had only been received by three of us. That solidified my worry and I knew I was about to be released as an employee, due to market conditions.

I was the last person hired. I did expect to be the first one relieved of my duties.

For now, I am on a month-long furlough with a possible extension to a second month, if the quarantine isn't lifted. I have decided to take full advantage of this time to take care of some tasks that I have been putting off around the house.

Interestingly, my husband has encouraged me to write. I guess I will have plenty of time to recall my childhood, as I go about my days waiting to return to work.

Recollections of memories can be cathartic or paralyzing, depending on the memory…

Going back as early as I can recall; most people would find it unbelievable that I can remember the moment of my birth. It seems like a faded dream now, but I can recall the brightness penetrating the darkness that had become a turbulent wave of events to expel me from the warm comfort, the constant heartbeat, and muffled sounds of my mothers' womb. I remember the piercing sensation on my body as I entered the cold environment.

We do not enter this world alone…or at least I didn't.

I had a constant companion up until the moment I learned to speak my first sentence. I don't know exactly how to describe it, other than it was a voice that spoke a language that was familiar to me, but unknown in this world. I could only hear the voice in my mind and the only way I could communicate with it was internally, in my mind.

It is a very odd notion, when I write about it now, to realize the relationship I had with this voice. The voice in fact was very encouraging, while assisting me through the early stages of learning. As I began to crawl and walk, the voice began to prepare me for its impending absence that I would eventually understand.

Teaching was its purpose to ease me into this life.

Soon, I began learning words and the voice warned me that once I was able to form a full sentence, the threshold of communication would be closed, and I would no longer be able to communicate with my internal companion. The voice was not allowed to remain with me, once I acclimated to the world.

Even as a small child, we can have arrogance... I remember communicating to the voice that I would never forget how to cross the threshold, but I was wrong.

The exact moment that I spoke my first sentence and understood what I said, the voice language was lost to me. I believe I was supposed to forget the voice entirely, not just the language. By mere chance, I held on to the memory of it. I count myself luckier than most to be able to recall my companion and those earliest memories of coming into this world. I have often thought of the voice and wondered if I would ever hear from it again.

To this day, the voice has been silent... Completely silent...

My upbringing did not offer me a sense of security, like my companion did. It was riddled with changes and heartbreak. Shortly after my first brother, Will, was born, my Mother (Anne) and Dad (Carl) separated. Their relationship was torrential, to say the least. Anne was young and it didn't help that she was free spirited and enjoyed a little ganja from time to time. Carl was an abusive and binge alcoholic, fueled by a disorder we now know as PTSD.

The two combinations did not mix well.

From the beginning of their relationship, Anne was burdened by her pregnancy with me. It didn't help matters that Carl's mother was not agreeable to the marriage. Their accord was doomed from the beginning. Carl married Anne because she was pregnant with me; he felt indebted to his responsibility.

They had been married for a little while, when Anne found out that she was pregnant with a second child. This was another strain on their already fragile relationship. Eventually, the tension became too much. Carl left after a horrible fight. His leaving left all of us in a vulnerable way.

After Anne finally gave birth to Will, Carl thought he would come back and work things out, but it didn't go as he had planned. During Carl's absence, Anne had met another man, so her heart was just not into the marriage anymore. Carl took us for a few weeks to spend some time with him, then we ended up going back with Anne.

I am compelled to remind the reader that this was the early-1970's, times were different, and parenting skills were not taught. There were no "how-to" books to provide a guide and no laws to encourage a protected upbringing of a child.

During the 1970's, people were expected to use common sense, a virtue that was sorely lacking in Carl. He would often leave us in the care of strangers, or alone at the house, or alone in a car when he had to run errands.

Leaving a child with a stranger during those times without performing a background check was nothing out of the ordinary.

No one questioned it.

We eventually moved to Bastrop, Texas with Anne and her new man, Nate. He had found a small trailer for us to live in as a family.

One blissful morning, while I was keeping myself entertained on the front porch outside, Anne and Nate were inside working on what I thought was cleaning the house. A curious smell began creeping out of the screen door...so I sniffed it. It had an earthy and intoxicating smell.

I was getting my first contact high on the front porch but didn't know it at the time.

Initially, I felt lightheaded and weightless. This feeling made me giggle at everything I saw and heard. As the effects saturated my senses, I began to feel heavier, so I laid back on the porch and watched the clouds and laughed all by myself, in a deep sense of euphoria. For a long moment, everything was serene, and I was not anxious.

To this day, I still associate the fragrance of marijuana with that memory.

Nate came outside to get me; he was curious as to why I was so giggly. Anne walked outside and realized that I was high. They both laughed and made fun of the situation. They were eager to show me something in the house, so they escorted me around the hall, to my bedroom, laughing the whole way.

WOOHOO!! It had bunk beds!

They had been working on putting up a set of bunk beds for me and Will. I was delighted! I couldn't wait to sleep on the top!

That night, Anne tucked me into bed and said a little prayer, "Now I lay me down to sleep, I pray the lord my soul to keep, if I should die before I wake, I pray the lord my soul to take."

If only we could have been more specific in that prayer, maybe, just maybe I would have woken up the next morning without a care in the world.

A sudden jolt, combined with the force of impact on the floor, woke me up a few hours into the night. I began screaming in pain and confusion. Anne ran into the bedroom to check on me.

I had rolled off the top bunk, in my sleep, and landed on my right arm, breaking it. Anne tried, but failed to console my pain. Nate realized that my arm must have been broken, as he insisted to take me to the hospital. The ride to the hospital was pure torture. Every bump and turn caused more horrendous pain.

By the time we got to the hospital, I had already passed out from the agony of the break. It would be a long wait before the Doctor could see me. In that space of time, my bones were already trying to fuse back together. It is amazing how fast a child begins to heal.

Upon examining my arm, the Doctor confirmed their worst fear and informed them that I would need to have my arm reset and a cast placed on it.

My arm would need to be broken again!...

I'm not sure any person could comprehend the shock of those words, unless they are being told it was going to happen to them. The events that played out from the time I fell from the bed, to the moment the cast was placed on my arm, were enough to cause any child a lifetime of traumatic scarring. It was the first, longest day of my life.

Tiny as I was, I put up such a fight that it took 6 people to hold me down while the Nurses strapped me to the table. I screamed, I cried, I pleaded. I fought the straps and kicked. I even tried to bite a nurse! I was too young to sedate, so I would have to endure the events while fully coherent. Anne kept telling me to look at her, which wasn't helping the situation.

How could I trust her? She was allowing these strangers to tie me down! She was going to let the Doctor break my arm again! I felt an intense burning in my arm, so I looked over and saw the Doctor sticking a needle in it.

Oh, the horror!!

The sight of that needle only intensified my fight, as I was extremely terrified of needles.

I just wanted it to be over with and I wanted the pain to go away. I passed out again. I couldn't say if it was from the struggling, or the pain. Either way, I fainted. When I woke, the Doctor was wrapping the cast.

He looked at me and said, "It's almost over, once the cast dries, you can draw on it."

What…I can draw on it? I thought that was neat, even though I was still angry at the Doctor. I liked to draw; I had been good at it from an incredibly early age. The Doctor finally completed the wrap on my cast. My arm was throbbing, but it was tolerable. It was finally time to go and I was relieved.

To get my mind off the experience, Nate suggested we go for an afternoon hunt. So, we piled up in Anne's station wagon and headed out to a dry deserted area.

Nate reminded me of an Indian. He was tall and dark skinned, with ebony black hair. He had a lean structure that was chiseled with muscle and he was incredibly agile. Nate sat us up around the car, as he took to hunting for snakes and birds. I was tired, so Anne sat me in front of her and braided my hair. She had made several hair-ribbons out of yarn, with pompom puffs on the end. She used the blue and white pompom to tie at the end of my braid.

I became bored, rather quickly, so Nate came over to show me how to hunt lizards. The ground was so dry that its crust was cracked into different sized shapes of dirt patties. I began pulling up the top of the crusts, like they were pizza pies, and then realized I could throw them like a Frisbee.

A past time that I still enjoy.

As the day waned, we loaded up and headed back to the house with a few quail and a couple of snakes. Anne kept the windows open, as we drove down the highway, to let the breeze cool our sun kissed skin. I stuck my arm out to feel the air tickle my skin under the cast. The wind cooled the heat that had built up underneath it.

My blue and white pompom hair ribbon had come loose, so I picked it up and held one end, sticking the other out the window to watch it dance in the wind. For a time, I forgot all about my pain and just enjoyed the dance of the ribbon. Every sensation of the moment was relaxing and surreal.

I decided to get risky and let both pompoms blow out the window as I held the center of the hair ribbon. I was fascinated that the wind made it look like magic as I would release my fingers and the ribbon stayed on my palm whipping in the wind behind my hand. Anne gave a brief warning to be careful not to lose the ribbon. I assured her, "I won't lose it. See! The wind is keeping it stuck to my hand like magic

No sooner had I uttered the words from my mouth, then the wind whipped around and peeled it from my open hand. I couldn't believe it! I stuck my head out the window and watched as it blew away, falling to the road behind us. Anne refused to turn around to go back and get it. "I warned you not to play with it out the window."

A hard lesson in heeding warnings…

I sat back down in the seat and pouted. After a while, I took a crayon and scribbled on my cast, in the light of the radio, as it played "Honky Cat" by Elton John. I drew a picture of my lost ribbon, which was my favorite ribbon. The loss of it still pains me.

I wish I would have listened to Anne.

On a sunny morning, after I got my cast, we got up and rode to the store. Anne and Nate got out, leaving me and Will alone in the car.

In Anne's ignorance and haste, she didn't realize what was being plotted against her. It had been several months since we had seen Carl. In his absence, Carl had collaborated with his mother to take us from Anne.

It was that morning that Carl followed Anne and Nate to the store, and he took advantage of her leaving us in the car unattended. After Anne and Nate disappeared inside the store, Carl and his mother quickly removed us from the vehicle.

My heart aches to think of the torment that Anne went through when she came outside to an empty car, finding her children missing.

I wonder… was a missing case filed?

Did she call the cops?

Did she realize right away that Carl had taken us?

I remember longing for her immensely. Why didn't she come get me?

Did she not love me anymore?

EDITH THE HARRIDAN

CARL TOOK US DIRECTLY TO HIS MOTHER, Edith, after the kidnapping.

Edith…god…I haven't uttered her name in years… Just to mention her name is an albatross.

It is my first memory of her. She was a bitter, intimidating woman. Very course, without tenderness, and a piercing look in her eye. She scared me. There was nothing remotely playful about her.

Edith was very irritated but tried to be hospitable for Carl's sake. It was noticeably clear that she did not like us inside the house. She would send us outside to play all day. In order to keep us occupied, she led us to a teeter totter and had her youngest son, Liam, play with us.

I guess I remember that moment most, because Edith took a Polaroid picture. I recall her instructing me with her acidic, bitter voice to smile for the camera. She was pretending to be nice for the occasion, in order to get me to comply. Edith taught me to fear the sound of her voice, immediately. I became highly skeptical of any display of friendliness that she showed towards me.

I think she used the picture to torture Anne, because I would find the picture, years later, in Anne's possession.

I was relieved to see Carl return for us later that evening. I didn't want to be in the presence of that woman any longer.

ABANDONED

WE WERE CONSTANTLY ON THE MOVE WITH CARL, never staying in one place too long. I assume he was living in New Mexico, but working in Texas at the time, because of all the traveling.

Carl was a paranoid man, as I said before. He would often leave us with strangers, while he would go off to work, or do other personal things to prevent Anne from finding us. At some point, Carl met a teenage woman known as Kathleen, who worked in the diner he would visit while in Monahans.

Later, Kathleen began babysitting Will and I on a regular basis. Initially, she kept us while Carl was at work, until one day Carl dropped us off at her house and he did not return for months.

Our extended stay with Kathleen caused a bond to form between us. She began to love us as her own. Kathleen was beside herself, being only 16 years of age and having unassured custody of two children.

What was she to do?

Kathleen's attempts to contact Carl were unsuccessful. She had no idea where he had gone. Carl just disappeared.

Eventually, we were introduced to her parents, who were very child friendly. They were kind and affectionate. I enjoyed being around them. Her mother, Grandma Earline, was naturally beautiful, kind and loving.

Grandma Earline was traditional in her look and her daily activities. I will never forget walking into her home for the first time. As I entered through the kitchen door, she was standing at the stove cooking a meal, anticipating our arrival. She was very kempt and modest, with tidy curled hair, a buttoned-up dress shirt tucked neatly into her skirt, while wearing heals. The best way to describe her is "Donna Reed", a real sweat heart who never spoke an ill word, or cussed for that matter. She was demur and patient.

She was the kind of woman I think I would have wanted to grow up to be someday, if life would have remained simpler.

Grandma Earline took me outside to show me how to find snails and how to be gentle with them, then she took me around to the front on the porch and showed me her mint bushes. She encouraged me eat some leaves. Then we went over to a plant that would close its leaves, if I ran my finger across the top of them.

(She was a professional at keeping children occupied.)

There was an electric organ in the living room that Grandma would allow me to play, when I was exceptionally good for her. It was not uncommon to walk into her house and see unusual animals being kept as a pet. She was particularly good with animals, especially birds.

I have always believed animals gravitate towards benevolent spirits in people. She was the perfect example of promoting this belief.

Kathleen's father, Lionel, was a force to be reckoned with when it came to dealing with adults. However, he was playful with children. His voice was booming and stern. His hugs were strong, warm and comforting.

The first time I met Lionel, he was sitting in his lounge chair in the living room watching the news. His hello sent me into a sprint towards him. I fell at his knees and propped my elbows on his legs to brace my face. I looked up inquisitively and asked, "Are you going to be my Grandpa?"

He looked lovingly down at me and responded, "Honey, I can be your Grandpa."

> (Grandpa Lionel would recall that very moment, every time we would see each other, up until the day before he took his last breath. As I write this memory, I took the time to call and speak to Kathleen and Grandpa. I recorded the call on my tape recorder for material to share in this Memoir.

> Grandpa Lionel had been ill for some time. Fortunately, I was able to visit him in October 2019, when my Grandma Earline passed away. The call was lighthearted, but my Grandpa was struggling. I was grateful that I had a few moments to speak with him.

> I get news from Kathleen just past midnight, the following day that my Grandpa had passed away.

> It is April 19, 2020 and we are still under COVID-19 quarantine. I am unable to attend his funeral, due to the travel restrictions of the quarantine and my heart is broken.)

My apologies for the departing, I shall continue the story...

Grandpa Lionel kept his head shaved to the skin and he would let me rub it and play like I was a fortune teller. When he had excess energy, he would pick on us and chase us around the house. The chase always led to a tickling event that would leave me sore and exhausted.

He had lots of stories to tell, as he had led a full life. One story sticks out in my mind was his meeting with Elvis Presley, while serving in the military. He was not a fan of the King. His recollection was that Elvis was a "pampered pansy boy" and his service was a sham to gain notoriety for his music. That still makes me laugh, considering all the hype around his legacy.

I was enamored by his grand collection of Indian arrow heads. He would often talk about where he found them. He would then deliberate over what the arrows were used for and what the weapon would have looked like. His prized possession was a large buffalo arrowhead. It was as big as his hands. I would linger over the arrow heads while he told his stories. He gave me an arrowhead as a gift. I still have it in my possession today.

Grandma Earline and Grandpa Lionel had married just two weeks after meeting each other. Grandma was fourteen and Grandpa was seventeen on the day of their wedding. Their story was and is amazing and still inspires me.

I admired them and wanted a life like theirs.

Our time with Grandma and Grandpa was short lived. Unfortunately, the inevitable happened, a loud knock awakened Kathleen at 3am one morning. To her surprise it was Carl at the door.

The knock woke me up and I listened to their conversation. Carl abruptly told Kathleen he was there to pick us up, because he needed to be back in Hobbs by 7am. She tried to talk him out of taking us.

After a futile plead, Kathleen reluctantly released us back to Carl, only after she made him promise he would never leave us alone again. Carl's promises to Kathleen were empty.

She had no way of knowing…

We drove the remainder of the morning back to Hobbs, New Mexico from Monahans, Texas. We arrived at a small box apartment we would call home for the next several months.

MEAGER EXISTENCE

I WAS HUNGRY AND THIRSTY ALMOST ALL THE TIME, while Carl would be absent from the apartment. Will was always crying and stinking of shit. Carl would leave in the morning and return sometime after dark. He would leave crackers and cheese on the table for us to eat. I was able to pull a chair to the sink and get us water to drink. Because I was still tiny in stature, I would make a horrible mess everywhere, trying to get water in a glass.

My hands were just too small. I would spill water on the cabinet and floor while climbing back down the chair. After a few weeks, I was finally getting strong enough to pull the fridge door open to get some bread and butter for Will and me to eat.

We would sit on the floor to eat and drink. Even sitting on the floor, I made a mess with my lack of coordination, trying to feed Will.

I can't recall how often Will would be stuck in a dirty diaper, or for how long, but I do recall the redness of his butt and the open sores that would bleed when I tried to clean him. I wasn't much bigger than him, so we were both in a bind as I attempted to care for him. I learned how to care for Will by watching Kathleen. I learned many things by watching the adults in my life.

By the time Carl would arrive home, there would be water, breadcrumbs, butter and shit everywhere. He would yell at me and spank me for making a mess. This went on day after day, for what seemed like an eternity.

One miserable evening, I became curious outside of my natural urges to eat and drink. I wanted to know what was in a tube in the bathtub. Will followed me into the bathroom. I began prying at the tube to open it, PRELL…aah…that fresh clean smell.

I can still remember the fragrance after all these years. As soon as I opened it, the smell filled the air.

Of course, I had to put my tiny little hands in that gel-like substance. Before I knew it, we had Prell shampoo everywhere! I placed Will in the bathtub to wash the shit from his butt. The Prell shampoo helped to remove it easier and it took the smell off him. I was so proud.

Surely, my dad would be proud too…

I heard the front door open and I ran excitedly to welcome Carl home. He immediately noticed the fresh clean smell.

"What did you do today, Mandy?" he asked, really meaning, "What did you get into?"

I started to sink emotionally, my soul crashing. I knew I was in trouble… "MANDY SHAWN! GET YOUR ASS IN HERE!!" he screamed.

That spanking was for using up the whole tube of Prell shampoo. I was too young to realize that a little bit of soap goes a long way.

After Carl simmered in his anger, he did praise me for not making a mess upon the kitchen and floor. I had been practicing, I had fine-tuned my cleaning skills and taught myself how to use a broom, after watching him clean up our messes.

Will was becoming more curious and able bodied each day. He was getting into everything. It was a hassle trying to keep him out of stuff, so I could stay out of trouble. Will was so curious that he was dangerous.

We never should have been left alone.

On a cold winter morning, Carl decided to take us with him to the store. This was a very unusual decision for him, considering he normally left us at home. We rode in his stick shift Ford truck. I was hoping to go inside with him to shop, but he decided to leave us out in the truck.

Not surprising, I guess…

Will was asleep when we pulled into the parking lot, but he began waking up to the slam of the truck door, as soon as Carl exited to go in the store.

At first, Will was calm and just looked around, then he slowly began moving about the cab of the truck. His surroundings were new, and he wanted to see everything. Will stood up on the seat and was looking out the back window and mumbling his baby language.

I was up at the window too, looking and taking it all in, as well. I became distracted away from Will, by watching the cars going back and forth across the street. It was a curious thing to watch the cars respond to the lights changing color.

As I watched the cars move with the light, I realized that the truck was moving closer to the road. I turned around to see Will playing with the gear shift. The truck continued to roll and was picking up speed. I was scared and I grabbed Will and hunkered us both down into the seat. I didn't know what to do. I held on to him tight and I closed my eyes even tighter.

I just wanted the truck to stop. In the distance, I could hear a loud scream. Car horns blaring and chaos all around as the truck continued to rattle as it rolled.

Then I heard a loud bang at the front of the truck. Carl had caught up with the truck, just as it centered the middle of the street with oncoming traffic. He hit the truck with his hand trying to grab it and stop it.

Carl's attempts were futile, the truck had momentum and it was too heavy. In the height of his distress, the truck finally came to a stop when it hit the other side of the street on the curb. To be honest, I don't know if he was more concerned about the truck or us.

Carl's reaction in the next few minutes would lead me to believe he was more concerned over the truck. He yanked me out of the truck and began spanking me.

It was all my fault for letting Will play with the gearshift...

CATHOLIC SCHOOL

OUR LIVES WERE CHANGING, and I was old enough to go to preschool. It was during the first year of pre-schooling that Anne entered back into my life. I went to stay with Anne for a brief time in Hobbs, New Mexico. Her attendance was only momentary.

It was a very confusing and unsettling time for me. Anne had enrolled me into St. Helena Catholic School. I had a feeling about the school from the very first day.

I hated it.

I wanted to spend time with Anne. I had missed her so much. Regardless, I had to go to school. At the time, my hair was down past my waist and Anne would braid it tightly every morning before dropping me off. The braids would be so tight that my eyes would lift slightly at the edges. Some of the kids thought I was Chinese. I didn't even know what Chinese meant!

The only good part of going to the school was getting to take my lunch with me. I had a Holly Hobby lunch box and Anne would put a Dr. Pepper and apple in it for me. My Teacher was mean, and she would spank our hands if we didn't please her with her requests. I didn't have any friends. I didn't know what a friend was, or at the very least know how to make one.

I was shy and introverted. I didn't trust anyone. How could I?

On the last morning that I would attend the school, I begged Anne to not make me go. She told me it would be okay, and she would pick me up at the end of the day. I cried and begged her not to leave me. I could tell Anne didn't want to leave me, but she felt obligated. So, she walked me into the classroom. Anne leaned down and kissed me, as I grabbed her tightly with a hug. I didn't want to let her go.

Anne hesitantly peeled me off her, as the teacher grabbed me strongly on my arm, pulling me away from her. As Anne walked away, the teacher kneeled and sternly told me to dry it up and to stop being a baby. I was afraid of her, so I stopped crying. There was a heaviness in the room. Maybe it was me...maybe it was the weather... All I know is I felt like I was going to suffocate.

I heard rain starting to hit the roof and I became increasingly anxious. I looked over and the door was still open, so I waited for the right moment. When the teacher was preoccupied with her favorite pupil, she turned her back to me. I ran out the door, leaving everything on my desk.

I ran as fast as I could down the hall and outside, under the easement. I stayed clinging to the wall as rain cascaded down, all around me. You see, I was horrified of thunderstorms. But, even the fear of the thunderstorm did not stop me from wanting to go home. It was thundering loudly, with bolts of lightning flashing; I held my ears and cried.

I was thinking on Anne so intently, and screaming out to her in my mind, so I wouldn't be discovered by the teacher. Just when I was in a moment of sheer panic and hopelessness, I heard a voice calling out to me down the corridor.

"Mandy! Come to me baby!" It was Anne.

Anne would later reveal to me that something was telling her to turn around and go back to get me.

I often wondered if she heard me in her mind.

We would spend the next few days together, before Will and I ended up with Anne's parents.

BUD AND FREDA

THE LAST THING I REMEMBER, before being with Bud and Freda, was that I went to bed at Anne's house and then woke up in their home.

Some information on my grandparents... Bud was an original Coors drinker, singer/musician and a welder who rolled his own cigarettes from a Prince Albert can.

Freda worked in the fast-food industry, she smoked Pall Mall with plastic filters and drank ungodly amounts of coffee. Freda's mother, Ethel, came to live with them, once they purchased some land outside of Hobbs. Ethel lived in a tiny trailer next to their similar home, until her death.

My earliest memory of Bud and Freda was a Christmas where Bud dressed up like Santa Claus and kissed Freda. I was so mad that Santa Claus kissed Freda that I told on them to Bud.

Freda played along with the ruse and begged me not to tell so she wouldn't get into trouble. I still told... How dare Santa Clause kiss my Grandma!! I got a riding spring horse toy for Christmas that year. I also fell off that horse and hit my head on the edge of the coffee table, scarring my eyebrow for life.

My next memory was the summer when Will and I went to visit, and

Bud was steadily packing camping gear and fishing rods into the camper of his red Chevy. He looked our direction and blurted, "I hope you brought your swimming trunks, because we are going for a boat ride!"

A real boat ride…WOW! The anticipation was palpable. We loaded up in the camper with Ethel. The single cab of the truck would not hold all of us at the same time. Which was fine by me! I wanted to ride in the camper any way.

We played card games and drew pictures during our trip to Brownwood Lake, in Texas. Ethel crocheted and would keep us busy. The ride was long and bumpy, but we didn't mind. We had all the windows opened, so the breeze would keep us cool for the ride.

We finally arrived at our destination and I could see the lake through the camper windows. It was huge! Water was everywhere. It was the most beautiful thing I had ever laid my young eyes on and that is the truth. I was awestruck from the scene.

Bud drove around to the boat ramp. He got out and readied his 1977 VIP boat to be launched. He was very proud of the boat, as it was brand new. He got in the boat and started directing Freda down the ramp.

I could hear in Bud's voice the frustration he was experiencing. He began yelling at Freda and she yelled back. That was the first time I had ever heard them talk to each other in that tone. Once the boat was in the water, Bud instructed Freda to meet him around at the campground.

We remained in the camper, as Freda drove to our camping site. Will and I were no longer worried about playing games and drawing. Instead, we were standing up on the seats, clinging to the windows to take in everything we could see.

As we pulled up to the campground, we were met by Bud's brother and his wife. They had already made it to the camp earlier that day. They had some children with them too; they were older than us. Their presence made the trip even better.

Bud pulled around to the bay in the VIP and we all ran to meet him. He started pulling out the life jackets that he had hidden away beneath the seats of the boat. We all put on jackets, in order to get in the boat. I couldn't wait to ride!

To memorialize the moment, Freda took out her Polaroid camera and snapped a few pictures. She was good at keeping scrap books. The day melted into the night, as we wrapped up the evening, while sitting around the campfire and roasting marshmallows on a stick.

I was tired, but I wasn't giving into sleep. I was having so much fun, I was afraid to miss out on anything. We stayed up until the coals burned low. I embraced the smell of the air and the crisp feeling of the night breeze softly caressing my skin.

The next day, we got started as soon as the sun came up on the horizon. I had been around the desert my whole life up until this trip. This was a brand-new sensation, in every aspect. The air felt different and it smelled different. I was falling in love with the feeling of being there. I was taking in my surroundings when Bud noticed me and asked, "Whatcha doin?"

I looked at him and replied, "I am making a wish."

He inquired, "What is your wish?"

Taking a deep breath, I responded, "I wish I could live here when I grow up and have a boat like yours."

(Wouldn't you know it… I grew up and that very wish came true! But that story is for the next book.)

Our trip was cut short, later that day, after Bud had gone to relieve himself behind a tall blade of bushes. Unknowingly, he had stepped in a bed of chiggers. The chiggers made their way quickly into his skin and managed to get into his crotch area. He was in a bind! Bud was extremely uncomfortable, and he had to seek relief fast. So, we packed up and headed back to Hobbs. We had planned to stay for a full three days.

Back at their house, Bud had bought us a little kiddie pool and he would fill it for us to play in, while he was working in his shop. Freda collected dolls with crocheted dresses and sold Avon at the time. They had a quaint little abode in the middle of Hobbs.

One of my favorite memories of being there was of playing on the ceramic donkey that adorned their front yard. The donkey had a little trailer on it where Freda had planted cacti. I used to pretend the donkey was alive and I was delivering cacti goods. Will would be climbing on the wagon wheels that decorated the entry to the driveway. Many times, you could catch us walking along the small rock fence that traversed the front of the yard.

Bud and Freda spoiled us. Freda didn't have any children of her own. She loved children, so she made things incredibly fun and I could be a child around her, without any worries. She would play dress up with me and I was her Avon model. It makes me laugh when I think of all those blues and greens she used to put on my face. I looked hideous, but I was too young to realize it.

My favorite part of the Avon bags were the tiny lipsticks. She would also have bonnets that were wrapped tightly and placed in tiny little containers that fascinated me. I was always wanting to open them and attempt to place the bonnets back in the container, the same way.

Freda had long hair down to her waist that we would twist until it would curl up into itself like little buns all over her head. She would wear it like that all the time. It made it easier for her when she was at work.

I thought Freda was beautiful when she would take down the buns. Her hair would fall all about her face in lustrous long curls. She was by no means a pretty woman in looks, but her hair was her grace.

Brushing and playing with Freda's hair was soothing for me. I know she enjoyed it too.

Everything did not remain happy and playful. There was a dark side to Bud that was only known by those closest to him. Girls were not safe around him. Especially young tender girls. They were his prey.

Freda had discovered Bud's dark side, early on in their marriage. She was pregnant at the time and Bud beat her senseless when she confronted him, which inevitably caused her to lose the child. Bud had a hold on her that she couldn't shake loose. Freda was subdued by the fear she had of what Bud would do to her, if she left.

Bud was married once, prior to Freda to my maternal Grandmother. His first marriage ended several years after they had three daughters.

There was a strain on the relationships, between Bud and his daughters. My mother, Anne, being his eldest child, was strained most of all. During our stay with Bud and Freda, Anne came to see us once, but Bud chased her off the property and she was not allowed to return.

MOMMA KATHLEEN

I WAS VERY AWARE AS A CHILD. I had to be aware, out of survival. I was aware of our parental absence and the lack of tenderness towards me and Will. We were a burden for others too, so we endured neglect. I was very protective of Will because he was my constant. I would protect and care for him.

I didn't know it at the time, but as fate would have it, Carl and Kathleen had crossed paths again. This time, Kathleen saw an opportunity to get us back in her life permanently. She was still working as a waitress, at the diner in Monahans. Carl came in and they exchanged small pleasantries.

Out of concern, Kathleen asked Carl where Will and I were staying. He told her we were back at his apartment in Hobbs. This caused Kathleen to feel very uneasy, and she reminded him that he promised her to never leave us alone again.

As a diversion from the interrogation, Carl noticed that she was no longer wearing a wedding ring. She had been briefly married to a young man for a few months. The marriage ended, almost as soon as it began.

Since she was no longer married, Carl asked if he could take her out to dinner. She brazenly responded, "Only if you marry me, so I can take care of those babies." They were married by the next evening and headed back to Hobbs.

33

Yes, even I found their story head spinning.

Meanwhile, back at the apartment, there was an older woman who had been checking in on us while Carl was gone for a few days, of whom I did not know. Maybe she was the neighbor…who knows. She was a friendly lady but offered little insight when I would inquire about our dad. She would respond by saying, "He will be back when he gets back."

Will and I were playing outside in the back yard of the apartment home one afternoon, chasing lizards and collecting pretty rocks underneath the shade of a tree. I heard the friendly lady call out to us. I knew Carl had returned home. When I looked up, there she was…Kathleen, standing in the door.

I began to move abruptly when Will grabbed hold of me and held on to me tightly, as to stop me in my tracks. I broke free of his grip and ran to the bosom of Kathleen. I looked directly at Carl and yelled excitedly, "You brought my Momma to me!"

Kathleen held me so tightly and I asked her, "Are you our mommy now?" Through tears, she said yes. She had married Carl and custody was in the works for her to become our legal Momma. I cried with tears of joy and the relief of belonging to someone who wanted me, someone who loved me. We held each other deeply and we cried together.

> (I was just a child longing for love, acceptance, and security. That moment is still so vivid in my mind that it still brings me to tears.
>
> I had to reach out to Mom and thank her and tell her how much I love and appreciate her. I had to step away for a moment

to regain my composure, in order to continue writing.)

As I child, I was prone to fevers. I believe Kathleen (Momma) coming into our life again was divine intervention at that time. One morning, I woke up feeling feverish and it wouldn't go away. Three days passed and the fever lingered. I had scarlet fever.

If it hadn't been for Momma's return, I believe I probably would have died that week. The fever was out of control and she called a doctor to come see me. When the doctor arrived, the doctor took my temperature and discovered that it had risen to 104 degrees.

I was so delirious from the fever that I felt like I was floating above myself. I could hear the doctor advise Momma that they had to get my fever down and get it down fast. I was in so much pain that I couldn't even move. I could see the fear and worry in Momma's eyes, as she was trying to help me. She was genuinely concerned and frantic. The doctor directed her to run a cold bath and add ice.

Momma picked up my tiny body and the pain was too much for me to bare, so I cried out. She tried to shush me and calm my aches, but her attempts were futile. Every touch and every movement felt like bone crushing agony.

Momma carried me to the bath and told me what was about to take place. I cried and pleaded for her not to put me in the water. She told me she had to place me in the water to help take away the fever. She had to get my fever down quickly.

After placing me in the bath, I immediately went into shock from the cold and passed out. I woke up as Momma was placing me on a bed of ice made of a black trash bag and covered by a blanket. I felt chilled and I shivered. Pain so much pain…I passed out again.

When I woke, I was sweating, the actions of my Momma and the doctor finally broke the fever and my body was beginning to heal. I wasn't allowed to get up until the fever was completely gone. I thought I would suffer that fever forever.

Momma and Carl had found us a rent house in Wink, Texas. After I had been well for a few weeks we moved. Momma wanted to move closer to her family and I am sure she needed her space from Edith. Carl had been hired at a Rig job that would take him out of town on an occasion and it helped Momma to live closer to Grandma and Grandpa.

Shortly after arriving in Wink, I was enrolled into Kindergarten and life with Carl and Momma began in full. Momma had a deep love for animals, just like Grandma, that I believe they both instilled in me. Momma had Carl build a rabbit cage, so that we could have a rabbit. They got me an albino rabbit and it was a sight to behold. Mom believed that giving me a responsibility would help me with my anxiety.

The house had a doll house out back. Will and I would play in it and pretend that it was a castle. I used to daydream about building a second story in it and filling it with real furniture. It was going to be so glamorous. I had such big dreams and a very vivid mind for such a little tyke.

We lived in the small home for a couple of months. My daily routine would consist of me getting up and feeding my rabbit and then walking to school. I would rush home after school to feed my rabbit and then Will and

I would head out to the doll house.

After a couple weeks of having my rabbit, I went out to check on her and there were little pink skinned babies everywhere. I rushed in to tell Momma and we were both excited. That excitement was short lived…

By the time I got home that afternoon, my rabbit had eaten the heads off all of her babies. I was horrified! How could she eat her own babies? The tears began to flow. I was devastated and my heart was broken.

Momma, being sympathetic, pulled me to the side and explained to me that sometimes these things happen. It didn't mean that my rabbit was bad, it was just that she didn't have the nurturing instincts that should come naturally. This, however, was my first experience with death, and it was brutal. A mother eating her babies heads… The experience would melt into my nightmares.

The sadness was replaced by disbelief, but I still loved my rabbit, even though I feared her to an extent. So, I continued to care for her every day for another couple weeks.

One Saturday, I went outside to care for my rabbit, but she wasn't moving. I ran inside to tell Momma and she came out to see what all the fuss was about.

My rabbit had been poisoned and it was stiff as a board. I overheard a conversation between Momma and Carl. The rabbit had blood coming out of its rear and Carl thought he may know who the culprit was and why. Carl had an ability to piss people off.

Because of the loss of my rabbit, Mom decided to get us a puppy instead. I can't say that I was ready to move on; she thought it best that I have something else to occupy my mind. That didn't last long either.

Once they realized the puppy wasn't potty-trained, the pup was sent packing to the next family. It took us waking up in the middle of the night, in a bed full of shit piles everywhere, to nail that coffin tight. I didn't mourn the puppy leaving. I didn't have a chance to even get attached to it.

About a week went by and we move across the road into a bigger house. I was happy because that was closer to school and I would get my own room. Momma was able to talk Carl into getting me a matching bedroom set. It was a calming sky-blue and green color. I had a twin bed, vanity table and Chester drawer to match. I was so proud of it.

A new responsibility was introduced to keep me occupied. I came home from school and Carl had set up a fish tank with black Mollies, Neons and a Coollieloach, and completed it with plants and pebbles.

It was a sight to behold and provided hours of entertainment. Something about watching the fish swim back and forth in that tiny tank was a pacifying relaxation for me.

Watching the fish calmed my storms and turned them into a sort of tranquility.

It was in that home that I learned that Tonka was more than a toy, it was also a boy from Japan who was now attending my classroom. I also learned that putty from a plastic egg made for the best passing of time when copying the comedy section of the newspaper (Heh heh, the original screen shot.). Hottie toddies are perfect potions for sore throats, potted meat tasted like vomit and the fish tank could be used as a looking glass to watch TV, after I was told to go to bed.

However, this was a tool which almost caused me severe distress when I watch my first horror flick, KING KONG in the reflection. Carl caught me watching through the fish tank glass, after I had already been told to go to bed. I froze with fear, thinking my ass was whooped, but instead he showed me mercy and told me that what I was seeing on TV wasn't real. It was all just make-believe.

> (I just realized that Kathleen had softened Carl. He should have spanked me for disobeying him. This was my first lesson from him that didn't involve physical punishment.)

My next lesson wouldn't be as kind. It was time to buy shoes for school. I had worn out the soles in my other shoes. Momma took me to the local TG&Y store to look for a pair of shoes. I wanted a pair of Converse shoes. The other kids were wearing them, and I wanted to be like everyone else. After looking for a while, we found a pair that I liked.

The shoe man took a measurement of my foot with a metal measuring device I had to stand on, as he pressed my foot down and pulled a leaver back to my toes. He quickly disappeared with the device in hand in the back. He returned with the last black and white pair of Converse shoes.

Momma looked at them with concern and told me she thought they would be too little. I disagreed with her and she let me try them on, uncertainly. I was right! They fit from heel to toe. They fit like a glove.

Mom shook her head and said that I should consider getting a larger pair, but there wasn't any more available. I told her adamantly that these would work. I wanted those shoes! I was going home with those shoes no matter what she thought!

To think a 7-year-old would know more than her mom… I laugh now, but it was no laughing matter then. She told me if I got them, I would have to wear them, because they couldn't afford to buy another pair. I agreed to her conditions and home we went.

I couldn't wait to wear them to school the following Monday. I was so excited! Monday morning came and I put the shoes on immediately. Hmm, they seemed to fit just a bit snugger than they did at the store. Maybe it was the sock I was wearing. I changed the sock…still snug. I thought that maybe they would stretch after I walk in them for a bit.

Off to school I went. About halfway to school my feet were in pain. The shoes did not stretch but my feet were beginning to swell from the tightness of the shoe. It didn't help that I was going through a growth spurt.

Oh my gosh, my mind raced. What have I agreed to for the sake of owning these shoes? My toes were tender, and both of my heels were wearing a blister. By the time I reached the school yard, I was in sheer misery.

But I couldn't tell my mom, that would mean she was right, and I had to figure something out quickly.

During class, I would slide the shoes off the back of my feet, in order to let my toes and heals rest from the pain. This went on for about a week. I was walking home on the last day, when my feet couldn't take it anymore. I sat down on the side of the road and pulled off my shoes.

I began crying from the agony, since the blisters had ruptured, and the socks began sticking to my sores. I felt overwhelmed and too scared to admit to my mom what had happened.

After a few minutes of sitting on the roadside crying, a car pulled up beside me. It was my teacher. She was bothered that I was crying and didn't have on my shoes. She asked if she could take me home, which I said yes to, since I was happy to ride instead of walking. However, the dread of owning up to my mistake was unwavering.

Momma was waiting at the door, as usual, and my teacher came around to help me out of the car. She and Momma both examined my feet, then momma looked at me with disappointment. My heart sank… She asked me why I didn't tell her sooner and I told her that I didn't want to get in trouble. She hugged me and told me that next time, I should listen to her when we buy shoes. I agreed and she tended to my feet.

I have since used the story to teach my own children the importance of how to purchase shoes.

My poor judgement was a punishment I never forgot.

FAMILY MALADY

WE BEGAN VISITING CARL'S SISTERS on the weekends to spend time with our cousins. He had two sisters that were married to two brothers and they lived next door to each other. One sister had two boys and one girl. The other sister had two boys.

Our arrival stirred up quite the commotion. All the children ran outside to meet us. The girl and I were about the same age. I was older than her, but not by much. She was curious about me and warmed up quickly. She dragged me inside to her bedroom so she could show me all her toys.

I had made my first friend and she was my cousin, Jill. We bonded instantly since were the only girls. That was the beginning of our time together. All my thoughts of her are fond.

Jill and I shared many laughs. I loved being around her. We could always be found, because we were always giggling. Her parents were doing well and were grounded steep in religion and "gave the appearance" of a very stable and happy life.

So, I envied Jill to a degree. She was spoiled with Barbie dolls and beautiful clothes. The clothes would eventually become mine, even though I was older. She was taller, but her hand-me-downs became something I looked forward to receiving.

Jill was the youngest of her siblings, with two older brothers. Her eldest brother, Dan had muscular dystrophy. We didn't know at first. He was on crutches, because he had trouble walking. But, it wasn't long before his condition deteriorated, and he ended up in a wheelchair.

We would often take turns with the other children, riding in Dan's wheelchair. When we got caught, we would get scolded by the parents for playing with the wheelchair and crutches. The fascination soon subsided, as we were around it more. As his condition diminished, Dan was set up in a mechanized wheelchair to assist him in getting around.

Dan was sweet, but he was a pervert. I suppose he inherited it from his father. I would realize this later. He would often ask me to sit in his lap and he would grab on my butt.

I don't know why I let him do it... Maybe it was for pity.

I only spent the night with my cousin a few times during that period. The first time I stayed with Jill, her father, Uncle Sputter kept coming into the room to check on us throughout the night.

At the time, I just thought Uncle Sputter was caring. I would find out later that he was molesting Jill. My presence prevented the action that night. I was in the way. Jill didn't want me to go home, but she couldn't tell me why.

I think Jill would have kept me if she could have, just to protect her from the attacks. I assume the sickness ran deep in the family, on both sides. Her father's brother, Uncle Spit, was also prone to the detestable actions.

The last night that I stayed with her in that house I was made to sleep in the living room on the floor, in a corner that was behind a couch. I woke up to Uncle Spit feeling my privates, underneath the covers. His hands were cold and shaky.

I tried to pretend I was still asleep, because I was scared. When he breached my tender split with his fingers, I flinched, and it spooked him. He quickly moved away. I couldn't sleep for the rest of the night; I was so shaken from what had just happened to me. I didn't understand it. I couldn't wait to go back home.

The following weekend we headed over to Uncle Sputter's house, again. This time, I wasn't looking forward to it. I was too ashamed of what had happened, and I was confused. I wanted to tell, but I was scared, and I didn't want to get in trouble. The closer we got to their house, the more depressed I became. I was not myself and I wasn't good at putting on a false front. Not yet, anyway…

The oppression of the situation came on swiftly. I was not happy, and I didn't have the comprehension to deal with what I was feeling. I felt dirty and less than a person.

Was it my fault?

Did I do something to cause him to touch me?

Was this something that was supposed to happen?

What if my cousins found out?

What would they think of me?

When we arrived, they were all there. Uncle Spit came over and hugged me. I shrugged away. His hug didn't feel right. My innocence was violated. I went outside and grabbed a bike to get away.

I rode around the yard and I wouldn't talk to anyone. The longer I rode the bike, the more I wanted to just keep going. Of course, I wasn't allowed to leave the yard or cross the street, so I was stuck riding back and forth.

My mind was consumed, and I just wanted it all to end. I made up my mind. I was going to go as fast as I could straight into the nearby ditch and end it all. Funny that a mind so young can think of such things.

My mind did...

I wasn't familiar with secrets; this was an express ride into the education of keeping secrets. This was a secret that I was too ashamed to know, much less be a part of any of the action. So, I did it. I told one of the boys' goodbye and he ran in the house to tattle on me.

By the time my mom was coming for me, the deed was already done. I had backed the bike up all away across the yard and I took off in a frantic peddle straight at the ditch. I crashed the bike so hard that it slammed me onto the middle bar and cut the inside of my leg and a portion of my inner vaginal lips. I had damaged myself, but I failed in the suicide attempt. I hit my head and had a concussion.

My momma picked me up and took me to the car. She was taking me to the doctor. I remember her telling me to stay awake. She asked me repeatedly what was wrong... I wouldn't answer her. My eyes focused on the green light from the radio on the dash as I began to fall asleep.

God, I haven't thought about that moment in decades...

I'm not sure what happened after that day. I don't have any recollection of going back to visit them like that again. I would occasionally see Jill at school, but she treated me differently. She almost treated me like a stranger. So, I stopped trying to speak to her on the playground.

I just kept to myself at recess.

MONAHANS

CARL AND MOMMA MADE THE DECISION to buy a house in Monahans. We rode up to the new house in a blue Cordova car. It was evident Carl was proud and there was an excitement in his voice, as he turned and said to me, "This is our home. It will be fully paid for by the time you're thirteen years old, Mandy."

Carl's statement made me happy. I couldn't wait to see inside our new home. It was a new feeling to have our own home. No apartment, no trailer, no rental. Finally, a real home.

As we approached the home, Carl pointed out the pomegranate tree by the entry. I had no idea what a pomegranate was, so I didn't know how to react. Momma noticed the puzzled look on my face and told me it was a fruit. She said once the fruit was ripe, we could eat it. Now I was eager with anticipation! I hoped it would be good.

On into the house we ventured, room by room. Wow, it was huge! So much space! Will and I ran from room to room. We could go around the house in circles as each room was connected to the next with only a door separating them. Rooms on the left, rooms on the right and rooms straight down the middle. The home had four bedrooms, two bathrooms, complete with a living room, den and dining room. I was amazed and thought of all the fun I was going to have living there.

Momma opened the back door to view the back yard. It had an old swing set and a small two-bedroom apartment. I overheard Carl and Momma talk about renting it out, in order to get extra money to pay towards our home. I wondered who would live there, but the thought quickly passed as I ran to play on the swing.

After a few days, we were settled into our new home. Life seemed to be taking on a more normal role and happy days were enjoyed. Carl was even more playful and at times would come to the den and wrestle with me and Will, until we tired him out.

The den was our gathering room and playroom. I would sit with momma in front of the record player and listen to her sing along with every song from Barry Manilow to Fleetwood Mac. Carl preferred Steppenwolf or anything Rock-N-Roll or Country. Television time would consist of Sesame Street, Electric Company, Pippy Long Stocking, Reading Rainbow and Saturday morning cartoons.

Some days we would go visit Grandma and Grandpa like a real family. The adults would often sit around the dining room table talking politics and taxes. I would take advantage of every opportunity to stand near and listen to their conversations. When the adults realized I was there, I would be sent away to go outside to play with Will and my new Uncle Neil.

Neil was Momma's younger brother and we became friends. We were only a few years apart and he had cool games to play. It wasn't long before he was off chasing girls and would be busy living his own life.

I was at the age of growth spurts and started getting debilitating growing pains. My legs would ache so bad that I couldn't walk on them. Momma would lay me down, then prop my legs up on pillows to alleviate the pain. I would get hot laying in the room at Grandma's so I would place my arm over to the side of the bed and place my wrist on the metal frame, which seemed to help cool me down.

After the growing pains subsided, Momma got me a pair of skates that summer and she showed me how to wear them. I was accident prone and very clumsy with the skates. I fell over and over again. There was a small sidewalk in front of the house that I would use to practice skating.

Momma taught me how to start and stop on the skates, but eventually she had other things to do and left me to my successes and failures. I can't tell you the number of bumps, bruises, scrapes and cuts I received trying to maintain my balance on those skates. But, I was determined not to quit!

I was going to conquer the skill of skating and that I did. I became quite good at skating, even teaching myself to skate backwards and in a circle. At times, I would daydream about being a professional skater.

(That was only a daydream, never to be fully realized.)

School was about to be back in session, and this would be the first time I would be riding the bus back and forth to school. Momma felt it necessary to show me the route the bus should be taking, so I would get home safely. I am assuming she had a foreboding feeling that I would get lost.

Her intuition was on point.

The very first day I got off at a school to get on the second bus for my route. I got off at the wrong school. I waited patiently for my second bus to arrive, but as each bus passed the kids began to get fewer and fewer, until, I was the last child left. I looked around puzzled and then the panic began to set into me.

After what seemed like hours had passed (probably no more than thirty minutes if we are being realistic, but I was a child and everything seemed like FOREVER!), a teacher emerged and asked me my name and where my parents were. Through tear-soaked eyes, and a stammering voice, I told her my name.

The teacher asked me what my parents name were, and I innocently replied, "Momma and Daddy."

"What bus number do you ride, dear?"

In the confusion of everything, I forgot my bus number. The teacher was becoming frustrated with trying to find out how to get me home. Another teacher came over to help. As they were discussing how to find out where I lived, and how to get me home, Momma drove up. The relief I felt to see her. She knew to come looking for me. She knew...

At this juncture, I feel I must embed the importance of my bond with Kathleen and try to emphasize the strength of it. I can only attribute the connection between us as kindred spirits, amplified with love and respect. I do not want to diminish it by labeling it as supernatural, but due to a lack of a better description it is extraordinary.

Throughout our lives, whether we are in the presence of one another, or separated by miles, we have always sensed each other. It only became more apparent as the years passed between us.

The rest of that school year went without a hitch. Thankfully... I would make it safely back and forth to school each day. My favorite part of getting off the bus in the afternoon was running up to the porch, picking a pomegranate from the bush to enjoy eating while I watched Speed Racer and Batman & Robin in the den, before I had to settle in and do my homework.

Carl had bought us a bean bag and I found it quite comfortable. Sometimes I would take a nap in the bean bag, instead of watching TV.

Momma would usually be in the Den, visiting with her best friend Ronda, or they would be in the dining room playing cards, when I would return home from school. It just so happened that Ronda and her husband Virgil lived next door in the house on the right. So, their daily activities usually involved coming to our house, or we would go to theirs.

I recall calling Ronda "Banana" ... I don't know why I called her that, other than perhaps it was because she was as skinny as a banana. Virgil was kind and playful. He seemed protective over us and I often caught him looking over at us to check on our activities. I came to trust and love Virgil, eventually referring to him as my Uncle Virgil. I always looked forward to his visits.

Virgil had a scar on his neck from a grisly accident where he was electrocuted, while on the job. I was surprised he lived through the accident, when he told me the tale. His scar was a reminder for me to never play with electricity.

I was getting better at reading; I was teaching myself new words by sounding them out, when I would see them anywhere. Uncle Virgil had his favorite coffee cup that he always carried around with him. I would ask him what it said, but he would always laugh and tell me I was too young to know. I was tenacious and set out to figure it out on my own.

So, as he sat at the table with the cup in hand, I fixated on the letters and began sounding out the word. He cut his eyes at me in surprise and quickly shushed me with a grin. (Okay, I won't sound it out... out loud any way...heh heh!)

In a matter of moments proceeding the shushing, I blurted out "BASTARD!"

Everyone damn near broke their necks when they turned and looked at me! (HAHAHA!! Sorry, I get a kick out of this memory. It gave me a good chuckle.) "What did you say?" someone asked.

"BASTARD!" I proudly proclaimed again.

"No, Mandy! You can't say that word!" Uncle Virgil exclaimed through a hearty chuckle.

Everyone agreed through their own laughter. I didn't realize it was a dirty word that only adults could say.

TENANTS

AN HISPANIC FAMILY MOVED INTO THE SMALL APARTMENT behind our home and they had a boy around my age, which made for a quick, but fleeting friendship.

As soon as the family moved in, the boy, Juan, made his way over to our home and knocked on the back door. He wanted to see if we could come out to play. I found him to be kind, so he was easy to like as a friend. I enjoyed listening to him talk. Juan had a thick Hispanic accent that made him interesting.

As we got to know each other, we would play on our swing set and spend the weekends running around the neighborhood, playing with other children living next to us.

Juan did do some bizarre things that made me question his mental faculties. One thing that stands out in my mind the most, is that he ate dog food. Juan was able to talk Will into eating the dogfood with him. I was grossed out! I absolutely refused to take part in the disgusting activity.

I would gag when he would pull some out of his pocket and snack on it like it was candy. He would laugh at me and show me the chewed-up bits in his mouth to watch me gag even more, as his abhorrent breath would punch me in the face. (Ugh, it still makes me gag!)

Nevertheless, we had lots of fun adventures, while he lived behind us. Often, we would run amuck around the neighborhood, playing games of tag and hopscotch.

The last memory I have with Juan was when we were pretending to be mountain climbers. We used the wooden fence next door as our mountain.

I was the last one to climb the "mountain" and just as I got to the top, it felt like someone hit me with a baseball bat near my armpit and I was knocked off the fence onto the ground.

The next thing I remember is being in my home and Momma tending to a wound under my arm. We must have aggravated a hornet.

This is where we realized I was highly allergic to stings, because I began swelling up… I still have a scar under my arm pit from that attack.

PARANORMAL HAPPENINGS

MOMMA CAME HOME WITH NEWS OF HER PREGNANCY. The news was thrilling for the whole family. I was hoping for a baby sister. Almost simultaneously to the news, events around our home started to become strange.

Initially the events seemed benign and hardly anything to speak of in conversation. Unexplained smells of powdered snuff would permeate the air around the home, on an occasion.

The middle room, on the left side of the house, which was used for storage had an old rocking chair in the corner that would rock slowly when Will and I would go play in there. Things would disappear, never to be found again. The list goes on…

Momma and Ronda often played cards in the dining room, when the men would be away at work. One evening, they had been playing cards for a decent amount of time, when Momma said in frustration, "Where is that Ace of Hearts when I need it?"

Her frustration was broken when the chandelier above the table made a clinking sound, as though it had been bumped. Both women looked up to see what could have caused it to move. Then they looked at each other with curiosity and shrugged it off, thinking it was nothing.

Momma looked back down to see the Ace of Hearts staring back at them from the middle of the table. Ronda had seen all she wanted to see and wasn't sticking around to see how the card had made its way out of the deck, so she was quick to excuse herself and go home.

Then the disembodied voices started... At first it was just a mumble or a sound that came out of what seemed like thin air. Most of the time, though, I would just shrug it off. It wasn't uncommon for me to wake up to whispers in the dark. I would quickly fall back to sleep thinking it was my mom and dad talking in one of the other rooms.

After a time, my Momma decided that it would be best for Will and me to exchange rooms. My room would now be on the left side and Will would take the right-side room. I was just getting my room set up the way I wanted it, when I heard a female say my name. I looked around and no one was there.

I responded by saying "Yes, ma'am?"

No answer...

I went to look for whom ever was calling me, but no one was there. Momma had gone next door to Ronda's house. I was beside myself wondering who it could have been that was calling out to me.

In the following months, little things that I had a personal attachment to would disappear out of my special hiding places, like my dresser or out from under my pillow. Mom would often ask if I had moved something of hers or if I had seen Will playing with it. I would always answer "no", but I assume that she thought I was lying because she would ask again.

Carl had some friends come to visit for the day, while I was at school. When I returned home that afternoon, I went to my room to change my clothes. When I opened my drawer, to my surprise my precious chunk of pyrite (aka fool's gold) was gone along with the change I had found in the cushions of the couch! I had been saving that for a trip to the store with mom for gum! I was devastated!

I immediately assumed that Carl's strange friend had taken it. Boldly, I darted out the door to meet the friend at the car. They were saying their goodbyes to Carl when I rudely blurted out, "YOU TOOK MY ROCK, AND MY MONEY! I WANT IT BACK!"

Carl almost fell over, in surprise, at my emotional outburst. The friend swore that he didn't take anything. Carl told me to hush, but I had no control over my mouth. "I DON'T BELIEVE YOU!!!" I continued, as Carl was trying to shut me down. Once again, the friend defended himself, "I swear, I would never take anything that didn't belong to me." Carl was embarrassed and getting visibly angry with me when I told the friend to empty his pockets so I could see.

Carl defended the friend. "Get your ass back in the house! NOW, MANDY SHAWN! However, the friend obliged and opened all his pockets to reveal nothing inside them. I was confused and began looking around in dismay. Where is it? Where had it gone?

Carl made me apologize to the friend and sent me straight to bed. I suppose I deserved it. I had no right to just assume this strange friend had taken anything. I never found my fool's gold or my change. That fool's gold was my ticket to the high life! Or so I thought at that age...

Was it paranormal? Who is to say? All I know is that things became unusual...very unusual. There were dark figures walking past windows, when no one was inside. Lights would turn on by themselves.

At times, I would be woken in the middle of the night to the sounds of footsteps like heals walking on concrete.

One night, I woke to the sound to see a small man not more than 4ft tall, wearing what I can best describe as a newsboy hat, casual suit and boots with a cane walk directly into my room.

The small man stopped in the middle of my room, and I became paralyzed with fear as I watched him. He looked directly at me and then began walking slowly in a circle around the cane. He continued walking in a circle around the cane until he just blinked out of existence.

After that night, whenever I would hear the footsteps, I would leap from my bed and jump in my elephant toy trunk to hide and wait for the footsteps to disappear.

On a visit to see Grandma Earline and Grandpa Lionel, I overheard Momma telling Grandma about some strange events happening to her. She had also heard the voices and noticed things disappearing or moving from places they belonged. I took a deep breath, feeling better that I wasn't the only one seeing things and decided to go outside and play ball with Will.

I wanted to put myself at ease and not worry about the adult matters.

Living in a haunted house was an experience that I will never forget. I still occasionally dream about the 4ft tall man. The dream always gives me a sense of dread. I continue to wonder why he visited and what his purpose was with walking around that cane.

The house itself still haunts my memories. If I am being honest, I miss that house the most.

Sometimes, I think the dreams are the house's way of reaching out to me… calling me back to its mysterious embrace. If it is still standing, maybe I will visit it again someday.

SELF-AWARENESS

MONTHS PASSED AND THE DAYS SEEM TO BLEND IN A HAZE. Carl was gone most of the time on a job. Momma's belly kept growing and her time grew near to give birth to her first child.

Will and I went to stay with Grandma Earline for a few days when Momma had to go to the hospital. Carl returned from a job in time to be with her and welcome our new brother, Phil, into the world.

Phil was noisy and needy, but cute, and I loved to tend to him. Momma said I was a natural nurturer. Her comment gave me a sense of pride. I went to my bedroom after she took our new baby brother to the den. I took a long look at myself in my vanity mirror, reflecting on the words Momma had just told me.

Vanity… As I continued gazing upon my reflection, my mind began to move into thoughts of the future. What would I be when I grew up? Would I be a mom? Would I be famous? I realized that I was easy to look at, knew that I had an acceptable appearance and would grow to be accepted in most circles.

My mind continued to be foretelling… it was a moment of transcendence, from being a child, to now looking into the future. I told myself popularity would not be my circle, but I would still be known. I would live a life of certain struggle, but I would rise out of the ashes and become more than people expected.

How did I know these things?

Were they memories reawakened from the teachings of my first companion, the voice? I withdrew from my thoughts and I crawled into bed for the night.

As time went on, I felt the tensions growing in the family. Carl was gone most of the time for work and he had taken, again, to drinking. When he would return home, he would go on drinking binges, until Momma confronted him on his problem.

Carl's actions quickly chipped away at their marriage. Carl became violent and disengaged. He would punch holes in the walls of our home. One night, during his rage, Momma had to leave, and she had to leave without us.

I was scared and I cried uncontrollably. I just wanted Momma. Carl made us sleep in the den with him on the pullout couch bed. I was unsettled and had a familiar feeling of dread rising in my core. I knew things were changing.

The next day, when I woke up, Edith was at the house. She visited with Carl and they began packing up Will's clothes. Edith was taking Will with her. I didn't want him to go but I had no choice in the matter.

As Edith was leaving out the door with Will, I asked her if I could go too, she quickly turned to me and said, "No!" Her response hit hard.

"But why can't I go?" I asked, hurt.

She replied, "Because you are not my granddaughter…"

Those words would haunt me for the next three decades.

Momma came home, after a few days of being away. I was relieved to see her and hoped that things were settled between them. Carl was different and things seemed to be okay.

With Momma back home and Carl away at work, I resumed my daily activities of school. Before I knew it, Halloween had arrived and even though Momma didn't have much money, she was going to make sure I had a decent costume for the occasion. All the neighborhood kids were getting plastic mask costumes of cartoon and scary characters. I wanted a mask, but Momma insisted my costume would be better.

Momma requested Ronda's assistance and they pulled together ideas to work with what they had available. They worked all day putting together the perfect layering of clothing. Momma made me stand on a stool as she worked, designing the fabric around me. Layer after layer, paying close attention to all the small details.

Ronda would cut and managed the materials as Momma sewed. I didn't know what a Gypsy was, but Momma promised I would like it. She tried to tell me a story about what a Gypsy was, in order to keep me occupied, while she worked. Curiosity was rising in my mind and I began to welcome the idea.

Ronda peeked around the corner after stepping out to her house. She came in with lots of razzle dazzle and shiny jewelry. I know I had a grin span the width of my face! I liked shiny things! She came over to me and they started placing the bracelets on my ankles, and wrists.

Momma was testing different clip on earrings to see which one complemented the costume best. Ronda placed several necklaces over my head to make a jubilant and layered assembly. Then Momma took a handkerchief and wrapped it on my head. To finalize the head piece, she adorned it with some beads.

Then the finale, makeup! I was going to get to wear makeup!! YAY!! I contained my excitement in my head, but it was hard. Momma defined my eyes with dark liner giving me cat eyes. Ronda picked the perfect shade of red for my lips.

Momma and Ronda stood back and admired their work. They smiled and helped me down from the stool. We went to the full-length mirror in the bathroom and I was so surprised! I didn't even recognize myself! I couldn't wait to show the neighbor kids!

We left out of the house for the evening and I was a hit! Everyone loved my costume. I did too. I was so proud. I got lots of candy!

I felt comfortable in the guise of the costume and I related to the transient lifestyle of the Gypsy story only too well.

The following week, I came home one afternoon from school not feeling well. I woke up the next morning with fever and sores. I had contracted chicken pox. Momma was going to have to take care of me by herself. I was riddled with chicken pox all over my body.

Once again, Momma cared for me until I healed. I asked her where Carl had gone and when he was going to be home, because he had been away for a while. Momma told me he was at work and she didn't know when he would be home.

It was all a lie; Momma had lied to me to protect me from the truth.

Carl had attempted suicide. He had swallowed pills and he was in the hospital recovering. The drinking and erratic behavior, combined with PTSD from his time served in Vietnam, had taken its toll on him and he was looking for a way out from his problems.

Momma knew she couldn't heal him. This wasn't a fever. It was an illness in his mind that he would have to escape by himself. He was damaged and Edith was his enabler.

Instead of getting the help he needed, Carl would run to his mother and she would fill his head with radical ideas and pit him against his wife. Momma also knew the toll his behavior was taking on their marriage, but there was no way she could explain that to a child.

Several weeks passed and Edith brought Will back home. Christmas was just a few days away. Carl had returned home at this point, as well. He seemed different and he would cry in Momma's lap. His cry was like a hopeless laugh. Such an odd feeling to hear a grown man cry. I found my heart breaking at the sounds of his wailing. I would hug him, and Momma would try to console his pain. I didn't know what else to do.

Time moved on, and soon Christmas morning arrived. Will and I woke up with anticipation. When we entered the living room, we beheld a cascade of presents dressed beneath the Christmas tree. I had never seen so many wrapped boxes. Momma sat us down and began handing out the presents one by one. We tore at the pretty packaging to get to the prize inside.

I had hoped for a bathrobe and house shoes. That was the first present I opened! I ran it into my room and hung it up in my closet right away. I had plans to use it right after my bath that evening. I also hoped for and American

Girl Doll and to my amazement, I got that too! I took her to my room and laid her on the foot of my bed with her changes of clothes. I wanted to play with her after my bath.

For a moment, everything seemed normal. I had hoped that life would get back to normal... Hope seemed to be out of reach. Normal was a luxury not afforded to us any longer.

When the day wound down, Carl left. I heard him argue with Momma in their bedroom, just before he left. I went to my room and decided to take my bath. As I rounded through the door, I realized my American Girl Doll wasn't on my bed. I looked around for it and asked Will if he had her. He didn't even know what I was talking about. He was too interested in playing with his new toys. I looked in my elephant toy box, but she wasn't there. I looked under my bed and she wasn't there either.

She was nowhere to be found.

Frustrated, I opened my closet to discover my bathrobe was missing too! I ran to Momma and told her about it. She went to help me look, but it was useless. Both of my prized gifts simply disappeared. I believed that whatever was moving stuff around in the house was responsible for stealing my gifts.

Those gifts were never found... never recovered...

TAKEN

AFTER CHRISTMAS BREAK, SCHOOL WAS BACK IN SESSION. It was my first day back at school and Carl came to pick me up. I was delighted because, my "Daddy" came to my school to pick me up! Plus, I didn't have to be in school for the rest of the day.

When I got in the car, Will was already with Carl, but Phil was not there. He took us to a café and bought us hot chocolate. The next stop was at a strange lady's house, where he left us until later that night. A familiar trepidation creeped into my soul.

Her house was a mess and there was an equally messy little girl there who wanted to play. The next few hours were filled with dread and I asked the lady when my Momma was coming to get me. She said my Momma would not be there to get me. So, I continued to play with the strange little girl. We took turns playing with her twangy toy piano.

Nightfall had come and there was a knock at the door. It was Carl; he was frazzled and in a hurry. He quickly placed me and Will in the car, as he took off in haste. I asked where Momma was and he told me she would not be coming with us.

We drove off into the night. He drove for what seemed endless hours.

He was driving frantically and turned down a dirt road. The road was long and solitary. I was perched up between the front seat and on the arm rest, watching down the road as the night waned. I would look at Carl from time to time and I could see his eyes well up with tears.

I asked him what was wrong and he responded, "You are too young to understand."

But I wasn't too young, I knew something was wrong. I didn't have a name for it, but I knew all wasn't right in our little world.

Carl continued to rush down the dirt road, then all the sudden a bull cow was in the middle of the road. Carl was going too fast to stop in time. He slammed on the brakes. Time seemed to slow down to nearly a halt, the next few seconds passing in slow motion. I heard a loud a screaming sound, as the brakes were applied forcibly.

An abrupt flash of white light crossed in front of the windshield, just as we impacted with the bull, causing the hood of the vehicle to slam into the windshield. The glass shattered back into the cab of the car, causing some debris to cut into my knee, before blowing me backward into the rear seat. Will was thrown to the floorboard, under the dash. Carl hit the steering wheel and cursed out with a yell.

The vehicle came to a halt and everything was abruptly silent.

Carl began to rustle around and cough out the impact on his chest, then an unsure cry came from Will. Carl reached over and pulled him out of the floorboard and checked his head. Will seemed fine, just a little shaken. Then he turned back to me and asked me if I was okay. I told him I was bleeding on my knee. He told me to just lie still; he had to get out of the car.

I watched him as he got out of the car timidly, in order to check around for the hurt bull. He pulled on the bull to get it to the side of the road, out of the driving path. After a struggle, he walked raggedly back to the car and checked the engine and lights. One light was knocked out from the impact. I could hear him cussing and carrying on in frustration.

Eventually, he was able to get the hood pushed down and connected. He got in the car, sat for a moment staring out the busted window, then started the engine. The car sputtered, as the engine turned over to run. Carl looked defeated. After a moment of hesitation, he put the car in drive and we crept the remaining few miles to a gas station located just inside the city limits of Lovington, New Mexico.

The wind felt brisk on my face, coming through the broken windshield. The ride was alarmingly quiet, aside from the sputter of the engine.

When we arrived at the gas station, Carl got out and went inside for a bit. Will began crying, so I crawled into the front seat with him to calm him down. Carl walked outside to the payphone and made a call. I guess Will and I fell asleep while he was on the phone. I don't remember the ride out to Edith's, but we woke up there.

Edith had moved from Hobbs to a rock house on a farm, with several acres, just northeast of Lovington with her second husband John. She still had Liam living at home. I came to know him as an uncle, but never referred to him as one, as we were only 3 years apart in age. We just called him Liam. He didn't share well and was a bully to me from the word go.

Carl wasn't anywhere to be found when I woke up that morning. I did not feel welcomed in this home. I knew Edith didn't want me there.

Right away she sat me down, staring at me with her piercing blue eyes glaring into mine, and told me that as long as I was staying with her, I would have chores to do. I wasn't to get out of line, or she would bust my ass. I believed her. She scared me.

How long was I staying there? Why couldn't I just go back home? Where was Carl? My future was uncertain then, anxiety became my constant companion.

My day would begin with following Liam out to the pens to feed and water the chickens. We would gather eggs, if any were visible in the nests. Liam would fuss at me and call me names, because I was weak, and a stinky girl.

Sometimes he would slap me in the back of my head, if I weren't moving fast enough. He would throw feed at me when I was struggling to carry the heavy bucket of water.

We would come in just in time for breakfast, after the chores. Everyone would wash up then gather around and sat at the table. John was always the first to fill his plate with food, then he would begin passing them around, until it would finally reach me at the end. We were not allowed to touch any bowl, until he had his portion doled out first, not unless you wanted to get your hand slapped harshly.

After every meal, I was to clean up the table and do the dishes. I had to use a step stool to reach over the sink properly. Edith was quick with her temper and did not hold back on the lashings. Every time I turned around, I was getting my ass busted. Liam would often tattle on me, just to get me in trouble. According to both, I couldn't do anything right. I walked around on eggshells and I began feeling very anxious all of the time.

I looked forward to my free time. When the chores were done, I was allowed to go outside. I would go climb a tree or walk the pastures. I needed to be by myself. It was the only way to shake off the constant bombardment of negative mental attacks from Edith and Liam. They would delight in talking about me in their presence, as though I wasn't even there.

I asked Edith when my Momma was coming to get me and she said, "You might as well forget that bitch, little girl.

"She isn't coming for you. Nobody wants you!" she emphasized.

"I am only tolerating you here, because my son asked me to take care of you."

She added, "If I had my way, you would go to an orphanage!"

Those words cut deep into my soul. I began crying and she started laughing and calling me a cry baby.

She sneered at me and said, "Get the hell out of my face." I ran outside.

Liam followed me calling out, "Little orphan Mandy, cry baby, cry baby!" all the way to the barn. He picked up rocks and sticks and threw them at me, as I ran away from them. I hid away and cried, wishing for my Momma or Carl to come get me. Edith yelled out the kitchen door, "Get your ass back in here. If I come get you, I will bust your ass all the way back!"

I hesitantly moped my way back to the house. She pinched me up by the arm and whooped me anyway.

Edith sent me to bed in the basement without any supper. I wasn't allowed back upstairs until the next day. When I walked into the kitchen, the dishes from the night before were waiting for my attention.

I couldn't wait to get away from there.

HELL ON THE FARM

I FOUND A CAT THAT WAS COMING AROUND THE FARM. I started taking care of it by feeding it scraps left over from the plates, after meals. The feral cat seemed to take to my company and began rubbing against my leg, eventually allowing me to pet its soft fur. I would enjoy spending time with the cat that I had affectionately named Morris.

Liam rounded the front corner of the house one evening and watched me as I was tending to Morris. When I raised up, after he startled me, he looked me straight in the eyes and sneered, "You know are wasting your time on that cat."

"It's going to die."

I countered, "All things die. Is it a waste to live?"

He called me a "Smart Ass!" then kicked me. He walked on past me and said, "Get your ass over here, we have to go to the barn."

It was time to get hay for the chicken coups. It was hot, tedious work, but necessary to keep the chickens busy and provide padding for the eggs to be laid. After we got to the barn Liam turned to me and said, "I want to see your pussy." I thought he was referring to the cat. I told him it was back at the house and he just saw it. He grabbed me and whispered, aggravated through his teeth, "Not the cat!"

He clarified, "Your pussy!"

"Show me and I won't beat you up." He continued with the threat,

"If you don't show me, I will beat you up, then I will tell on you."

I was afraid and felt I had no choice. I was defeated, with no way to get out of this scenario. I hesitantly began unbuttoning my pants. He expressed his urgency, "Hurry before someone sees us."

I closed my eyes and pulled my pants down below my private area. He walked over and touched me. Then he said put your hand on my dick. I told him, "I don't want to touch it."

Liam grabbed my hand and put it on him. It was hard and it surprised me. I opened my eyes and saw that he looked different than my brothers. I saw my brother's peewee when I changed his diaper and it was weird, but I never thought anything about it.

Liam's member looked like a worm. I asked him why it looked like that and he pushed me away from him. He put it back in his pants and I pulled up my own. He told me that he hadn't been circumcised. I didn't know what that meant. He threatened me again and told me if I told anyone about what just happened, he would beat me till I died.

I believed him. So, I never told anyone... until now.

The next morning, I heard John out in the front barn yelling at Liam to get in there. He ran out to see what John needed. John had found a nest of rats and he needed Liam to dispose of them. Liam was all too willing to dispatch the mice to an early grave.

Liam called out to me and I went to assist him. He handed me a bucket and he told me to hold it still. I placed the bucket on the ground. He picked up a potato sack and began pouring the contents into the bucket. It was the nest of mice.

I asked him why he was pouring the mice in the bucket and he said you will see. He turned and picked up a hammer and he began slamming it back and forth between the walls of the bucket, chasing the mice around, while pounding them to death.

It was morbid and I turned my head from the horror. He grabbed my face and made me watch, as he continued to torture the helpless creatures. Tears began flowing down my face, and he began laughing, while calling me a cry baby. I couldn't stomach the persecution and began to retch at the sight. He was sadistic and found pleasure in killing the mice. He found pleasure in watching me agonize over their death.

With the final blow of death to the last mouse I thought that would be the last I would suffer of such an event.

The next morning, after breakfast, I went outside to feed Morris. I was met with an empty bowl and no Morris.

I called out, "Here Kitty, Kitty!"

Still no Morris... I decided to place the scraps in the bowl and continued with the remainder of my chores. Once my chores were completed, I headed out to go read a book in our club house.

The club house was a small building that was once a chicken coup that had been retired, and then pushed to the side. All the kids used it as a fort or club house, depending on the scenario of what we wanted to play that day.

It had a small bench in it, so I thought it would be the perfect spot for me to prop up and get some alone time.

It was bright outside, so my eyes had to adjust for a minute, once I entered in the small darker area. As I entered in the opening, I felt something hit my head and I looked up and, to my devastation, saw it was Morris. He had been hung from the ceiling with some baling wire. I fell to my knees, disoriented from nausea and shock. Liam had killed my cat. Killing the mice had just ignited his taste for murder.

After some time, and a lot of crying, I composed myself and pulled Morris down from the ceiling. I could tell he had suffered by the contortions of his body. I dug a small grave and buried Morris.

I looked up to heaven and asked, "Why, God?" I heard no reply.

What makes a person take pleasure in the torture of creatures? Even after all these years, my heart still aches for those little mice and my mind is still scarred from the atrocity I beheld with Morris.

I walked back to the house in a numb state of mind. Liam was sitting on the front porch and he watched me as I approached him. "What's the matter with you cry baby?" he inquired.

"Cat got your tongue?" he began laughing in a maniacally satiated tone that sent chills up my spine.

I didn't react. I walked past him, into the house, and down to the basement. Edith called me up for dinner and I told her I wasn't hungry.

She said, "Hungry or not, you still have dishes to do after everyone eats."

I obliged and then went straight to bed.

Another day in hell... I took a deep breath and got up to begin the day. Edith was upstairs and told everyone to get ready to ride to town. It was grocery shopping day. We all got ready and began to head out to the car. I saw a bike in the driveway and as I attempted to speak up about it, Edith told me to shut up and get in the car. Obediently, I did as I was told.

Edith started the engine and put the car in reverse. She began backing up when there was a loud scraping crunch. She slammed the car into park and got out to see what she hit. She came back, cussing at us for leaving a bike in the driveway. I spoke up and told her that I saw it and was trying to tell her, before we left.

Boldly, I reminded her that she had told me to shut up. That statement incited a fury in her. She turned around and slapped the hell out of my face.

"You have anything else to tell me?" She asked, as she dared me to say another word.

I shook my head no and looked down.

I didn't utter another word, until I was asked a question, for the remainder of my stay. I just did as I was told and observed. (I was living up to the adage, that children should be seen and not heard. I kept my interactions as limited as possible to chores and meals.)

In my spare time, away from chores, I would spend as much time as I could climbing the trees around the property. I loved to sit in the shade on the branches, as the wind breezed through, cooling my hot skin.

On an occasion, when Liam felt like being a normal kid, he would take us to the pond to fish. Some days, we would go to the barn and play Cowboys and Indians. This was fun for me, because we would climb up the rafters to the top of the barn and jump off into a loose pile of hay. I felt like Superman, even though I was a girl.

But, soon, another workday out in the dusty field came. This time we were moving large irrigation pipe. It was heavy work in the dusty field, under the beating heat of the sun.

We started the day early. I packed the water and tea jugs for the first portion of the morning. Edith would come out to the field, around lunch time, to bring sandwiches and a fresh tea with a refill of water for the jugs.

This day seemed to be unusually taxing and the water was utilized rapidly.

We all expected Edith's arrival with the refills, but on this day she would be delayed for unknown reasons. I began feeling the effects of the heat and my mouth became sticky, as my lips started to crack. I was very thirsty.

We went to the truck to see if Edith had delivered the water, but nothing yet. John could tell that we were all needing a break, but we continued to work until Edith arrived.

Finally, we could see her in the distance as the dust kicked up behind the car. I was at the point of feeling faint when she drove up to us. I went to help her gather the goods out of the car, never-the-less, I still had to wait until John and Liam got their portion of the refreshing water.

Edith drove off and I turned to see Liam guzzling up the last portion of the water. He had done it on purpose. He looked at me and smugly stated, "I figured you already had a drink."

I couldn't even form spit at this point. I was dehydrated and the heat was making it worse. After laughing at my desperation, he reached over the back of the truck and grabbed the other jug and handed it to me. Without hesitation, I put it to my mouth and began to drink the tea…

Only it wasn't tea. It was a jug of gasoline. I ingested just enough to knock me out. The next thing I know, I was in the cab of the truck and I began to vomit as John raced me back to the house. The look on Lances' face was something I had never seen before this point. He was afraid… He was very afraid.

John took me in the house and told Edith to take care of me. She knew John was pissed and all the sudden she didn't look so intimidating. She seemed daunted!

Edith didn't question John and there was a look of concern, as she saw him bolt out the door, yelling for Liam. Then I saw her break for the door, as I heard a sudden loud pound of belt against flesh. John was whooping Liam for nearly killing me.

Edith tried to stop John from continuing the beating of Liam… she was unsuccessful. John turned to her and called them both out on how they had been treating me. He told her if she had anything else to say that he would have her grabbing her ankles as he whooped her ass. After hearing this, I vomited one more time, before I passed out again. But, this time with a bit of vindication, that those two had gotten a portion of what was coming to them.

I don't know how long we had been at the farm, before Carl finally showed up one day. I was so relieved to see him. I asked him if we could go home and he said it would be a little longer. I begged him to take me home, but he said couldn't. He left us a few more of our things and some bikes to ride. I didn't really want the bike after the incident with the old bike getting run over by Edith.

The events from the last few days was about all Edith could tolerate and she wanted us gone. If Carl wasn't going to be able to take us, she was going to find an alternative option to get us out of her hair. Or, should I say, me out of her hair. She favored Will and she had no qualms about letting it be known.

Edith called Bud and told him to come get us. The call was abrupt, and she didn't mix her words when she told him she was tired of having us there. We weren't her responsibility and if he couldn't get us, she would call and have us turned into the state. I was sitting outside on the front porch during this call. I know she intended for me to hear every word.

Finally, a chance to leave. An escape! Freda arrived in her silver Ford Falcon just a few hours later. She was a sight for sore eyes. There was no friendship between Freda and Edith. Edith put on a false front and pretended to be doting and caring as she quickly escorted us out to the car.

Edith spoke kindly to Freda, but I knew she was a viper and as soon as Freda drove off, Edith would begin the treachery. Edith was deceptive and not a friend to anyone.

TEMPORARY RELIEF

Bud and Freda had just settled on some new property outside of Hobbs. We arrived in time to help plant trees. Bud purchased some horses for recreational purposes, since the last time we visited. Sunflowers grew wild in the back field, between the trailer and the horse pen, so we always had fresh seeds with which to snack.

Will and I spent most of the days outside playing and piddling around in the yard. We found our favorite spot to be under the porches, because of the shade and cool breeze that would blow through them. We made the space beneath the porches our hideouts. When we made friends with the nearby twin neighbors, Mikey and Mickey, they too would join us in our hideouts.

Some nights, I would go spend the night with Ethel in her tiny trailer. It was like camping out to me. She was kind and enjoyed my company. I would sit and ramble about everything and she would patiently listen, as she enjoyed her powdered snuff.

The snuff had a heavy sweet smell. It reminded me of the smell that occasionally penetrated the air back at home in Monahans. I wanted to try it and she let me. I almost threw up immediately! It was nothing I thought it would be and I couldn't get it out of my mouth fast enough! She found my reaction very amusing and laughed uncontrollably.

The day would turn into night and she would prepare for bedtime. She had heavy quilts that would make me fall asleep fast and her trailer was always cool. She didn't have a TV, but she would listen to the radio all day and all night. I was simply fine with her lifestyle. It was okay by me.

Freda worked outside the home at McDonalds for the first portion of our stay. Bud was the in charge adult of our care, while Freda would work her shifts. Bud was semi-retired, only working on an occasion when someone needed something special made of iron. He was a master with welding and building things. In the evening, Freda would bring us treats left from her shift. I thought that was special.

When Freda was off work, we would spend the days playing and she would encourage the artistic side of me, once she realized I had a knack for drawing what I looked at with precision.

At first, they thought I was copying my art by placing the item under the paper and drawing over it. Then Freda had an idea and began testing my abilities by giving me different things to draw. Once they sat and watched me draw without cheating, they knew my talent was authentic.

Bud and Freda were amazed and wondered where the talent came from, since no one on either side of the family displayed an artistic talent, aside from the music Bud played.

Freda was offered a new job opportunity to make more money. This was a plus for them to help support us, since we were staying with them for the moment. She began working at Long John Silvers. I really liked that she went to work for Long John Silvers, because of the chicken and the crunchies she would bring home for us to devour.

It was a rare, but equally anticipated treat to go visit her while she worked at Long John Silvers. The establishment was decked out with aquatic still life, Pirate hats, swords and peg legs, casting nets tied to a helm and treasure. I would pretend to be a pirate and fantasize of life on the ocean.

We loved getting to wear the hats and bibs, as we enjoyed the atmosphere and ate our food. I felt special that my Grandma was working there. Sometimes, when business slowed, she would get to come sit with us and eat her meal. I really enjoyed spending time with her in the restaurant. I believe she liked to brag that we were her grandchildren too.

SIMON SAYS SUGARFOOT

A COUPLE OF WEEKS PASSED, AFTER OUR ARRIVAL AT BUD AND FREDA'S, before the traumatizing events at Edith's begin to fade. Spending time with our friends Mikey and Mickey next door made life more bearable. The boy twin, Mikey, was a friend to Will. They would go play in the fields and tear up things.

The girl twin, Mickey, was my friend and we would sit in her room most days and listen to music on her record player. She would tell me about boys she liked at school. I would indulge her, just as Ethel indulged me.

I didn't have stories to tell Mikey, like she told me. I would just keep her going with questions, so she wouldn't ask me anything. She didn't mind. She loved to talk about herself. She was remarkably interesting. After all, she was a twin!

With Freda working all the time, Bud would usually keep himself busy with welding in the shop. Business started slowing down for him, so he would interact with us more. The twins would come over and he would sit on the porch, playing Simon Says with us. Bud played the part of Simon.

This game became our evening routine. One evening, we were in the middle of a game, before what was fun and innocent began to take on a more ominous tone.

Bud began calling out Simon says commands, encouraging more deviant actions, "Simon says, "Slap each other on the butt."

Another command, "Simon says, boys kiss a girl on the cheek."

Then Simon commanded Will to kiss the twin girl on the mouth. It was a quick kiss and they both giggled, but Simon didn't say to stop kissing. I began feeling nervous and very insecure.

Bud turned to me and Mikey. Simon says the two of you kiss. Mikey leaned in to kiss me, but I turned my face away and he planted the kiss on my cheek again. This irritated Bud and he called out the command again.

The game was abruptly interrupted when Freda pulled into the driveway. Her timing couldn't have been better, because I felt very uneasy about having Mikey kiss me.

The fun was over for the evening. It was time to call it a night. We had big plans scheduled for the following day. We had to go back to Monahans to gather some of our belongings.

Bud had a conversation with Carl about going to Monahans and picking up some of our belongings from the house. Bud decided he would make the trip and told Freda he would take me to help with gathering our things. Freda agreed and decided to keep Will, so he wouldn't be a frustration for the trip.

Bud and I got up early that morning to head to Monahans. It was still dark outside of our place. We listened to the radio, as we drove down the road. Bud decided to stop at a diner and grab us a bite to eat, before getting out of town.

We stopped to eat flap jacks and I drank chocolate milk with the meal. Bud treated me with favor. I knew that he loved me. He looked at me across the table and told me that I looked just like Anne. I didn't know if that was a compliment or a detraction. I just continued to eat, and we carried on.

I watched Bud as he drove the old red Chevy truck down the road. I paid attention to everything. Bud had a CB radio in the truck that would play static messages occasionally. Every now and then he would pick up the CB and call out to the truckers as we passed. He referred to himself as Iron Daddy and I thought that was odd. I finally had the nerve to ask him why he kept saying "This is Iron Daddy, come back."

Bud laughed and told me it was radio talk. That was his handle on the radio. That is how other drivers knew him. I asked him if I could be a part of the radio talk and he was quick to get me onboard.

He said, "First, we need to get you a name to go by, so the other drivers will know who they are talking to on the radio."

I agreed and we started brainstorming about names. He finally came up with using my nickname he gave to me.

"SUGARFOOT!" He spouted.

I responded, "What?"

He said that can be my handle. I said with a shrug, "Okay, if you think it's good enough, then I am fine with it too."

We had fun the rest of the drive to Monahans, while playing on the radio.

Before we knew it, we were in Texas. Pulling up to the house in Monahans was surreal. I pulled what would be my last pomegranate from the bush. I entered the house. It had been so long since I had been there. I had grown up a bit and things looked smaller to me than I remembered.

The house was in disarray and looked like a Tasmanian Devil had had his way with the place. The smell from the ripe trash nearly knocked me over to the floor. Bud told me to grab everything I thought was important and to make it quick.

Being rushed didn't afford me the time to reminisce about living in the home. I did wonder if our unusual occurrences would happen while I was in the house, alone. But, there was nothing. The house was silent and still. No disembodied voices, no smell of the snuff powder, no sounds…That, in itself, felt eerie and made me a little sad.

I grabbed a trash bag and an empty box and filled them till they couldn't hold anymore. We placed the bag and box in the Camper, on the back of the truck. I went back in and filled up my Elephant toy box and asked if he could help me carry it to the truck.

The toy box barely fit through the door of the Camper, but, somehow, we managed to get it in there. Just a few more things, a lingering final look, and then we were back on the road.

As we were leaving from Monahans, I mentioned how I would like to drive someday. Bud looked at me and asked, "Why wait when you can drive now?" I immediately got butterflies.

Wow, this was happening! I was about to drive for the first time. Bud informed me we would pull over, just outside of Monahans, at a truck stop and he would show me what to do.

We pulled into the first rest area, where Bud put the truck in park. He got out of the truck and told me to scoot over a bit. I placed myself behind the wheel, but I couldn't reach the foot pedals and see over the dash at the same time.

I was just a little too short to be able to drive by myself. Bud had an idea… I could ride in his lap and do the steering and he would shift the gears and peddle.

I felt a little better that I was going to have some help. I wanted to drive, but I knew I wasn't ready to do it all by myself. Bud gave me a few pointers as we completed some test runs around the rest area.

The impromptu training was valuable and appreciated. Bud decided I was ready, so we eased out onto the highway and began our drive back to Hobbs.

Initially, everything seemed innocent enough. However, after Bud would shift the gears, he would make a grinding motion with his hips underneath me as I sat in his lap. Uneasiness set into me and a tension began creeping up the back of my neck. I attempted to scoot down his lap, closer to his knees, but he grabbed my hips quickly and held me tight in place.

"Now pay attention to the road, Sugarfoot."

He continued with a shudder in his breath, "We don't want to wreck."

I focused back on the road, gripping the wheel tight. I felt a movement under my butt cheek. I felt trapped between the steering wheel and Bud. I kept telling myself it was all in my mind and I was just nervous. I was lying to myself. I could feel his breath on my neck and his movements became more pronounced.

"Boy, this road sure is bumpy." Bud said, trying to play off the fact that he was dry humping me from behind. I could feel him pulsing in tiny movements underneath me. Even though it felt like a long time, his actions were over after a few minutes.

Bud let out a groan, when he finished, and followed it up with a cough to cover it up. The awkward silence was broken with a call out on the CB.

Bud was good. He knew how to manipulate the situation and make it seem like nothing happened.

What should have been a moment remembered as a rite of passage is stained with violation and disgust.

LOVINGTON

CARL PICKED US UP FROM HOBBS, JUST BEFORE SCHOOL STARTED. We moved several times during the next couple of years, from New Mexico to Oklahoma, then back to New Mexico. We lived in Enid, Oklahoma, with Carl's cousin, for two months of the beginning of my Second-Grade year, before moving back to New Mexico.

When we arrived back in Lovington. We had moved to a newer model home, located on Avenue M. There was a small house in the back yard that we used as a club house. The neighbor boy across the street would come to play on an occasion. Carl was bringing new people into our lives, as he continued his flight of fancy women and divulged in his drink.

One evening, Carl had brought over a new woman. She had brought her children with her. Carl and the woman had plans for the evening, so she left her children with us, to keep us company. What a fun evening we had together.

I had a record player. It was a disco case with lights that would play in the background when the music started. The record player was amazing, and it was my favorite toy. The case was hard and white; it closed like a suitcase. When I opened it up, the background in the top part of the case was where the lights would dance brightly.

I couldn't wait to show it off to the new kids. We went into my room and I put a 45" record on to play. I had a few records; however, my favorite record was FUNKY TOWN by Lipps Inc.

After warming everyone up to a dance night, we turned out the lights and pretended we were dancers on Solid Gold and Soul Train. We danced all over my room. We danced on the bed, on my dresser and on my vanity chair. We had more fun than was allowed by law.

To this day, when I hear that song FUNKY TOWN, I reminisce about that night. It was that night that I began writing in a diary. I wanted to savor the memory.

School was back in session, but this time I had to walk to school. We lived 5 blocks away from the school, yet it seemed like miles to my little legs. I was in the second grade and I was attending Ben Alexander Elementary. I was incredibly nervous as I walked to school.

When I arrived, all the kids were standing in the hall, waiting for the school bell. I had to go to the office, to find out where my class would be.

I was led to my classroom and as I took my seat, I could feel all the other children looking at me. I brushed off the feeling and contained my composure, as the teacher introduced me to everyone.

Soon the bell rang for breakfast and everyone lined up to head to the lunchroom. This is where I learned that I was going to be last for every event going forward in my school years, because I had been cursed with the last name of Woods.

"Line up children, beginning with the letter A to Z in your last name," directed the teacher.

I was the last child in the line for breakfast, lunch, school yard activities, and to get up in front of the class to read essays. I was last for everything. Basically, this meant I got what was leftover, if anything was left to be had.

I would be left out in activities, if the other children took longer than expected, which would run us out of time for everyone to participate. I was the last to be picked for teams when we played sports.

There was a silver lining though… Being last to read my essay meant the teacher's attention span was stretched, listening to everyone else and she would pass the essay, just because. I did not mind this at all! I became comfortable in being last. This kept the spotlight off me.

Because I was last in everything, I was a loner. I didn't have any friends, because who wants to hang out with the girl who always comes in last. On a particularly cool and windy afternoon, during lunch break, I had finally made my way onto the playground. I found a place over on a bench to sit and watch the other children play on the swings and other playground equipment.

After a few moments on the bench, a boy, Scott, (who was what would be considered a popular boy) walked over to me and placed his hand on his hip, as he looked down on me in judgement. I looked up at him with curiosity.

Scott asked me my name and I replied, "Mandy."

His composure changed as he taunted, "Well Mandy, I don't like you."

Shocked, yet trying to save face, I replied, "I don't care. You don't know me."

I continued, "Maybe I don't like you!"

Wrong answer!

Scott pulled off his glove and slapped me across the face. I swear, you could hear a pin drop, as every kid on the playground turned to witness the slap.

I reacted immediately, as I went after him and we scuffled back and forth. He pushed me away and I went in with a solid punch to the face as he went down.

The crowd of children gathered and a roar of "FIGHT! FIGHT! FIGHT!" was chanted. I was not going to let this boy get the better of me, even if he was popular. As we wrestled on the ground, I was pulled off Scott by a teacher that sent me directly on my way to the office.

I hadn't been in school a full week and I was already labeled a bad kid, because a boy wanted to bully me. I received three swats and a stern talking to by the principal, before making my way back to class.

I meekly entered into my class and waited for the bell to ring. Kids began clamoring back into class. As they passed me, I could hear snickering and whispers.

A couple of the kids gave me a high five for punching that kid. Scott deserved it! I found out later that he had bullied many less privileged children. I was the last one he messed with. Heh, I guess I taught him a lesson!

Because of my defensive actions on the playground, I was punished for the next week. No lunch recess: I would have to wait in my classroom and read during this forty-five-minute break. HA! They though it was punishment for me. I enjoyed having quiet time to myself, without the judgement of my peers.

On the second day of my punishment, a girl by the name of Sophie walked into the room to join me in detention. She did not sit still, nor did she read like she was supposed to do. Sophie was nosey and she got into everything.

I was afraid she was going to get caught and get us into more trouble. But, she knew how to get away with things. By the time the bell rang, she had sat in her chair, pretending to be there all along with her book opened to a random page.

I was impressed.

Sophie's misbehavior continued for the remainder of the week. She knew everything there was to know about the teachers' desk and all its hidden papers. She looked in every kids' cubby and took what she wanted, when she found something of interest to her.

On the last day, Sophie turned on the radio and we listened to music. After a couple of songs, Sophie got up and peered out the window at the kids on the playground. After belittling everyone she could think of, she turned around and began dancing to "Into the Night" by Benny Mardones.

I watched Sophie in wonder, as she continued dancing. Then, she shocked me, as she placed herself on the corner of a desk and began grinding her private on it. She looked at me and said, "You should try it, it feels really good."

Nervously I said, "Um, I think I will pass."

Sophie laughed at me and told me I was being silly. Confused, I thought to myself, "No, you're the silly one!"

The song concluded when "Eye of the Tiger" by Survivor hit the airwaves. Now this was a song I didn't mind participating with in dancing. She and I danced our hearts out! We danced on the chairs and tables just like the night at my house with my disco player.

The bell rang and we quickly jumped into our seats, still breathing heavily from the dancing. Our teacher entered the room and looked suspiciously at us…we both giggled quietly at each other.

Sophie and I became friends for a brief time, after that week. We would play hopscotch and soccer on the opposite side of the playground, away from the popular children.

We eventually got in on an addictive game of marbles. I was good at the game and won many awesome marbles. Sometimes we would break out and play Jumping Jacks. We eventually moved on to playground equipment.

I was small and built for the Monkey Bars. I could swing myself around and hang upside down for long periods of time. Sophie wasn't as limber as I was, so she would stick to soccer and swings.

As life moved forward, we would eventually go our separate ways.

ELEMENTARY PAINS

THIRD GRADE WAS A BLUR, AS TIME PASSED. Fourth grade came on fast and I was moving through the motions. New opportunities arose, such as Cafeteria and Office duty. It was an honor to be chosen for either of these tasks.

My turn arrived one day; I was chosen for cafeteria duty. This was exciting, because now I got to be first in line for lunch. I was released from class to go help in setting up the cafeteria.

When I got to the cafeteria, the lunch ladies told me to go make a tray and eat before we got started. I couldn't believe it! The food was fresh and there was strawberry and chocolate milk!!

I never had the chance to get flavored milk before, because I was always last in line. I drank and ate my fill before my duty to serve began. It was somewhat empowering to stand on the other side of that serving line.

Getting to determine how much someone received and what part of the food they received was cool.

I did such a great job in the Cafeteria that I was called next for the Office. This was an exceptional honor. We were responsible for answering the phone and taking messages.

We also had to write excuse notes for the children coming in late or back from a doctor's appointment. I had completed my 3rd day in the office when a new girl, Anya came in to assist.

I was going about my usual duties when she interrupted me and asked what would happen if we flipped a switch on the PA system. I was baffled, as I looked at her with disbelief. I told her straight away that we were not allowed to touch the PA system. THAT WAS THE #1 RULE!

"Awe come on!" she encouraged.

"We can't! We will get in trouble!" I retorted.

"I just want to flip one switch." She continued, "How about this one that says Girls Bathroom?"

I couldn't believe she wouldn't leave it alone. "You are no fun!" she pouted at me. "I am fun! I just don't want to get in trouble." I defended.

The moment was tense, and I turned back towards the counter to relieve some of the pressure when I heard a click... I spun around so fast that it seemed like slow motion. Anya had a menacing grin on her face as she went directly for the speaker and said, "Get out of the bathroom!"

I yelled at Anya, "NOOOOOOO!"

Then we heard my voice echo down the hall from the girl's bathroom.

I stopped breathing and looked at Anya as her eyes were as wide as mine. What did we just do? We sat frozen for a second as we waited. In the distance, we could hear heavy footsteps coming quickly down the hall. Anya quickly flipped the switch back and we pretended to be busy. Mrs. Bell, the fifth-grade teacher rounded the corner with her intimidating stature and presentation.

She demanded, "Who did it? Who touched the PA System?"

I looked at Anya and she immediately denied anything had happened. Mrs. Bell was no fool and she wasn't taking any bullshit. So, she grabbed both of us by the arms and sent us straight away to our classroom and revoked all our cafeteria and office privileges for the remainder of the year. I never spoke to Anya again after that day. I didn't like her.

Because I had been a victim of circumstance in the office, I was once again placed in detention. Ugh…only this time, I had to write 100 sentences before I could go to lunch that said, "I will not disobey the office #1 rule." I had to do this every day for the entire week.

On Friday, I was in a hurry to finish my sentences because I needed to be out on the playground for an epic game of hopscotch.

I hurried to the cafeteria, grabbed my tray and rushed over to the table to scarf down the pigs-in-a-blanket. This was one of my favorite meals! I got the first one down and began on the second one, when I bit off more than I could swallow.

In my haste, I swallowed a piece of the pig-in-a-blanket that got lodged in my throat. I realized I couldn't breathe. I looked around frightened as I watched the last kid run out of the cafeteria towards the playground.

I was all alone…choking.

I tried to get someone's attention by throwing my plate to the floor, but no one was coming to see what happened. I began to panic, as I realized I was going to die of suffocation, unless I did something and quick.

I remembered watching a reel about the Heimlich Maneuver and began pushing in my stomach with my fist as hard as I could push. It wasn't working, so I had to get creative. I slammed my chest and stomach on the edge of the table. I felt something move in my throat, so I slammed myself again as hard as I could muster.

One more time...SLAM!!!

This time, I hit the table so hard it felt like I broke a rib... IT WORKED! I was able to dislodge the sausage and bread out of my throat.

Those next few breaths were the sweetest breaths I had ever taken. I composed myself and wiped the tears from my eyes. My throat, stomach and chest hurt from the abuse it had just sustained, but I was alive. I walked slowly outside, just in time to hear the bell ring for us to return to class.

No one saw my suffering, no one saw my heroic act. I walked away a different person that afternoon.

Death had me by the throat and I defeated it...all by myself.

WOMAN CHILD

SUMMER ROLLED AROUND AND CARL SURPRISED US by taking Will and I to spend time with Kathleen. They had come to an agreement on visitations and I was so ready to see her.

We had been on our visit with Momma for about a week, when Will was out in the backyard playing. I yelled at him, asking if he wanted play ball with me. He was all too willing to play.

Kick ball was one of our favorite things to do. I just hated that he wasn't particularly good at it. Will would often kick the ball out to the side, instead of straight.

In an attempt to help his skills, I kicked the ball straight and he caught it. Will was getting better at something at least. He squared up and kicked the ball back to me. The ball came directly at me!

"YES!! That was good!"

"Now do it again!" I said encouraging him.

I kicked the ball back to him and he caught it again.

"Two for Two! You are on a roll!"

I yelled across the yard at him. He squared up again and kicked the ball hard. This time it came directly at my stomach and hit hard. I caught it in amazement. I was so proud of him.

"One more time. Let's see you do it again."

This time, when he caught the ball, he paused with a look of fear in his eyes. I looked at him in bewilderment and asked, "What's wrong?"

He began screaming, "I'm sorry! I'm sorry! Please don't die!"

I was confused. I didn't understand why he would say that to me. Then I looked down to follow his frightened gaze. Blood… I saw blood running down my leg. I immediately became woozy from the sight. I bent down to find the source of the blood. It was all over the middle of shorts, between my legs.

Will took off running to get Momma. I became hysterical with the sight of him running away. What was happening? Was I dying? Oh NOOOO, my favorite white shorts are ruined. I wondered if I was going to die in them!?! I fell to the ground devastated and curled into a fetal position.

Momma and Grandma ran up and began checking me with haste. After a few frantic moments, I heard a laugh of relief.

Momma eased, "There is nothing to worry about baby."

"You are going to live."

I was befuddled. How was I going to live if I was bleeding bad enough that it was running down my leg?

Grandma added, "Looks like our baby girl is turning into a young woman."

What?? What did this mean? I was confused.

Momma told Grandma she wasn't expecting to have this conversation so soon. She didn't realize I was already this far along in the process of growing up. I was still confused.

How does bleeding have anything to do with growing up?

Had everyone lost their mind??

What was happening???

Momma gathered me up and carried me inside the house. She took me to the bathroom while Grandma eased Will's mind. We went into the bathroom; Momma began explaining what was happening to me.

I was becoming a young woman.

I had started my menstrual cycle and the changes I was going through would accelerate, until I fully became an adult.

I breathed a sigh of relief… Thank God… I wasn't going to die. I wasn't exactly thrilled about this happening every month for the remainder of my adulthood, though!

It was gross!

Momma laughed and assured me I would get used to it.

Our time with Momma came to a quick end and she had to return us back to New Mexico. We met with Carl at the Ranch House and had lunch together. Carl informed us, while we were gone, that he had moved from our home on Avenue M, out to a place in the country.

I was not happy about the move, even though I had no say in the matter.

We did not go directly to the new place, after Momma left to return to Texas, Carl took us to stay with Bud and Freda for a little while. He said work was keeping him busy and he needed some more time to get the new house settled for us to come home.

I was looking forward to seeing Freda. It had been a little while since we got to visit, and I had so much to tell her. I wanted to see Freda most of all. I was getting older and now I could show her my skills in putting on makeup and doing my hair. I missed our twin friends too. I figured they probably had grown up so much that I wouldn't recognize them.

When we pulled down the drive, I saw the twins bust out of their house to run and meet us. This was exciting and the reunion was a pleasant one. We spent the whole day catching up on all the happenings since we had last visited.

As the evening rolled in, Bud suggested we play Simon Says as he sat out on the porch and, of course, everyone was willing. After a good thirty minutes passed, a cramp entered my lower abdomen and I had to leave the game suddenly. I went inside, saying I needed to use the bathroom.

I found Freda in the kitchen and nervously asked her if she had any feminine napkins. She looked at me with bewilderment before it clicked as to why I needed that from her. She bent her head down and in disbelief questioned, "You have begun your menstruations already?"

I shook my head in a yes motion and she quickly whisked me back to her bathroom.

She was beside herself.

She looked at me and said, "Oh honey, you are so young to be having your period already."

I asked her how old I was supposed to be, before having a period. She didn't know the answer, so we both agreed that maybe I wasn't too young after all.

I went back outside after cleaning myself, but the twins had already been called to go home.

The following morning, I had to ask Freda for another feminine pad. Bud overheard our conversation, even though I was attempting to be discrete.

When I finished in the bathroom, I went to the kitchen table to drink up the orange juice that Freda had poured for me. Bud looked up over the newspaper and stated, "So you are beginning to become a young woman."

I looked surprised at Freda and she shushed Bud and told him that those were personal matters not to be discussed at the breakfast table.

I was embarrassed.

Freda sensed my shame and reassured me it was nothing to be ashamed of and all woman must go through it. I finished the last drink of my juice, then rinsed my glass to go on about my business.

Will and I went outside to play, as soon as Freda left for work. We were waiting for the twins to wake up and come join us. We decided while we waited, we would work on our Fort and get it ready for company. We collected rocks and wood planks to build a table and seat spaces.

The twins arrived and began helping us work on the Fort. We were busy bringing the items to the Fort, when I heard my name.

Bud called out to me to return inside to help him with something. I obeyed his request and returned to the trailer.

Once inside he said, "I want to play a special game with you."

"It will be our game and we can't tell anyone about it."

I was curious and said yes, with a shrug. He took me back to his room where he closed the door and locked it.

He began grooming me. "Now, that you have started having a period, it's time that you make the next step to become a real woman."

He turned to me and assured, "It's my privilege as your Grandfather to help you to the next step."

He continued, "You are going to have to trust me." He crouched and looked me in the eyes with his hands on my shoulders and asked, "You do trust me, don't you?"

I felt nervous but replied timidly, "yes."

He made me swear to keep it our secret, with a threat that if anyone found out I would get in a lot of trouble. He knew what he was doing. He had done this before... He had all the manipulations down to a science. I was at his mercy, with nowhere to run.

To employ my submission, he told me about Anne. He had to assist her into woman hood too. So, since he helped her, he had to help me. How could I fight him now? He told me to lay back on the bed and relax. I did as I was told.

Bud pulled my shorts and panties off and spread my legs out as he ran his fingers along my legs up to my middle. I was looking at the ceiling just wanting it to stop. I could hear his breath become jittery. I swallowed and closed my eyes as he continued to rub his finger between my lips.

"Mandy, look at me." He demanded. I hesitantly opened my eyes, then looked at him; he had his member out and in his other hand, stroking it.

It was shocking to see; it was bigger than Lances'. It looked like a mushroom. I looked away towards the window quickly. My reaction made Bud nervous and he quickly made me look at him.

"You look at me. DO NOT LOOK AWAY!"

Bud wanted me to see him. He wanted that control. He began rubbing his member between my legs. He would ask me questions that I didn't want to answer. He continued to rub with more pressure. The actions were causing him to breathe rapidly and he started shaking.

The pressure started to hurt. I recoiled in pain. He grabbed me and told me to relax. I told him it was hurting me. He became frustrated and stopped. He sat me up on the bed and said we will try again later, but he needed me to do something for him, since it was my fault that he was in pain too.

Bud made me open my mouth and he tried to stick his member in it. He couldn't, my mouth was too small. He became more frustrated and told me to turn over on my stomach. He laid on top of me and began humping between my cheeks. The next few moments didn't last long. I heard a familiar grown and then felt a warm sensation on my skin.

"Lay still. Do not move." He commanded.

I felt a rag rake across my skin and then he told me to put my clothes back on.

I got up and just stood there in his presence, not knowing what to say or do. He looked at me and made me swear not to tell anyone again, with a threat of trouble and punishment. He then told me that if anyone found out, he would have to kill them, because it was a secret no one needed to know. Once he was sure I wasn't going to tell anyone, he sent me outside to the yard.

Instead of going to play with Will and the twins I just went and hid under Ethel's porch. I could still feel a stinging burning pain between my legs that made my cramps worse. I cried. I was trying to process what had just happened. I now had a bigger secret. I now shared a common situation with my birth mother, Anne. I now have a beginning of understanding her.

> (I must admit writing the previous section has taken me nearly a week. Working through the emotions and realizations of what happened that day have been taxing and I almost pulled away from writing the book entirely. The truth can be unbearable to accept. These memories disturb me and reawaken emotions long forgotten, even after all these years. I had to take a week away from writing to regain my emotional composure to complete this section of my life. I digress...)

Freda returned home and called us into dinner. Bud told her to let us eat in the living room on the TV trays. This was his treat. His disposition was playful. He was being tender and nice to me. I didn't know how to feel about it. He was keeping me occupied. (Thinking about it now, it was his security to keep me occupied.).

Freda asked me if I wanted to learn how to drive. I hesitated at first, but I realized, I had grown a little and I didn't have to sit in her lap. She didn't scare me like that, I trusted her. I said, "Sure..."

We walked outside and Freda sat me in the front seat of her Ford

Fairlane. Yep, I had grown. I could sit at the edge of the seat and reach the pedals now. She instructed me on what I needed to do, then she went around and sat in the passengers' side.

Believe it or not, I was a natural. I had paid attention when I was riding in the cars to see what the adults were doing, so I could do it when the time came. It helped that it wasn't too long ago that Bud had allowed me to drive from Monahans back to Hobbs.

We drove up and down the dirt road, until I felt comfortable enough to get out on the highway. Freda had a lot of belief in my abilities. This made me feel empowered and confident. I was very fond of Freda and I loved her for her patience with me.

That Saturday, Bud had gone to town early. Freda was at work for her first shift, so Ethel was in the living room listening to the radio and crocheting when I got out of bed. She directed me to the cupboard in the kitchen to find some cereal for Will and myself.

Freda kept the cereal cabinet full of the best cereals. The shelf was lined with a variety of flavored choices such as Fruity Pebbles, Lucky Charms, Boo Berry, Count Chocula, and Cookie Crisp. I made a choice after several minutes and poured us both a bowl of Cookie Crisp.

I heard the engine of the Chevy roaring, as Bud drove up the gravel drive to the Trailer, just as we finished our cereal. Will was the first out the front door, as I was cleaning up our dishes from breakfast. I could hear excitement in Will's voice, as I approached the front door. Motor scooters…Bud had bought us motor scooters.

To say I wasn't thrilled would be a lie. I forgot about all my shame for a moment and was caught up in getting to ride a scooter. Bud helped me up on the scooter and he sat on the back of me, as he taught me how to drive the machine.

I felt uncomfortable with him behind me, but I had no choice if I wanted to ride the scooter. We rode the scooter up and down the gravel road from one end of the property to the other. It was an exhilarating experience to ride that motor scooter.

After many attempts, I finally conquered the skill of driving the scooter myself. I was proud and riding the scooter gave me a sense of freedom, not to mention I felt like a badass.

The twins came over and I took turns giving them rides for the remainder of the afternoon.

Another surprising morning came, as I woke to the sound of horses neighing. I looked out the window and there they were. Bud had bought horses. Two mares and one was pregnant.

The mares were mother and daughter. Britches and Biddy were their names. A new responsibility, I came to love. We all gathered down at the corral to watch as Bud and his brother, Uncle Pete, released the mares out into the field of the corral.

"Do you like what I got for you, Mandy?" Bud asked with a smile.

I could tell he was proud; he was showing off in front of his brother.

"Can I ride on one?" I asked instead of answering his question.

"In a few days."

Bud responded while adding, "The mares have to get used to the new home and they have to get used to being around you."

No problem, I would spend every waking moment down at the corral. Time at the corral was my escape. After a week or so, Bud brought home a saddle. Finally! I had my chance to ride Britches. Biddy was not as willing to let people ride her. She needed to be broke, but she was pregnant, so it would be awhile before anyone could ride her.

Bud helped me up on Britches and walked along side, while I rode her. Eventually, Bud trusted her enough to let me ride alone. I was becoming skilled at riding Britches. I was learning how to maneuver her where I wanted her to go. Bud would sit at the gate and watch me. I kept thinking to myself, one day, I am going to get on Britches and ride through that gate and off into the sunset. No one would ever find us.

I thought of doing that often.

Biddy gave birth to a mare; we named her April. She had one blue eye and one brown eye. She was so beautiful! Her eyes reminded me of a boy with different colored eyes that I had met briefly in Monahans. It was fascinating to watch April get up and move around. Everyone in the country block came to welcome April into the world.

The evening of April's birth was filled with live music and celebration. Uncle Pete and a few of Bud's friends came to visit. We gathered around the living room, sitting at the adult's feet, while Bud and his company played guitars and sang country songs.

The twins were staying the night, so when we had enough music and our bellies were filled with food, we decided to retire to the bedrooms and call it a day. I was exhausted from all the activities and fell asleep as soon as my head touched the pillow.

Waking up the next morning refreshed and ready to start the day, I woke Mickey and we headed to the kitchen for a bite to eat. The weather was very windy, so Bud told us we needed to find something to do inside, until the wind died down.

We went back to the room and got an idea to jump on the bed. We were having a lot of fun until we heard, "Stop jumping on the bed!" coming from the front room. We fell to the bed, then began giggling uncontrollably, because we got caught.

We meandered from my room, to Will's room, to see what they were doing.

They were playing with some toy soldiers and quickly let us know, "NO GIRLS ALLOWED!"

Quickly I responded, "Ugh, FINE!"

Mickey and I made our way back into the living room when I discovered the photo albums nestled in the shelf on the bar between the living room and kitchen. We pulled them out to gaze through the pages of Polaroids.

After lingering over the memories for several minutes, we had continued to prowl through the shelves, before we found a deck of cards. A card game was a welcomed distraction.

I sat on the floor in the living room slumped between the couch and the coffee table. Mickey sat opposite of me, as we played Go Fish. Will and Mikey came to join in the game, once they heard the fun we were having.

I wanted to tell them, "NO BOYS! GIRLS ONLY!" But I held my tongue.

Bud came to watch the game and he sat on the couch next to me. I felt an immediate uneasiness. I did not want anyone to know what he had done to me. My nerves made me react with an itch on my neck. Like a nervous twitch.

Bud noticed me itching my neck and he placed his hand on my neck and began rubbing it. This did not help my nerves. I began looking at everyone to make sure they did not notice what was going on.

They were oblivious.

Bud eased in closer and was engaging in the game to keep the other children distracted, as he slipped his hand under my shirt around to my chest and began rubbing on my titties. The coffee table was just tall enough to conceal his violation. He whispered in my ear; this will help them grow.

The phone rang.

Thank goodness! Bud got up and went to answer the phone. This gave me so much relief.

I decided I was done playing the game and I wanted to go outside. Everyone was happy to join. We cleaned up the game and began heading outside. Bud called out and told me to stay, as he sent everyone else out the door.

"Mandy, can you go to my bathroom and get a brush?" he asked.

I obediently went to get the brush. As I turned around and entered the bedroom from the bathroom, Bud came through the hall entry and closed the door behind him.

I seized up with fear for what was coming next.

I had hoped that the first time was the last time. That was just my hopeful ignorance. Bud was more aggressive this time. He walked directly up to me and pulled my shorts down. He told me to lay on the bed. I refused and he physically made me lay down on the bed.

This time he placed his mouth on my privates and began kissing on me. I felt disgusted and began to cry. My reaction angered Bud. He told me to hush and relax. He raised up and began rubbing his member on my privates. I closed my eyes. He insisted I look at him.

Once again, he began to press in on me. I tried to move away; he held my hips and told me to relax. I began fighting to get away as the pain increased. He was becoming frustrated and held me harder as he pushed harder. I cried out and he placed his hand over my mouth hard to quiet me.

A loud bang on the outside of the house made him stop. He pulled away from me to check the source of the sound. The kids were playing ball by his room. He yelled out the window for them to go further away from the house. The distraction made him nervous.

While he was distracted, I got up and quickly began putting my shorts back on to myself. He turned and asked what I was doing.

"I want to go play." I responded.

"We are not finished here."

"We have to finish what was started." He insisted.

In rebellion I retorted, "I don't want to do this anymore!"

"It hurts and I don't like it."

Once again, he forced me onto the bed on my stomach.

"You will do what I tell you to do or you will be sorry." He continued.

"I will hurt everyone you love!"

"Do you want that?"

Bud pulled my shorts down again and pressed his member between my butt cheeks and began stroking back and forth as his bated hot breath hit my neck. He relieved himself on my back and got up haphazardly.

"Next time we will get the job done." He assured me.

"You just need to relax and let me inside you." He said as he cleaned me up.

I closed my eyes and wished I could be somewhere, anywhere, but on his bed.

I left his room defeated. This time the pain was unbearable. I went back to my room, closed the door and went to bed, crying myself to sleep.

I woke up to Freda's voice and gentle nudge.

"How are you feeling, honey?" she asked.

"Your Grandpa told me you had a headache."

"Do you need anything?" She inquired gently.

I was in pain, but not in my head. Bud had lied to Freda to cover his act.

Bud was good at being duplicitous. Engaging and playful in the company of others. Behind closed doors he was a deviant slug. His arrogance knew no bounds as that night, he made me sleep with them in his room. I did not want to, but Freda encouraged it. I crawled in the bed on the outside of Freda, but Bud was not having it.

He made me get in the middle of the bed so that I would be between them.

I could not relax. I could not sleep. I clung to Freda and tried to keep some distance between Bud and myself. Freda fell asleep fast. I thought Bud was asleep, so I began to relax and drift away. I was awoken by a hand pulling on my hand. Bud had pulled my hand over and placed it on his member. He began pumping himself in my tiny hand.

I could not believe what was happening. I was frightened that Freda would catch us and hate me. A few moments passed and he finally got up and went to the bathroom. I took the opportunity and left the room quickly. This time, I went and got in bed with Will.

Morning came, after a long tortuous night. I hesitantly made my way to the kitchen. Freda asked me why I left her bed and I looked at Bud. He met my eyes with a threatening gaze. I felt tension, as I reluctantly told her that the room was too hot, and that I couldn't sleep. She understood and resumed reading the paper and drinking her coffee.

Freda reminded Bud that his youngest daughter, Brenna, would be visiting later in the day. I had met her briefly as a child, but had no real recollection of the moment. I did know who Freda was talking about. I was interested in seeing her, after all she was my Aunt Brenna and the youngest of Anne's siblings.

> (It is not easy to reflect on this memory. It has physically made me ill and I had to run to the bathroom and vomit. After getting out a good cry, I pulled myself together to move through this moment.
>
> I realized, I never healed from what Bud had done to me. He knew what he was doing, he knew how to disguise his sin by taking me, while I was having my menses, in order to cover his

violation.

No one would ever question the blood now. I never accepted what he had done to me. He didn't just molest me... He raped me. I just pushed it back and covered it up and tried to forget it. That was how I dealt with it. Reflection has made me realize how it severely affected my level of intimacy in all my relationships.

It is a very curious thing the behavior of compartmentalizing traumas. The trauma becomes hidden by pushing it away, deep in the recesses of one's mind, but the pain lingers and seeps through various aspects of a life, as it is lived.

For me, the rape and molestation are a cut that never healed; a lie I was forced to live at a very tender age. It was a lie that I have been burdened with my entire life. There is no retribution, no salvation, and no justice that can be obtained.

I was robbed of something I will never get back...my innocence...my virtue. Those events are a stain that will never be lifted as it is seared into my personality and character.

I can't talk to anyone without judgement. Even those afflicted with the same traumas do not have the capacity to understand, or help, because they too are damaged.

I have carried it as a cancer that slowly eats its way through my life, affecting every emotion I have ever felt.)

GETTING SMOKED

Aunt Brenna's arrival was surreal. She brought her two children with her for the visit. She had a boy, Salomon and a girl, Ava. The girl, Ava, was close to my age and we bonded almost immediately.

It was a much-needed distraction from the previous days' events.

As the visit lingered, Ava and I wanted to spend more time together. We came up with the great idea for her to stay the night with me. Freda agreed and told us we could even stay out in the Camper for the over-nighter. We were thrilled! We immediately ran out to make the Camper our new abode for the evening.

Aunt Brenna had a gentleman call on her and she was in a hurry to go meet with him. Ava and I had the Camper straightened out and the beds made. We sat and talked for hours about everything…almost everything.

I didn't tell her that I was experiencing pain between my legs. I would never tell her. I would never tell her what had happened to me, just the day before, even though she was easy to talk to and I wanted to tell her everything. I had to protect her. If she knew the truth, it would put her in jeopardy.

I couldn't do that to her.

Ava and I carried on in conversation until the wee hours of the morning.

I am not sure what possessed us, but we started prowling around the camper to see what we could find. She found a box of cigarettes. It must have been Freda's forgotten box. It had three matches inside a match fold. We looked at each other and giggled thinking how lucky we were to find the matches.

We hesitated, looked at each other, than decided we would smoke it!

First, we were clever, or so we thought. Quickly we opened all the windows. We didn't want the smell of smoke filling the camper.

We thought we were adults…haha!

We finally lit the cigarette after wasting two of the matches by lack of experience. I took the first puff…

"Ugh! It was horrible!!

"Why do people do this?" I asked.

She laughed and said, "Let me try!"

Ava agreed with my summation, it tasted horrible and it was a terrible idea.

We tried our best to clear out the smoke from the windows and quickly hid our evidence in an old coffee can. Just as I noticed a car pulling up the drive.

"Who is that at this hour?" I asked.

My cousin squealed, "It's my mom!"

"OH dang, oh dang, oh dang!!" I whispered.

"Act like we're asleep!" she whispered back.

We jumped in bed and covered our heads.

> (I should regret this memory, but I don't. I did regret it at the time… I realize now it was the first time I had done something

I wasn't supposed to do, but the decision was mine. It was my decision to do something bad, not a decision that was forced or a control placed over me.)

Wouldn't you know it, Aunt Brenna got out of the car and walked straight to the Camper.

Her timing could not have been better. BUSTED!!

As soon as Aunt Brenna opened the door, she could smell the smoke. We were not as clever as we thought we were. My cousin tried to lie and tell her mom that the camper already smelled like smoke, but that didn't work.

"Come on, you are going home." Aunt Brenna told my cousin.

"I knew I couldn't trust leaving you here."

I got up and tried to change Aunt Brenna's mind.

Aunt Brenna would not hear me.

I know she saw me as a bad influence.

DEAD MAN'S CURVE

UNEXPECTEDLY, CARL WAS IN THE KITCHEN THE MORNING following Ava's departure. He had returned to get us. Bud was not happy about it and he was speaking strongly to Carl. Bud's reaction did not persuade Carl to leave us there. We were sent outside, while the men continued talking.

Will asked, "What is going on?"

"Daddy is here to take us home." I told him.

Will didn't want to go home. He enjoyed living at Bud and Freda's. For him, life at our grandparents' home was comfortable and somewhat normal. He had quickly grown accustomed to their daily routines and felt at home. He was protected from the consternation I had endured.

Bud wasn't interested in little boys.

We were startled by a loud commotion. Bud and Carl had elevated their conversation and Carl began packing our things.

"Get in the car!" He yelled out the door to us.

I grabbed Will by the hand, but he fought me wanting to stay. "Come on, brother!"

"We have to go now." I insisted.

Will wouldn't stop fighting me, so I had to pick him up and carry him to the car.

Carl came out the door with Bud following suit. Bud was yelling profanities at Carl and telling him he better not ever bring us back!

Bud never wanted to see our faces again. He threatened Carl with calling the cops. Bud told Carl not to ever ask for his help again. Freda ran to the car and gave us both hugs and kisses and told us how much she loved us. Tears were streaming down her face. Will was crying too.

Was I supposed to cry? I didn't know. I wasn't sad to leave... I was READY to leaven

Carl got in the car and threw his middle finger out the window into the air as high as he could reach, as we drove down the dirt road for the last time. As we drove out the gate and made a right turn, I looked back at the property and I realized I was leaving Britches, Biddy and April behind.

I asked Carl if we could go back and get my horses. He told me no, because we had nowhere to keep them or the means to take care of them. Carl encouraged me to forget all about them.

That broke my heart and then I began to cry.

The drive was long and quiet. We arrived in the country just past a curve that was affectionately and rightly dubbed "Dead Man's Curve." Carl had rented a country home out in the middle of a cacti field.

We finally got to see the house he had told us about when we returned from Texas. There was one house maybe a block away on the same property. This would be our new home for the next couple of months.

After we got settled, Carl noticed that I seemed uncomfortable as I would adjust myself frequently and go to the bathroom often. Bud had given me a yeast infection. Carl stopped me and asked me what was wrong; I honestly told him that I hurt. He asked me to describe it, so I told him how it felt.

He took me to the doctor after making a call. The doctor gave him a prescription and nothing else was said. When we returned home. Carl made me lay on the couch and he placed the medicine on my privates.

I was filled with dread at first, but he put it on me and nothing more. This made me feel comfortable and the pain and itching began to subside.

Daily routines returned to the mundane. Carl would go to work, and I would be left in charge of caring for Will. Alone again… I began to embrace moments when adults were not around. Will and I would often find our way out into the field chasing lizards, while Carl would be at work.

When Carl would return home, we would eat dinner and he would wash some laundry and throw it on the bed for me to fold. Will wasn't any help. He would throw the laundry around the room and jump on the bed. SO FRUSTRATING!!

I would get a few clothes folded and Will would run through the pile and knock everything down. GRRRR!! This would incite my rage and I would tackle him down and threaten him. He would calm down for a bit. Just long enough to allow me to make some headway before annihilating everything again. I would run into the living room and tell on him. Carl would yell, but nothing would be accomplished.

Carl whooped me a few times for not getting the laundry completed, but I guess he realized it was really too much for me to do on my own and he just left the clothes on the bed for us to dig through when we wanted something.

Carl was still up to his drinking and leaving. I was used to it and didn't pay any mind to it. I was tall enough now to cook on the stove, so I was capable to take care of myself and Will, as long as there was food available. We mostly lived on Ramen noodles or spotted ham and cheese sandwiches.

An old fear worked its way into my life again. Carl came home and he had been drinking.

"Mandy Shawn, get in here." Carl called out to me.

I had been coloring with Will, in our room. I ran into the living room to see what he wanted, and he told me to get on the couch.

I asked him, "What for?"

He asserted, "Don't ask me questions, do as I say!"

So, I did. He told me to pull my shorts off, so he could check me. I told him I was feeling better. I didn't need to be checked. He wasn't listening and made me pull my shorts off of myself. Will ran into the living room and Carl scolded him and sent him back to the room.

As I laid on the couch, Carl began rubbing the medicine on my privates, but he didn't stop. He looked at me and asked me if it hurt when he did this, or if he did that, as he continued to pretend to put on the medicine. I was uncomfortable and distressed that he was doing this to me. I thought that I was away from it; I thought I had left that all behind.

The next couple of nights followed suit. Carl came home drunk, fondled me for a disproportionately long time, than sent me on my way. I was grateful he did not penetrate me. Then he didn't come home for two days.

Instead, his middle brother, Don, showed up and stayed with us.

When Carl finally returned, he had my baby brother, Phil. I hadn't seen him since going to Momma's house and I was glad to see him again. The next thing I knew we are on the move again.

I welcomed the change, since we would be moving into town this time.

INNOCENT REGRET

WE HAD MOVED INTO A NEW HOME ON AVENUE K IN LOVINGTON and we had new neighbors and new babysitters. When I think of it now, it is funny that Carl began using babysitters for us at that stage in life, as he had left us alone very often as toddlers.

Will had a crush on a girl across the street, Michelle. She and I had become friends, because Carl would ask her sister to watch us from time to time. She was fun and spirited. I thought we would be friends for the rest of our lives. But, life has a way of separating people.

We shared clothes and played games together outside. Michelle had a pair of yoyo heels that she gave me. I felt so pretty when I put them on, because they made me tall. She would paint my fingernails and toenails "to accentuate my beauty".

We watched the movie "GREASE" and decided we wanted to be part of the "Pink Ladies" club. We dug through our closets looking for old jackets. When we found the jackets we needed, we took painstaking detail in making them perfect for the club. I venture to say that we took all day drawing and sewing on those jackets. It was worth it.

We wore those jackets proudly, as we walked up and down the block. I fantasized about growing up to be Olivia Newton John. I bought her LP record "PHYSICAL" with some money I had earned. I placed it on my record player, and I would dance around the house, pretending to be her when I was alone.

Fun times…

Carl had been going through women like water pouring down a sink. He seemed to have a different woman come to the house almost every day. On days he was alone, he would be at home sober, so we would sit in the living room and watch television shows with him.

A new television invention had come out called 3D Television. We were excited to try it out. First, we had to purchase the special 3D glasses that had one blue lens and one red lens, in order to watch the show.

The 3D show would play on Friday nights and we would gather around to watch it. Thank goodness that craze didn't last long. I don't think it was good for our eyes. I enjoyed watching Friday Night Tracks, Soul Train and Saturday morning cartoons. That was about all the T.V. I needed. Most of the time, I preferred to be outside with the neighbors.

One evening in December, a few days before my 11th birthday, Carl went out and left me to watch Will and Phil. I asked him if we could sleep in his bed since it was cold in the house. I didn't expect him to come home till the following morning.

Carl wasn't bringing the women home anymore. I think he would just stay the night with them instead. He said it would be okay, so that night Will and I slept in his warm room.

I don't know what I was thinking…

I groggily woke up to Carl bumping around in the dark. I knew it was him, because I could smell the liquor. It was strong, like he had taken a shower in whisky. After turning on his 15" T.V. that was propped on a table, at the end of the bed, he picked up my brothers and took them into the living room.

I fell back into a deep sleep. I woke up to a pissy smell and a penis rubbing on my lips. Carl had my head in his grip and stuck his finger in my mouth and made me open it, so he could stick himself in my mouth. I tried to fight it, but he was forceful.

Once he had his member in my mouth, he tried to push it in and out but once again, my mouth was too small, and my teeth raked against his skin. I gagged and started crying. He stopped and got up. He looked back at me, but didn't say anything. I just continued to cry.

Carl left that night and I didn't see him again for several days.

FIRE IN OUR MIDST

MY 11TH BIRTHDAY HAD COME AND GONE WITH NO CELEBRATION, no cake, nothing...

Christmas morning arrived and we woke up to a few presents under the tree. Carl had an announcement that we would be moving again. He had finally found a home that he took out a loan to buy. The new home was located on Avenue N, just a few blocks away.

Christmas break had concluded; school was back in session. I went to school that morning and Carl came to pick us up from school that afternoon. While we were at school, he had moved our things to the new house. We settled in quickly. We were getting good at change.

I had the furthest back room with all my stuffed animals set up nicely. By this time, Carl had been able to take custody of my youngest brother from Momma. Both of my brothers shared the middle room. After a couple months, Carl made us exchange rooms and I took the smaller room, allowing the boys to have my larger room.

Carl would sleep in the living room on the couch. He had a room of his own, but he never used it. This was now the normal routine for him while he was home. He had stopped drinking.

Carl told me one afternoon that he would never drink again. It was his promise to me. I think it was his way to make amends for what he had done. We never spoke about it. We just carried on as though nothing had ever happened. Such a heavy burden of secrets I had to keep. He had no idea that he wasn't the only one.

I lived closer to another girl, Gracie. She attended the same class with me, so we began walking to school and home together every day. I looked forward to meeting with her in the mornings for our walk, because her mom would make fresh tortillas and refried beans with scrambled eggs for us to eat before school. I can still taste her cooking when I think about it.

Time seemed to carry on without a hitch and life was calm for a season. Carl bought us a VCR so we could watch rented movies. ET the Extraterrestrial was one of our preferred videos to watch when nothing was on the television. We finally got a microwave, which made my life so much easier until Will stuck a fork in it and ruined it.

Home to school and do it all over again was our routine. Carl wasn't working on Rigs anymore. He had taken up a job driving trucks. This would keep him gone for days on end.

To make ends meet, while he was gone, I would collect all the change that we would find in the couch that had fallen out of Carl's pockets when he slept. I would use the change at the local Allsups to by candy, or necessities when he was out on the road. Sometimes, I had a good little chunk of change to spend and my brothers loved Allsups day!

Shortly after arriving to school one morning, I got called over the PA system to go to the office. There was talk of smoke in the sky, in a nearby neighborhood, and the teachers were genuinely concerned.

My 5th grade teacher, Ms. Bell asked me if I had noticed the smoke on the way to school. I told her I hadn't noticed anything, and I didn't think twice about it. I sat there as other children were questioned. Then a call came through on the telephone and the other children were dismissed.

Ms. Bell held me behind and told me that it was my dad on the phone; he would be there shortly to pick me up. This was unsettling, as Gracie would be waiting for me to walk her home after school. Ms. Bell assured me that I would not need to worry about Gracie. I was curious why my dad was coming to get me.

"Did I do something wrong?" I asked inquisitively.

"No, you haven't done anything wrong." Ms. Bell assured me.

"Mandy, it was your home that was on fire."

"The smoke came from your home." She informed me as she kneeled to my height, grasping my shoulders.

I reacted, "There is no way it was my home."

"I just left it, and everything was okay."

I looked up at her and she consoled me. "

"What about my baby brother?!??" I screamed, as I realized he had been left there with Carl, asleep on the couch. I panicked with despair, as reality had set in. Ms. Bell was attempting to settle me, as Carl rounded the door. He fell to his knees and grabbed me tightly. I stood there in shock, looking around the room and feeling dizzy.

"Where is Phil, Phil??!?" I asked loudly.

Carl looked up and told me he was safe in the car with a friend. His response eased my mind, but now I realized we had nowhere to live. I thought about all my stuffed animals, as we drove away from school. It broke my heart to think they suffered in the fire.

My stuffed animals were as real to me as my brothers. One stuffed yellow bear, Tinkle Bear, was the most important to me. She had been with me and traveled everywhere I went, since the day I was born. She was a yellow snuggle teddy with bells in her ears. I feared for her most of all. Carl told me after the smoke settled and the remains dried out from the water, we could go back and look for her.

I asked Carl how the fire started, and he relived the moment in detail. He was asleep on the couch. He woke up, because Phil was hitting on him while saying, "Fire Daddy."

At first, he thought our baby brother was just playing. Then the smell of smoke creeped into his nose. He looked up at the ceiling and noticed the smoke billowing across it. This sent Carl into a panic. He stood up and wrapped the sheet around his waist. He followed the smoke down the hall to my brother's room.

The door was closed.

Carl reached up to open the door, in order to investigate further. When the door cracked open, the force of the fire meeting with the oxygen from the hall caused it to slam open on him. The flames wrapped around Carl, singeing the hair on his head, face and chest.

The sheet caught fire and Carl was swift enough to get it off himself, as he sprinted towards the front to grab Phil. He admitted that opening the door had caused the fire to ignite uncontrollably.

Will had taught Phil how to strike an old lighter that Carl had left as a toy for us. We never thought anything about it. We would strike the lighter to watch the sparks fly. We found it mesmerizing in the darkness.

Unknowingly, Phil had gotten hold of a lighter that was full of fluid. He had crawled under one of the beds in his room and tried to burn a thread that was hanging from the underside.

He was more than successful in burning off the thread.

That single thread led to the loss of our home. Carl thought he would be able to come out on top because the house was insured. He thought we would be able to recover our losses. However, there were forces working outside of our interests.

The bank that the house was insured through filed bankruptcy a couple months after the fire. It took what Carl had left in his checking and what little he had saved in his savings, and closed up shop. (He was never able to recover what he had lost.)

By the time Carl had finished telling me about the house fire, we were pulling up to a farmhouse in the middle of nowhere. I asked, "Where are we?"

He replied, "We are at your Grandmother's new home."

My chest immediately became tight. I challenged, "Why are we here?"

Carl informed me without hesitation, "You will be staying here until I can find us another home."

In disbelief I said, "NO! NO! NO! This just cannot be true!"

"Can I just stay with Michelle?"

"I don't want to stay here."

Carl looked at me in annoyance, "You don't have a choice in this matter."

The dread poured over me as we walked up to the house. I was not looking forward to this reunion.

Walking inside I could feel the tension build in my chest. How would we be received? I knew Edith did not really want us there, she felt an obligation towards Carl. Just as I suspected, she was not happy. She made Carl promise that he would look for another home quickly. Carl pledged his promise and left us there.

Thankfully, this time he was true to his word. We only stayed there for a few days before he returned to get us.

EVA THE TRAMP

CARL HAD FOUND US A PLACE TO STAY OUT ON THE ARTESIA HIGHWAY, in a trailer park. The trailer park had two houses on the left side, on the way into the area. It was a quaint area and it was filled with other children our ages.

We made ourselves comfortable in a 3-bedroom trailer. (It was more like a 2-bedroom with a large middle closet)

I had the middle room; it was so small the twin mattress had to be placed on the floor and partially in the closet. I had just enough room to squeeze a tiny end table on the side to use as a prop for my personal items.

About the same time we moved into the trailer, I had picked up a cough that was getting worse by the day. At first, the cough was just an inconvenience. Carl bought some cough medicine to help alleviate the symptoms, but it did not help.

The cough persisted. I would hack until I passed out from lack of oxygen. Carl was at a loss and didn't have the money to take me to the doctor. If I moved, I coughed. If I ate, I coughed. If I breathed, I coughed. I was so incredibly miserable.

Nighttime was the worst part of suffering the aggressive cough. I would run myself a cold bath to sit in. That seemed to help and give me some relief.

My chest, throat and back were sore from the exhaustive coughing.

Carl had met a young red headed woman by the name of Tammy and she came to live with us in the trailer. The first night she stayed with us, I had a vicious coughing attack after going to bed for the evening. I hacked so much that it made me weak. I crawled out of my room into the hallway for some cool air and then I puked and passed out.

Tammy immediately realized that I was sick with the Whooping Cough and told Carl he had to take me to the doctor. It was a miracle that my brothers didn't get it too. Apparently, it is highly contagious.

After I recovered, I got to spend some time with Tammy. I liked her and I hoped that she would stick around for a while. Tammy was fun and active. She would dance with us in the living room to Van Halen, Darryl Hall and John Oats, Blue Oyster Cult and everything in between. Good times...but, just as suddenly as she had entered our lives, she left.

We woke up one morning and she was gone. I never heard from her again and we still don't know why she left.

Tammy was soon replaced by a much older lady by the name of Eva (should have been EVIL), that had two children. She seemed nice enough at first but that would all change soon. Eva had two children and they were abominable. Carl courted Eva for two months before they got married. They came into our home and took over everything!

When I first met Eva, she was a blue eyed, raven haired, willowy beauty. The morning after their nuptials, I decided I would be cordial and deliver them breakfast in bed. I was not prepared for what I was about to see. As I sat the tray down next to the bed, Eva turned over to face me. What I saw was startling.

She had no eyebrows or eyelashes, and a portion of her hair was missing.

"WHAT THE HELL?!??"

(A completely uncontrolled reaction to what I was looking at…)

My reaction set the dominoes in motion. Apparently, Carl had never seen this side of Eva either. He was just as shocked as I was, but he was more in control of his emotions. Carl quickly dismissed me from their presence. I was happy to oblige. I actually felt sorry for Carl. He had married that scary woman and now he was stuck with the consequence of his rash decision.

Eva's children were master manipulators and just horrible humans.

If they were even human at all…

Her daughter was spoiled and tattled all the time. She would take whatever she wanted and never got into trouble for anything. Her son was just as bad, if not worse! Despite their high thoughts of themselves, they were riddled with scabies.

That family brought those filthy bugs into our home and they penetrated everything we owned. We had to bomb the trailer and put lotion all over our bodies to get rid of them. I don't know which was worse, the whooping cough or the scabies!

The list of indignities that they brought into our home are too many to say. That would be a book by itself. To highlight their malicious behavior, one morning while getting ready for school, her son, David was in the kitchen stirring a pitcher of Kool-Aid. I rounded the corner into the hallway coming from my bedroom and saw him just as he spilled the pitcher of Kool-Aid all over his clothes and the ground.

I did not expect what happened next. David had run to tell Eva that I pushed the pitcher over on him! I was nowhere near him! I was at least 12ft away when it happened. Of course, Eva believed him over me.

That was expected.

An ass whooping came shortly after David lied on me and I was dubbed an evil child. Hmm, the "evil child" label was more fitting for her son, David. I did not trust that boy after that incident. To be frank, I couldn't believe someone would do something like that and live with knowing they had lied to get someone in trouble.

To this day, I am still shocked that people can be so devious.

Thank goodness, things between Eva and Carl began to spiral downward quickly. I must admit, Edith had something to do with it. In retrospect, I think Carl may have unleashed Edith on Eva, just to get rid of her. However, Eva didn't leave empty handed. She left with a brand-new Station Wagon; Carl had bought it for their wedding.

Oh well, c'est la vie! You will not hear any complaints from me!

I was glad to see them go!

Carl was able to get over Eva easily too. A month had not passed before we were moving into the second house on the left. Along with a new home, Carl had a new woman.

New woman, new house, new start on number…oh hell, I already lost count. Summer had arrived and things seemed to be looking up now. I was a little apprehensive when the new woman, Carolyn, stepped into our lives.

Can you blame me?

CUNNING CAROLYN

CAROLYN FIGURED ME OUT QUICKLY. She needed to get my approval, or so she thought. Little did she know, my thoughts didn't count for shit. I wasn't going to tell her that piece of information though. I enjoyed watching her figure me out.

We quickly realized that we both enjoyed art. She was a painter and decent enough in her craft. She also wore fake nails. I guess that wasn't too bad considering her hair, eyebrows and lashes were real. THANK GOD!!

Carolyn seemed to enjoy dragging me around with her everywhere she went. I didn't seem to mind tagging along either. One day, we decided to have lunch at the Ranch House. After seating ourselves, I noticed one of the waitresses was familiar. Then I realized, it was EVA! I pointed her out to Carolyn.

"Well, we are going to sit right here and eat our food and watch her feel uncomfortable." Carolyn giggled at her comment, as did I.

Half-way through our meal, I had to excuse myself from the table to use the ladies' room. What I did next was totally deliberate and completely out of character for me. As I was sitting on the toilet relieving myself, I read the scribbled writings on the wall and decided I was going to leave a little message behind too.

I built up the courage and grabbed a pen out of my purse. I wrote, "Eva S is a Tramp!" in BIG BOLD LETTERING. I walked out and met with Carolyn and we left without incident.

Two days had passed since my bold graffiti had been left on the wall. I had forgotten about it to be honest. Then a phone call came for me and Carolyn yelled out the door, "Mandy, phone call for you!"

I ran in with anticipation that it might be some good news from somewhere…truthfully, I didn't know what to expect. Who would be calling me? Low and behold it was Eva on the other end…

Holy shit! She knows…

"Mandy, I have to ask you, did you write Eva S is a Tramp on the bathroom wall at the Ranch House?" she asked adamantly.

I tried to deny even knowing about the graffiti, but I am a terrible liar. After a few minutes of hostile inquiry, Eva told me that another girl was about to get in trouble. But, she wanted to make sure, before they did anything to that other girl, that no one else was involved.

I finally admitted the truth, I done it. I couldn't allow another person to get in trouble for my actions. After all, I knew what that was like and it was not fair. After admitting the truth, I realized that Eva had just manipulated me.

There wasn't any other girl. IT WAS ALL A LIE!!

Then my admittance turned to anger, and I lashed out at Eva. I told her everything I hated about how she had treated me and my brothers. I told her to every degree how she had raised horrible corrupt children that were just like her.

I continued to tell her that I should have written more on the wall to warn other unsuspecting men. Then I hung the phone up and never heard from her again. GOOD RIDDANCE!!!

After hanging up the phone, I turned around and saw Carolyn was standing there listening.

"I can't condone the way you spoke to her, but I can't blame you either." She scolded.

"We will just keep this phone call to ourselves and if she tells your Dad, we will just say it never happened."

Wow, I didn't know what to think, but I was grateful she wasn't going to tell on me. In that moment, I did realize that people can manipulate for good and for evil.

Depending on the circumstance...

My moment was short lived, due to a crisis going on outside. Our landlord had been digging up the septic system for the Trailer Park. The excavation had left a wide deep crevasse down to the open septic tank. This opening had been there for a couple weeks, without any barriers.

My brothers were outside playing, when I went inside to take the call. I didn't think anything about leaving them out there. They had played outside by themselves many times before. Will ran towards the door screaming that our baby brother had fallen into the sewer. My first reaction was to run and get my baby brother! Carolyn called out for Carl.

I arrived at the crevasse and tried reaching down to get my baby brother. He was struggling to hold on and he was scared. I couldn't reach him. I began slipping forward, when I felt a hand pull me back away from falling in the crevasse too. It was Carl. He told me to go inside and get some towels.

I stood back, horrified that my baby brother might die. He was slipping under the putrid liquid. Tears began flowing from my eyes. I could barely see, as I ran back to the house. Panic took over me, while I looked for towels. The next few minutes felt like hours.

A crowd of people had gathered around to assist Carl, as he was attempting to retrieve his child. My baby brother had sunk under the surface and had lost consciousness by the time Carl was able to reach him. I was paralyzed, as I watched through the screen door, when Carl laid his tiny lifeless body on the ground.

Everyone stood silently.

Carl began performing CPR, a skill that he had learned during his military training. It was a sight to behold when my baby brother began puking up the rancid water.

He was alive!

Carl brought my baby brother to the house and told me to run a bath for him. I had the responsibility of calming him and cleaning up the mess. The moment of relief was also short lived, as Carl began yelling at me for leaving him outside without supervision.

I was taken aback for a minute, as I tried to process his logic after all the times that he had left me and Will alone without supervision. I guess my baby brother was a little more important to him.

I would come to realize our baby brother was favored among the three of us.

VACATION

CARL AND CAROLYN HAD PLANNED A WEEK OF VACATION and hunting with our neighbors, Sheila and Jim, who lived in the front house on the left. I was glad for the distraction. Carl had become close friends with Sheila and Jim. They met each other after Carl joined a local biker club known as the Desert Rats.

Sheila had three children, two girls and a boy from a previous marriage. Her eldest daughter, Stef, became my best friend. She reminded me of a mini Olivia Newton John. She wore sweat bands and had a short pixie hairstyle. She was the coolest chic I knew. We were excited to get to spend a week together on a hunting trip.

The road was long, but just as we were getting restless of the travel, we arrived at our destination. The area had many trees and a field. We were surrounded by nature's beauty, a sight different than the desert area that we lived. We began setting up camp. Carl had brought a tent for us to sleep. Jim was a little more upscale with a small camping trailer and two four wheelers.

Once camp was set up, we were free to explore. Stef and I headed out into the wilderness with nothing more than our wits. We spent hours walking around and finding neat hiding places.

We were in search of pixies and fairies.

Our young minds were amazed with fantasy. We found a windmill that had a cow tank next to it. This would be our secret swimming hole. As it was getting late, we decided to head back to the camp. We probably would have stayed longer, but we were hungry, and we could smell the food being cooked on the campfire.

When I think about it now, I am surprised we did not get lost in that wilderness. We went everywhere without a compass.

We made it back to camp safely and the adults were visiting merrily around the campfire. They had been drinking and the music was playing loudly on the car radio. As the sun set, the cooler temperature made the wind unbearable. We decided to turn in for the night. I couldn't wait to get warm. I got in my sleeping blanket, huddling and shivering all night.

The next morning arrived and the women decided it was too cold for the children to sleep in the tent. So, they made amenities in the camper for all the children to sleep and stay warm throughout the night. I was so glad. I was still chilled to the bone from the previous night. Stef and I layered some clothes on, before venturing out again. I had so many layers of clothing on that my jeans fit tight and it was hard to breath for a few moments.

Thank goodness the jeans stretched a bit, unlike those damn Converse…

The men got the 4-wheelers out and decided to let the kids play on them. I had never ridden a 4-wheeler before. It should be easy since I could ride a motor scooter all by myself.

Ooof, I was wrong!

I had no idea how powerful those machines were, when engaged. We started out by riding on the back with an adult driving. Then they decided to let us have a turn by ourselves.

Fresh from the start, I killed the 4-wheeler. As soon as I engaged the throttle, it popped a wheelie that knocked me off the back onto the ground.

Second try...

I regained my composure, but forgot to pick my foot up and place it on the pedal (I was on a 4-wheeler, not a motor scooter, HUGE DIFFERENCE). It was too late by the time that I realized my mistake... Once I released the brake and turned the throttle, the back wheel of the 4-wheeler grabbed my right foot and drug me under the machine as it plowed straight over my body, planting my face in the dirt.

Yeah, that's right, I ran over myself...

Thus, ending my 4-wheeling career...

I was ready to move on to the next adventure. Will must have had the same thing in mind after he ended up treeing his machine. The adults had an adventure of their own in mind. They decided we (meaning the children) had to cut the 4-wheeler out of the tree. By cut I mean chop with an ax. Will had managed to run the 4-wheeler between the "V" split of a tree, and it was not willing to break free.

The men decided since it was a kid that got the 4-wheeler stuck, it would be kids that got it out of the tree. By the time we finally cut that thing loose, I had blisters on my hands the size of quarters.

Damn, that was some hard work! I have hated 4-wheelers ever since.

We ended the day in another celebratory fashion. We sat around the campfire and made smores. Stef and I had taken some time to collect sticks to roast the marshmallows. The adults were inebriated and playful.

Carolyn passed me the bottle of Jack Daniels and told me to take a swig, "Here, you earned it!" The adults laughed and cheered when I took a quick shot. The smell was inviting, and the liquid was warm on the way down, causing me to shiver at the bitter aftertaste. It made me feel grown up for the moment. I appreciated the gesture. Stef quickly followed my lead.

The adults thought it funny to break us in on their nightly adult rituals. They gave us a beer and we pretended to enjoy it. Beer was not my choice beverage, as it had a bitter twangy taste that required a development I had not yet acquired. Needless to say, we were all giddy and the night was relished.

Four days into camping, everything had become pungent. The body odor from lack of bathing, combined with smoke of the campfires was not a pleasant aroma. Sheila was voicing her need for a bath, when Stef told her about our secret swimming pool. We hadn't literally swum in the tank, but we thought about it. Sheila decided it would be a good idea for us females to go down and attempt to bathe, after she gathered up some bathing supplies.

Carolyn wasn't interested in bathing in a cow tank, so she stayed behind.

We finally approached the solemn tank, located in the middle of the field that was surrounded by a tree line. Sheila was apprehensive, as she walked up. She was looking around for critters and snakes. She looked over the side of the tank and said it should work. I looked over the tank and I could see algae growing in it.

(I feel it is important to let the reader know that by this time in my life,

I had watched the movie "JAWS" which had instilled an unhealthy illogical fear of sharks in my mind. It also didn't help that I watched "SWAMPTHING" and had a reoccurring image of a grotesque hand reaching out of murky water.)

Along with algae, I imagined numerous other things growing in the tank. I didn't want to show my fears to Stef and Sheila, so I tried to remain calm. Sheila was fine with getting in the water. She climbed up the windmill and crossed over the pole that reached out over the tank. She carefully hung her clothes on the pole, then she dipped herself down into the water.

"Oooo! It's chilly in here!" She told us, as she quickly washed herself. I dreaded the cold water, not to mention every scary creature that was waiting to grab me in there.

Next, it was my turn. Stef had already claimed the last bath. In support of me going first, Stef decided she would go up and wait on the pole for her turn.

"Okay, fine… my turn."

I took a deep breath and I climbed across the pole. I had a clever idea that I would just hang one hand on the pole, and bathe with the other hand, in order to keep my body above the surface of the water.

It took me a few minutes to talk myself into getting into the water. I could see the algae clearly now from the top of the tank and it seemed benign enough. Mustering up as much courage as I possibly could, I finally dipped myself down in the water. EEK! It was cold, but tolerable.

As I quickly soaped down and tried to rinse off, my mind was filled with trepidation. I began to imagine creatures of the deep, when I felt something brush my leg… "AAAAAAaaaaa!"

Wouldn't you know it, I lost grip of that damn pole…

To say I panicked, is an understatement. I damn near walked on water! When I lost grip, I fell deeper into the water where a strand of algae had wrapped around my leg. I came up out of that water like a screaming banshee shrieking "HELP ME! HELP ME!!!", while clawing my way hastily to the side of the tank.

Every bone in my body was telling me JAWS was at the bottom of that tank, working his way up to the surface to eat me. Every strand of algae that brushed against my leg made me think of some dead cold hand grabbing me.

Stef found my reaction hilarious and she began laughing uncontrollably, which didn't play out fairly for her either. She suffered from the inability to control her bowels when she got tickled in laughter.

Generally, Stef would pee herself when caught up in heavy giggling, but this time the giggle would be monumental, as she perched on the pole, watching me die in my agonizing fear. She pissed and shit all over the back of her leg and the pole.

Needless to say, I felt horrible for Stef after I made my way to safety, however, I didn't feel too bad. It took some of the attention off of me and I was able to recover some of my dignity.

That swim in the tank made for an eventful morning and a most cherished of memories. After Stef was able to pull herself together and rinse off, we made our way back to the camp. We laughed the whole way back, reminiscing about our experience in the cow tank. The rest of the week went without incident. By Sunday, we were all worn out and ready to return home.

I was just ready for a real bath without sharks and dead hands!

DEAREST DINAH

As mentioned earlier, Carl was prospecting for a local biker club known as Desert Rats. On an occasion, we would go out to the club house with him and hang out with the other kids that went with their parents. The club was in a small two-bedroom trailer house that had been converted for club use. It was a special feeling to be able to walk inside and see how the badass adults hung out.

Entering the front, the living room had been converted into a makeshift Bar with pictures and magazine covers plastered all over the walls. A large mirror hung across the back of the bar, reflecting everything in the room. Photo albums lined the bar with pictures and newspaper clippings. The club usually had a small crowd of prospects and members hanging out, engaging in stories of their past activities and plotting their next adventures.

Walking down the hall, to the back, opened into another bar with a few pool tables. When the adults were busy with club duties, the kids were allowed to play pool. Or should I say, attempt to play pool. As kids, we were clumsy and uncoordinated. That didn't deter us from trying. When we accidentally made a ball in the hole, it was a lauded feat by all who bore witness.

The club house is where I was befriended by an older lady by the name of Dinah. She was the girlfriend of the Club Leader Jon. Dina was 19 but she treated me with respect and as an equal, not just a child. She spoke to me on adult things and she eventually knew some of my secrets.

Our friendship began by accident I suppose. The Club was having a weekly meeting and I was told to take my brothers to the house and watch something on the VCR. Dinah was in the house, curling her hair and getting ready for the day. She stopped what she was doing to help me find a video tape that was kid friendly. Dinah popped the movie in and went about her business. After a bit, I heard some knocking around in the kitchen.

I peeked around the corner to see Dinah was cleaning up from breakfast. I grabbed a broom and started sweeping to help her. This impressed her. Dinah observed, "You are more mature than most girls your age."

She continued, "I guess you have had to grow up faster than most."

I looked at her puzzled, "What makes you say that?"

She carried on with the chores as she confessed, "You have been helping your Dad raise your brothers, haven't you?"

Up until that point, I never really thought about it…but she was right.

"Yes, I suppose I have." I said in agreement.

"It is really tragic for a child to have to grow up so fast. I should know." She lingered.

That conversation opened into many deep confessions between the two of us. She knew me. I was a shadow of her, just in another life. Even though we shared many things, I still couldn't confess everything. I know she held back too.

I could have told Dinah everything and she would have kept all my secrets. I could trust her, and I knew it in my soul. I know she felt the same about me. We had an unspoken understanding between us.

As our friendship bloomed, Dinah spoke to me on many topics of womanhood. I treasured her wisdom. I looked forward to our visits when the Club had meetings. She would often drive me into town to go get a slushy at the Allsups Store where she worked. Sometimes we would sit in the bathroom and she would talk to me while teaching me to curl my hair. I trusted her so much, I even let her cut my hair.

Carl and Carolyn found a rock house out in the country, located half-way between the club house and Lovington. I was anxious to move there, because I would be closer for Dinah to swing in and grab me when Jon was gone.

The house was beautiful. The rooms were large. The kitchen had an island, which was amazing. That was the first island kitchen I had ever seen. I even had a room with my own bathroom. I was so proud! I was training for track, so the dirt road was a perfect place for me to practice my runs.

This was going to be perfect! Or so I had hoped.

CAMARO VS DEAD END

MOVING OUT IN THE COUNTRY PLACED US CLOSER TO EDITH. Carl began making weekly trips to visit, with Edith, bringing all of us along with him. He would load all of us up in his 1974 Camaro Z28 and we would head out to Tatum. I never looked forward to the visits.

The good thing was that Edith would stay preoccupied with Carl and Carolyn and I wasn't subservient to her, since I wasn't staying with her. I would still help with the dishes, if we ate with them, but I didn't have to do them all by myself. Liam had to be nicer to me too.

One evening, after visiting with Edith, we headed home late. Carl and Carolyn were discussing the conversation of starting a small chicken farm at our new house. I listened in as they continued.

My place in the car was in the back seat on the ridge of the seat divider. I had to keep my brothers separated in the car, because they would get restless and fight with each other. This position in the car made it easier for me to listen to the adult conversation.

We turned off the highway 206, heading west on the first dirt road heading home. Carl was so wrapped up in the conversation that he didn't realize how far we had travelled down the road. He had a heavy foot and sped everywhere we went. I was watching down the dirt road, when I saw the traffic T coming up quickly.

I screamed in fear, "DAD, STOP!!!"

Carl and Carolyn turned in unison to see we were going too fast to stop in time. The next few seconds were all too familiar. Carl had slammed on the brakes, but this time we didn't hit a bull.

This time we hit the ditch and flipped the Camaro end over end.

The sudden impact sent me forward, the flip of the Camaro plunged me back into the seat and tossed me like clothes in a dryer. The windshield was filled with white light and I could see everything around me in slow motion.

Carl slammed forward, shoving the steering wheel into the dash. Carolyn's arms were flailing in the air and I saw her head hit the roof, before she was knocked back into her seat.

My brothers remained in their seats, because Carl had installed seat belts for them to keep still, while he drove. The sawed-off paddle, Carl affectionately referred to as a "Nigger Knocker" flew up from the floorboard and whacked me in the collar bone, just before landing on my brothers' head. I heard a crack and I felt a sudden sharp pain.

All the chaos came to a sudden stop. Complete silence…

I could barely breathe. The pain in my shoulder was making it hurt to draw any air. I looked around and my brothers were silent from shock. Carl and Carolyn had been knocked out by the sheer force of the impact. I began to panic.

I called out, "Dad… Dad! DAD!!"

I grabbed his shoulder and shook him as I called out to him, "DADDY!!"

Carl began coming to and reality brought him front and center. He sounded frantic, as he checked on everyone. He had to wake Carolyn and it took a few minutes to get her to come around to consciousness.

After everyone was accounted for, and able to move, Carl had to crawl out of the driver side window. The crash had damaged the front and sides of the Camaro, sealing the doors shut. Carl tried to pry the door open once he was on the outside without success, he had no strength and he was severely hurt.

Carl did what he could to help all of us get out of the Camaro. We all stood there in shock, as he assessed the damage to the car. Carolyn was furious. She began screaming in uneasiness, "What the hell are we gonna do, Carl?"

Carl looked around…We were in the middle of nowhere, out in a pasture at the end of a dirt road, in the middle of the night. We were without any way to get in contact with anyone.

Refusing defeat, he decided we would walk the rest of the way to the house. We were about a mile or two from the house, so he thought we could do it. We could walk at a comfortable pace and get there within the hour, or so, and call an ambulance, once we made it to the house.

The walk was long, dark, and solemn. I could feel the desert breeze cool the sweat on my brow. My baby brother cried and I tried to console him. I would normally carry him, but I couldn't lift him up in my arms. I hurt too much. Everyone was in pain.

It seemed as though we were never going to make it to the house. The road was long and unforgiving. Walking on the dirt and rocks in the pitch of night made my feet hurt. We were all miserable. Just as I was about to give up in pain, we could see the house.

Finally, we made it in the door and Carl went to the phone and called for help. He was hurt and so was Carolyn. I felt sorry for them. Carolyn lost her glasses during the crash and she had had to walk the whole road blindly.

An ambulance came to the house to assess us. Carl had to call Edith to come get us. Both he and Carolyn had to go to the hospital. Carolyn had a concussion and cut above her eye. Carl had hit the steering wheel so hard that he needed to be X-rayed for possible breaks in his chest and ribs.

I was not happy to see Edith when she pulled up at the house. Thankfully, we only stayed for the remainder of the night and a portion of the next day.

Edith dropped us back at the house when Carolyn made it back home. Carolyn was not feeling well, so she went to lay down and I tended to my brothers. Carl had to stay at the hospital for a couple days, so he could recover from his injuries.

(I was sore for a couple months with my shoulder. I would later find out that I had received a hairline fracture in my collar bone from the hit of the sawed-off paddle board)

Carolyn seemed different after the wreck. She didn't engage with us much, so I continued with my duties and took care of my brothers. She stayed secluded in her room, painting and sleeping. She seemed irritated when she had to do anything for us.

We went about our days as though everything was okay, even without the presence of Carl. It was the last day of school of my fifth grade year and my brothers and I were listening to REM on the radio. We were waiting for the bus, making plans for what we were going to do afterschool, for start out our summer.

We didn't know that the last day of school would also be the last day we would be at that house.

As the bus pulled up in front of our home after school, we noticed Edith waiting in the driveway. She was there to pick us up and we went to stay the remainder of the summer with her. We had become her free summer help for the farm.

FARM LIFE

I AM NOT SURE EXACTLY HOW LONG CARL HAD TO STAY at the hospital, we hadn't seen or heard from him since the accident. I asked Edith when he was coming to pick us up. Edith was quick to get back into her mean-spirited attitude when she replied, "Don't get your hopes up little girl."

"Your daddy won't be coming to get you anytime soon." We had been given up to her, by Carolyn.

I was now Edith's indentured servant. I was to return to my former chores, with additional work at assisting with the livestock, the garden, and the harvest. In return for our work we were given three hots and a cot.

There was no such thing as sleeping in on the Farm. We were up at the crack of dawn to eat a hearty breakfast and then out the door to begin the day. Our daily activities broke down into the following:

6:00am Breakfast and cleanup.

6:45am Feed and water chickens.

7:30am Slop the pigs.

8:00am Feed and milk the cows.

9:00am Assist John in the fields that needed attention. Fields were cotton, milo, wheat and alfalfa. We would help to irrigate, plant or harvest the fields depending on the day.

Yes, I did pick cotton. I picked a lot of cotton and it was hot backbreaking work. I hated it!

12:00am Return to the house for lunch.

1:00pm Collect chicken eggs.

1:30pm Tend to the gardening. This consisted of planting, weeding and harvesting depending on the season.

3:00pm Feed and water chickens again.

3:45pm Slop the pigs.

4:15pm Feed and milk the cows.

5:15pm Boys returned to the house to relax, while I assisted Edith in the kitchen with supper.

The boys would play and watch television, but I was expected to be in the kitchen, helping to prepare dinner. I would clean the dining room table from the ashes and newspapers that Edith had collected on it throughout the day. Once the meal was ready, I would set the table with plates, silverware and prepare tea for drinking.

We would all sit at the table after John sat down first. He would begin dishing his plate and then pass the food clockwise. Our seating arrangement was John, Edith, Liam, Will, my baby brother, and then I was last.

After dinner, I would clean off the table. Edith would help me store the leftovers, before I would be sent to wash the dishes. In the beginning, it would take me some time to get the dishes completed. After a week, I realized the faster I got the dishes done, the faster I could have some me time, before bedtime.

The boys would end the evening by either playing a game, or going outside to relax in the crisp night air. Liam had grown up some, since living on the old farm on the highway, going to Denver City. He was still an asshole and a bully, though. But, he engaged with me differently now and he would invite me to play along in board games and outside night activities.

The preferred board game was Monopoly. He would play the banker and he would always win.

I know he cheated…

We made one game of Monopoly last for a whole week. That game was fun. We would just pick up where we left off from the previous night and play through till bedtime.

Another nightly activity would consist of going out to the first irrigation motor and lay in the cool soft sand. It had built up in front of the motor over time from the pressure of the water hitting the ground. We would lay on our backs and look up at the stars.

I don't know what it was about the New Mexico night sky that made it so beautiful, but it was a sight to behold. Maybe it was the sparse population that didn't pollute the skyline with lights. The night sky was always lit up with stars. Some nights we could see the Milky Way. I enjoyed these nights.

Liam was tolerable during these moments, as we wondered about what was out there in space and then we would share our dreams about the future. He rarely allowed my brothers to spend time with us when we went to lay in the sand. I think it was his way of trying to connect with me.

Occasionally we would find free time during the day when John had to go back to work on the rigs. Liam took us all around the 660 acres of property. We had to be shown where all the electrified fence was installed, so we could avoid it.

Of course, Liam didn't tell us this initially.

Liam had another intent in mind. He took me and Will over to the eastern side of the farm, where the cotton was planted, known as the North40. There was an old one-room farmhouse they used for the storage of empty mason jars. An old barn was located adjacent to the farmhouse that John used to store some of the hay. One of the rooms he also used as a hot house to season and dry out his meat.

We piddled around the area for a little while, before Liam urged us out to the cotton field.

The three of us were playing around kicking and throwing rocks when Liam dared us to touch a wire fence.

I was hesitant at this dare.

I already didn't trust him.

Will was a little more gullible. When Will agreed to touch the fence, it prompted Liam to change the dare. Instead of touching the fence he dared Will to piss on the fence.

> (I obviously wasn't dared to piss on the fence, since I was a girl.
> In addition, I must confess, I tried to piss like a boy once… to
> my dismay I was only successful in pissing down my leg into
> my shoe. I lacked the necessary appendage and skill set…sorry
> for the interruption. Carry on.)

To encourage Williams' compliance, Liam acted like he pissed on the fence and nothing happened. Liam secretly knew that the fence was on a pulsating interval charge. He could look at the end of the fence and wait for the red light to disappear on the charge box in order to piss on the fence as though it was safe.

Will shrugged his shoulders and pulled out his pecker and began pissing toward the fence. He was just shy a couple feet.

Liam pushed him forward and said, "Try harder."

Will, wanting to prove his courage, did as he was told and pushed a piss stream out higher and farther. Just as the stream began losing steam, it contacted the fence at the same time the fence was charged sending a shock straight up the stream to Williams' pecker! He yelped in the highest volume known to man, piercing my ears. He simultaneously began dancing and jumping uncontrollably in a circle, while yelling and patting his privates as if to put out a fire, "OOOWEE!!!"

The sight of his reaction was hilarious to behold. That was a lesson Will would never forget.

That fence was not done teaching life lessons.

I was its next intended victim.

On hot days, we would play in the water that ran through the irrigation ditches. One portion of the ditch was wide and deep enough for us to swim back and forth. It just so happened that the particular area for swimming had the electric fence crossing directly over it, just six inches above the water. Liam had taken the time to show us how to swim under the fence without worry, by counting to three.

We each took our turns successfully. After a few passes, I was confident in clearing the fence. It was my turn again, so I took a deep breath, went under water and began swimming. When I had counted to three, I raised up out of the water and wouldn't you know it, just in time to connect my forehead directly with the fence

All I remember is feeling like I ran my head into a brick wall and a flash of bright white light crossing my eyes. I woke up to Liam slapping my face, while yelling my name.

"MANDY!!"

"MANDY!! WAKE UP!!"

I didn't know what happened, or how long I had been in this state.

Liam looked at me and asked me how many fingers he was holding. I thought that was strange, but I replied. He sat back in relief and told me he had thought I was dead. He told me he was yelling at me to stay down, but I raised up and there was a loud zap that he witnessed, as the shock hit my head. He went on to tell me how I fell into the water and how he had to pull me out, before I drowned. He said it took him a few times to get me to wake up.

"That was one hell of a shock!" he stated. "I could hear it hit you." He continued to admit that it scared him.

That was the last time I swam in that ditch.

Our days ran together during that long summer. Break dancing was a popular pastime, and I was amazing at performing the Centipede and the Millipede. Of course, I was still limber at the time. Edith would allow us to move the furniture out of the dining room and break dance in the room, while we cleaned, waxed and buffed the wooden floor.

Liam would invite one of his friends over to practice break dancing and they would usually own the room, not allowing Will or myself much practice time. We would sit by the wall and watch Liam and his friend perform for us.

One day, I decided I was going to push my way onto the dance floor...

BIG MISTAKE!

Liam took to beating me without mercy, back to the wall. The beating hurt bad enough, but the humiliation was the worst part. His friend bore witness to the whole event. Then, I had to endure listening to Liam brag about the beating he gave to me.

Thus, my break-dancing career ended before it even began.

John had a stray female dog that had given birth to pups. He interrupted the break-dancing session with the pups in a potato sack. He told Liam to go take care of them. I wish I hadn't been there to know what came next. Liam took the pups out to a rock pile and beat them against the rocks killing every one of them. I was devastated.

My reaction... I vomited...

The sound of the pups screaming in pain still haunts me. My response irritated Liam, and he beat me again for being weak.

I crossed some thresholds while being on the farm; driving a stick shift was one of those thresholds.

Liam took me out to the field and began teaching me how to drive the Old Blue, which was a Dodge Truck. I needed to know how to drive by myself, in order to help more around the farm. I knew how to drive an automatic, but a standard five speed was a completely different machine, all together. I was eager to learn to drive a standard five speed.

Driving was something that seemed liberating to me, especially without sitting in someone's lap.

My first attempt at driving Old Blue was almost my last attempt. Liam began by showing me how to push the pedals and shift the gear stick. I watched him closely, as I wanted to be sure not to make any mistakes. He then instructed me to shift the gears as he pushed the clutch.

Once I became comfortable with the shifting, Liam felt like I was ready to get behind the steering wheel. He had the bright idea to stand on the driver side, with the door open, as he held onto the door and the back of the seat to instruct me as he walked.

I gathered my courage and placed my feet in position.

Liam instructed, "Now, do exactly as I say!"

He took a deep breath and tried his best to remain calm, "I want you to put your left foot on the clutch all the way to the floor and hold it."

"Make sure the gear shift is in neutral and start the truck." He continued, "Do not release the clutch until I tell you."

Gathering myself, I did exactly as I was instructed. SUCCESS! The truck was now on and I was holding the clutch to the floor.

"Okay, now I want you to put the gear shift in first and began applying pressure to the gas pedal, as you slowly release the clutch." Liam continued, giving advice.

I aimed to do precisely as he had instructed. Only, we did not realize that the clutch had a kick back that was stronger than my tiny leg could handle. As soon as I began to release the clutch, it kicked out and caused me to lay down on the gas pedal, which in turn shot the Old Blue forward at a high speed. Liam was running, as he held on for dear life, while Old Blue picked up speed.

He began yelling at me, "Hit the brake, HIT THE GODDAMN BRAKE!"

The excitement of the whole situation made my mind go blank and I couldn't remember which pedal was the brake.

"THE MIDDLE PEDAL!!"

"PUSH THE MIDDLE PEDAL!!!" he screamed.

The whole time I wasn't even paying attention to where I was going… I found the middle pedal and I smashed both feet onto it, which caused Old Blue to come to a sudden stop, slamming Liam into the driver side door. The engine of Old Blue killed over and Liam fell to the ground, with his breath knocked out of him.

"OH, you done it now!" he seethed at me through his ragged breath.

Liam regained his composure and pulled me out of the seat with a fury. He beat the shit out of me. He called me every name in the book. He was not happy with my failure and he sure let me know it.

We would have to try again, until I got it right. I was almost too sore and too afraid to attempt it one more time. I am grateful that he didn't give up on me, but I could have done without the ass whooping.

Once I finally had it down, he allowed me to drive back to the house.

That summer the beatings between Edith and Liam mounted up in the numbers. Edith had Liam make her a whooping board. When we got a whooping the first time, our name went on the board. A tick line was added to your name for every whooping received, after your name was added.

Wouldn't you know it, my name was the first on the board and I had tick lines nearly halfway down, before anyone else was even added to the board. I received a whooping for everything.

If I looked at Edith wrong, if I missed a spot on the table, if I didn't wash the dishes properly, if I took too long doing the dishes, if I didn't sweep and vacuum under the furniture, you name it, I got whooped for it.

After the horrific death of the pups, Liam took to picking on me again. I had hoped we were past that phase in our relationship. He would often instigate Will into picking on me too. Both would often gang up on me with the teasing and picking. Liam found personal pleasure in watching me get into trouble.

The more they picked on me, the more nervous I became, which would incite their rage against me.

I couldn't do anything right.

CARL'S RETURN

CARL SHOWED UP AT THE HOUSE ONE MORNING, out of the blue. I was thinking we were going back home. I was so glad to see him. He had no idea, or least I think he had no idea, what had been happening, during his absence.

I saw him pull in, while I was cleaning up after breakfast. He came inside and made quick with the greetings, before telling Edith he was there to pick us up and leave. I was so freaking happy! I went into the room and told my brothers. They didn't share in my excitement. They liked staying with Edith, but then again, she treated them with favor.

For example, just the week before, Edith had gone into town to buy groceries, with all three of the boys, leaving me at the house to complete my chores. While they were gone, she took them to Dairy Queen, before coming home.

When they arrived home, the boys were still indulging in their ice cream in front of me. When I asked where my ice cream was, Edith looked directly at me and sneered, "Do you really think you deserve one?" She pfft at the thought.

That is when I knew she had no regard for me as a human being. Once again, I digress...

Carl called out to me to get ready to leave. I gathered up what few personal things I had to take with me. My brothers half-heartedly did the same. Quick with the goodbyes, I headed out to the car and waited for the rest of them to join me. I watched the house, as we pulled out with a fear that Edith would come outside and make Carl leave me there.

Not much was said on the road back into Lovington. We stopped in to see Jon and Dinah for a visit, or what I thought was a visit. I was happy to see my friend; it had been too long since we last spoke. I could tell something heavy was weighing on her mind, so we went out back to talk.

Dinah told me about Carl living there with her and Jon. I had no idea that Carolyn had left Carl. Dinah told me the reason we were sent to stay with Edith had been because of Carolyn.

Carolyn had given Carl an ultimatum to get rid of us, or she would leave. Carl chose Carolyn over us…

This news hurt me deeply. I thought Carolyn had liked us.

Dinah went on to tell me that after the wreck, Carolyn had started acting differently and would lash out at Carl during Club meetings. I assumed Carolyn had sustained more than a mere concussion in the wreck. Dinah and I both concluded Carolyn may have had real brain damage from the accident.

Carolyn had left Carl a week, or so, before Carl came to get us. He thought she would return, but she never did. I couldn't even muster up sorrow for Carl. I felt like he got what he deserved for abandoning us to Edith.

Carl woke us up on the third day to tell us that Kathleen was coming to get us for a couple of weeks, but he made us promise not to tell Edith. I was thrilled at the thought of seeing Momma again. I hadn't seen her for some time. She would get to call us from time to time, but as soon as she would contact us, our address and phone number would change.

I thought it very odd that Carl was allowing us to see her all the sudden, and even more oddly, was his request to keep the visit secret from Edith. I spoke to Dinah about my skepticism. She enlightened me to the true nature of the relationship between Edith and Carl. I guess she had a better understanding of what was going on, because she could see things from the outside looking in.

Dinah was very intuitive and could tell a lot about a person when she met them. She did not like Edith from the moment she met her.

Dinah explained the relationship between Edith and Carl was what is now termed "co-dependent". She didn't have a word for it at the time, but she described their behavior to the tee. Carl was Edith's first-born son and she never let go of him completely. Carl never cut the cord from Edith either. When Carl would get into a relationship, Edith would become jealous and sabotage his relationships either directly or indirectly.

If Edith felt a real threat, she would turn Carl against his companion by getting in his head. Carl was her puppet and he didn't even realize it. Dinah went on to explain that Edith was a bitter, viperous, jealous, manipulative woman.

Dinah was right.

I had lost track of time during the conversation with Dinah, when there was a knock on the door. Kathleen was standing on the porch when I opened the door. She was a sight for sore eyes. I hugged her hard and for a long time. We both cried. I know she was surprised when she saw me, because I had grown. I was 11 years old now. She hadn't physically seen me in a while. My brothers joined in the hug.

Momma quickly gathered our things and we said quick goodbyes to Carl. He wanted her to stay and talk. She did not linger.

I know Kathleen was Carl's regret. I think he loved her, but he ruined it and he knew it.

SWEET REUNION TEARFUL GOODBYE

WE HIT THE ROAD, HEADING TO MONAHANS. Momma and I had so much to catch up about each other. We talked so much that we made it to Monahans, before we knew it. Momma had remarried and had had another child, a baby sister. I was delighted to meet her. We gathered everyone up and headed over to see Grandpa Lionel and Grandma Earline.

This trip was going to be special, because we also got to visit with MeeMaw and Pappaw. They are Grandpa Lionel's mom and dad.

Seeing everyone was like a dream. I knew I missed everyone; I just didn't realize how much. We gathered around the dinner table and talked until we were blue in the face.

All of the grandparents had so many questions. I tried to keep it light and didn't elude to the horrors that I had endured. They were fascinated with how much I had grown. The conversation eventually turned to the length of time we would be staying with Momma.

I looked at Momma and asked her if she could keep us. She said she was trying to get us to come home to stay. I hoped beyond hope that she would be successful. Momma went on to tell me what she had experienced with Carl and Edith over the past few years.

Edith would threaten Momma when she called to speak to us. I knew Momma was telling the truth about Edith threatening her; I had overheard her on the telephone bragging to one of her friends about how she treated Momma.

Other times, Edith would call Momma to further antagonize her heartache. This knowledge made Edith more terrifying to me. She had no boundaries in causing someone pain.

Our conversation was interrupted with the arrival of Manda. She was a family friend that lived around the block from Grandpa and Grandma. Manda was a couple years older than me and a few years younger than Momma. She would visit every opportunity she had available.

Momma had somewhat taken Manda under her wing and they became close, spending time together as often as possible. Manda and I became friends during the visit.

Momma, Manda and I would sit and have coffee together in the mornings and converse over breakfast. It was a welcomed change of pace. I didn't even mind the small list of chores that I had to do to help around the house. At Momma's house, I wasn't treated like a red headed stepchild. I was treated with dignity and I knew I was loved.

Momma even gave me some freedoms and allowed me to hang out with Manda. In the mornings, after our coffee talk time, Manda and I would go walking and stop at her house for a quick refreshment to cool off, before heading back over to my Grandparents home.

Even with all the distractions of the visit, I had a lingering dread that Edith would find out about the visit. I knew her wrath would come down on me. I tried not to think about what would happen, but the fear of the possibility caused tension in my spine and chest. I would take a deep breath and shake it off, so that I could enjoy the visit as much as possible.

Reality was quick to rear its ugly head and the visit was over, before I was ready. I begged Momma to let me stay and I could tell it was breaking her heart to send me back. She didn't have any means to keep me. Carl and Edith had made sure to tighten the reins of Momma's rights, in order to prevent her from having full custody of me and my brothers.

The drive back to New Mexico was not long enough for me. I cried nearly the whole trip back. I didn't know what was waiting for me, once we returned. Momma pulled up into Jon's driveway and Carl came outside to meet us. I helped get my brothers out of the car. Carl wasn't really interested in our return, as much as he was interested in talking to Momma.

Carl didn't even hug us hello. It was then that I realized he hadn't hugged us when we left either…

Momma kept the visit with Carl as short as possible. I stood at the door, watching through tear stained eyes. Carl was begging her; Momma wasn't going to have it. She had moved on from him. Momma knew what Carl was about and that was not the life she wanted. When he realized his pleading would be of no use to him, he turned into a madman and began cussing at her.

Momma broke away and came into the house to hug all of us, while telling us how sorry she was that she couldn't take us with her. She was crying now. That broke my heart even more. I held onto her tightly. I didn't want to let her go. Carl came in demanding that she leave. She had to peel all of us off her body. Everyone was crying, but Carl was furious.

Momma ran back to the car and backed out down the driveway looking at the door as we all stood there watching. I didn't leave the doorway as I watched her drive off down the highway. I watched until I couldn't see her any longer, then I watched a little more to see if she were emboldened enough to turn back around for us.

My hope was broken by Carl's voice to get my ass out of the doorway and to close the door.

I flopped down on the couch. I asked where Dinah had been during all of this and Jon told me she had taken on overtime down at Allsups. I thought to myself, at least I can look forward to seeing Dinah.

I was doing the only thing I could think of to get over my heartbreak.

GOD FORBID THE CHILD

THE NEXT MORNING AS I WAS FEEDING MY BROTHERS A BOWL OF CEREAL, Carl came in and told me we would be going back to Edith's for a time. He couldn't have us all living at Jon's home, since there really wasn't enough room for all of us. He needed some more time to get back on his feet and get us our own place.

This news was not what I wanted to hear. I was desperate. I told him that I didn't mind sleeping on the floor. I didn't need much space and I didn't have anything of value to keep, except for my yellow teddy, Tinkerbell.

I went on to plead my case and told him I would even let my brothers sleep on the same pallet, so they didn't take up the room on the couch. My pleas were in vain. Carl wasn't moved by my plight. That afternoon, we headed north to Tatum.

The anxiety built up inside my chest as we got closer to Edith's house. When we pulled into the drive, there was a strange truck parked by the front gate of the yard. I was curious to whom the visitor might be.

We walked around to the back door because everyone entered through the back. The visitors were the neighbors just west of the property. Peter, his brother and his father had stopped into visit with John.

I knew Peter, we had gone to school together in Lovington. He was kind and funny. We spoke on an occasion at school, but I was too shy to make conversation without his persistence. His presence did relieve some of my anxiety and broke the ice of our arrival.

Carl made his visit short and left without saying goodbye. Peter and his family stayed to eat supper with Edith and John. It was interesting to see Edith interact with the company. She seemed lighthearted and easy. She was very engaging and obliging. It was strange to see her in that capacity.

Peter was able to break my fixation on Edith and we went outside to play. I inquired about their relationship with Edith and John. Peter informed me that they were the new neighbors in the rock house at the end of the dirt road, by the highway. I was surprised that he lived so close.

This was good news for me, because now I would have a friend.

School was back in session, only this time, I would be attending Tatum instead of Lovington. The first day of school made me nervous. I thought to myself that I should be used to the changes by now, but I was introverted with an insecurity complex. So, meeting new people scared me. I thought at least I would know at least one person...Peter.

I walked with my brothers and my uncle down to the bus stop at the end of the dirt road. A bus was coming up the road and I watched it stop at Peter's house, before it turned and headed back to Lovington. I was immediately fearful that the bus had left us, and that we were in trouble. Liam assured me that we did not miss the bus.

I was confused.

I just saw it drive back the other direction.

Liam told me I was stupid and that the bus picking up Peter was a bus for the Lovington schools. Our bus was coming from Tatum.

"Wait…so Peter isn't going to school in Tatum?" I asked in confusion.

Liam shook his head in disgust and said, "No, you idiot!"

Now, I was at a loss…

The only thing I had to look forward too just left in front of my face. This realization didn't make the bus ride a favorable one. I had already planned to sit next to Peter, when we got on the bus. Now where was I going to sit?

All the kids looked up at us, as we entered the aisle to find a seat. I was uncomfortable and I could feel my face flush from the rush of heat and embarrassment. No one wanted to scoot over and share a seat. Liam had a seat near the back, and I went to sit with him. He told me I would have to find another seat, because he didn't sit with nerds.

Finally, a kid opened a space next to him for me to sit.

I guess he felt sorry for me.

I didn't speak to anyone for the entire ride to school. When we arrived, I was escorted to the office to find out about my schedule. The office assistant took me around and showed me where all the classes, cafeteria and gym were located. Then, she escorted me to my locker.

I must have had a look of panic or confusion on my face because the office assistant giggled then said, "Here let me show you what you need to do." I had never had a locker before this. This was my first. It was located on the bottom tier; good thing too, because I was short!

I was then led to my first class. I didn't have to introduce myself this time. When I entered, the class was still in the process of getting seated and the teacher took me to my assigned seat.

After a few bustling minutes of chaos, the teacher calmed the class down and requested everyone's attention. Class began and I noticed the kid in front of me had beautiful golden locks of hair that resembled Farrah Faucet. The hair was in perfect form with waves of feathered back bangs. I was hoping she would be kind, once we met.

The teacher passed back forms for us to fill out for the office and when the kid turned around, I realized she was a HE! I was completely confused. His name was Roger, and yes, he was kind. I knew from the moment he turned around that he was different. I did not realize at the time how different, but it was no matter to me.

We became friends.

Roger allowed me to hang around with him and he even took the time to introduce me to other kids. He introduced me to a Tina and a Misty. We would hang out around lunch and break. I eventually met other kids during our Gym periods, due to sports.

I met a Spanish girl by the name of Juanita. She was already wearing make-up and she had awfully long nails. She had a sister that was a grade below her. Between Roger and Juanita, I had friends. This made me feel more comfortable and made me look forward to attending school. I didn't look forward to the bus rides...

Our daily routine hadn't changed much from the summer routines, apart from school time. Our mornings started at 5am to tend to the animals. We had to be back in the house by 6:15am, in order to get dressed for school and have breakfast.

I tried to tend to my chores as quickly as possible, because I was beginning to take more concern with my looks and wanted to have plenty of time to give myself a whore's bath and curl my hair.

When I say whore's bath, I mean that I literally washed myself with a soapy rag throughout the week, until bath day. My brothers and I were only allowed to bathe on Sundays. Edith would run a bath for the boys to take their bath first. I would then have to bathe in their left-over filthy water. Edith said we had to conserve water, because they were on a septic system and it would fill the tank up too quickly, if we all had our own baths.

I never really felt clean after bathing in their water. I was permitted to run some hot water in the bath to warm it, when it was my turn, but I could only run so much. I figured out quickly that I could pull the plug to drain the dirty bath water and just shower under the running water. It was the only way I could clean myself properly. I had to do it quickly, so that I wouldn't get questioned on why the water was running.

I know that I had smelled of pig shit and cigarettes and I wanted to do everything I could to take it off me. I have often wondered if any of the kids at school made fun of me for smelling like a farm animal behind my back.

Edith began voicing her suspicions about where we were, during our time with Carl. I could hear her voice echoing into the hall, as I bathed. I had already sworn my brother to secrecy, so that we wouldn't get into trouble. I hoped that they would keep our secret. When Edith would ask Will what we did, while we were away, he would just shrug and say, "I don't know."

I couldn't understand why it was so important to her. Why did she even care what we did? Still, I had a dread that she would find out we went to see Momma. I would lie awake at night with fear in my mind that she would discover the truth. My stomach would ache in pain from the worry. I began to pray to God to keep our secret safe.

Late one evening, after being on the farm a couple weeks, I heard Edith talking to Carl on the phone. The conversation was not pleasant, as she was questioning him. I could hear Carl speaking abrasively to her on the other end. She scowled and called him out, "You have a sharp tongue when you are on the other end of the phone!"

She rebuked him, "How dare you speak to your Mother that way!"

Then, in agitation, she dared him to come say it to her in person. The conversation ensued in a bitter feud.

Edith pulled the truth out of Carl. He admitted he had allowed us to go spend a couple weeks with Momma. Edith cursed him to high heaven and slammed down the phone.

I quaked in my bed, as I heard her shriek in anger. She then stomped her way to our bedroom and furiously pulled me out of bed, by my arm.

"YOU LIED TO ME LITTLE GIRL!!" she yelled violently.

I just stood there frozen. "Didn't you!"

"You lied!" she insisted.

Yet, I hadn't lied to her. I just never admitted what we had done.

I tried to distance myself from her, when she continued scolding me. She continued to yell, "You are going to suffer for lying to me."

I defended, "I never lied to you."

In panic, I said, "I never told you anything about it, because Daddy told me not to say anything!"

Her anger exploded, "You are going to pay for this!"

"You are going to pay dearly!"

She forced me to the couch and made me look in the mirror that hung just above it. "Now bend over!!" she demanded.

I bent over and placed my hands on the seat of the couch.

"Look in the mirror!" she commanded.

I hesitantly looked up.

Edith began beating me with the board, as she cursed me and Carl. When I would look away, she would force me to look in the mirror again. I began crying in pain. She continued. Liam came into the living room to join in the taunting. "Liar! Liar!" he chanted. "LIARS GET WHOOPINS!" he jeered.

Edith beat me mercilessly. Liam laughed at my anguish. She took all her rage out on my ass. I went to bed bruised and broken. At least, I wouldn't have to worry about her finding out the truth anymore. The worst of it was over.

The pains in my stomach became excruciating over the next several days. In the beginning, I kept it to myself and just suffered it. After a few days, I couldn't tolerate the pain anymore and I went to Edith for help. She rolled her eyes and told me I was probably overreacting for attention.

I ran to the bathroom and vomited.

It was at this point that she gave me some Milk of Magnesia. It helped. I was good for the rest of the day. The following morning, I went to school and was getting sick after eating food. I ended up in the Nurse's office three days in a row. The Nurse contacted Edith with her concerns. Edith had no choice but to take me to the doctor.

During the Doctor visit, Edith was questioned on what kind of stress I was experiencing at home. Edith lied. She told the doctor that I had an easy life and I was well cared for in all matters.

If the Doctor had made me turn around, during the examination on my stomach, he would have seen the bruises that were still healing from the beating I had received on my backside. I wanted to scream out that she was lying, but it was no use. I had to go back with her anyway.

The Doctor diagnosed me with ulcers. He voiced his worry that I was too young to be suffering this ailment. He believed I needed to be monitored closely. I felt like he suspected her deceit.

A prescription was written, with a reminder that I would have to be back in a couple weeks to make sure the medicine was helping to heal my ulcer. The Doctor would also be checking my stress levels at that time. Heh, heh, he had her pegged!

Unfortunately, that didn't stop Edith from continuing to add stress to my tender situation. She complained the whole way to the pharmacy, and all the way back, about how much money I was costing her. She made it clear that Carl would have to pay her back for the expense.

When we returned to the farm, John was in the dining room sipping on some afternoon tea. Edith sent me to my room and proceeded to make fun of me for being weak.

"I suppose we have to coddle the little Prissy."

Those words uttered from her lips burned in my mind. I began thinking of her demise and wishing ill upon her head.

Weeks turned into months and we had not even received a call from Carl. Halloween and Thanksgiving had passed. Christmas was just a few days away. All the relatives would soon be arriving to partake in the festivities, except for Carl. Edith and I had painstakingly placed out all the decorations for the holiday. Christmas was her favorite time of the year, not so much mine. I did admire the way Edith would take such care in making sure everything was perfect for her family to enjoy the visit.

My 12th birthday was also coming up, just days before Christmas. I dared not mention it; I knew better. Edith was always quick to make me feel unworthy of any thought or feeling, so I learned quickly just keep my mouth shut.

Just a few weeks prior to the Christmas holiday, John was discussing finances with Edith and they were both fretting the loss of income. I recalled back to Thanksgiving when Uncle Sputter was preaching about God. He would provide in time of need, so I thought it would be a good idea to reassure Edith with God's commandment to not worry.

Edith slapped my face and hissed, "Don't you ever speak of God to me!"

She stood up and squinted her eyes, glaring down at me, "You are just a stupid little girl and you have no idea what you are talking about."

She continued to scold me, "You need to mind your own damn business and stop being a busy body."

"You are so nosy, it's SHAMEFUL!"

That was it…that shut me down. Her strike was deep and debilitating. Her conditioning had broken me. I walked around on eggshells and jumped to her every command. I dared not listen to any conversation she had, for fear of her abuse. I was sent to my room.

In my defeat, I needed to lash out. I began writing a letter to Carl.

It was hateful…

"Dear Dad,

Why haven't you called us? Where are you? Why did you leave us here with Grandma? She doesn't want us here. Why did you take us away from Momma? She loved us and cared for us. I wish I would have died in that car accident; I would have been better off.

I HATE YOU!

I HATE THIS LIFE!!

I wanted to write a good letter to you. It's not my job to reach out to you. It's your job to stay in contact with us, protect us, and take care of us. You have abandoned us over and over, while you run around and play. You are a horrible man!! You are a horrible father!! We are just children. How can you break our hearts like this, time and time again?

I don't care about anything, anymore. I don't even care if you come get us anymore. Maybe one day Grandma will be mad enough at me that she will snuff the life from me. She has already taken my hope.

Whatever you are doing now, I hope you die. I DON'T LOVE YOU ANYMORE! I want you to just FUCK OFF!! I hope you have a terrible life and every woman you ever meet breaks your heart!

Merry Christmas…

Your Daughter,

Mandy

Sealed. Delivered.

The only known address I had was Dinah and Jon's. I knew Dinah would get him the letter, if she saw it. I didn't care what consequences came with the letter. I had made my bed and I was going to lie in it. I was going to be mistreated, whether I wrote that letter or not. I simply didn't care anymore.

December 23rd arrived, and my brother was already up with Edith. He was playing in front of the TV, when he looked up at me and said, "Why didn't you get a birthday too?"

I immediately looked at Edith. Her reaction wasn't shocking. She brushed off her forgetfulness by blaming my behavior on the postponed birthday.

"We will make a cake later to have after dinner, for your birthday."

"What about her presents?" asked my brother.

Edith looked at me and told me to pick one of the three presents that was under the Christmas tree for a birthday present.

Everyone got three presents on Christmas. If I opened one for my birthday, that would mean I would only get two presents on Christmas day. I hesitated and thought better of it. However, Edith encouraged me to go get a present.

I think she had a moment of shame for forgetting my birthday and this was her way of making it up to me. But, then again, it could have been her way to stick the knife in a little deeper, in order to short me on Christmas day, in front of all the family.

I guess I will never know.

The last Friday of the Christmas break came with a surprise. Carl pulled into the driveway. I was sitting out on the front porch, enjoying some alone time. I can't say I was happy to see him. I had supposed he was coming to scold me for the letter.

To my amazement, he got out of the car and came straight up to me, fell to his knees and wrapped his arms around my waist as he buried his face in my stomach and asked for forgiveness. He began to cry and promised me he would do better. He was coming to take us with him. I couldn't believe my ears! We were leaving the farm! I hugged him and told him it was okay.

Edith came outside and Carl hurried me along to grab our things. They began to fuss at each other. Edith belittled Carl for coming to get us after all this time, "Hell, Carl, you might as well just leave them here."

As expected, she remembered what a burden I was and started in on Carl for money. He pulled out his wallet and obediently paid her for the doctor's visit. That wasn't enough to satisfy her temperament. She continued in on him.

I hastily got my brothers to the vehicle. Once we were loaded up, Edith yelled out to my brothers that she loved them. She didn't say anything to me.

I didn't expect her to either.

We drove off, down the road. I had expected to stop at Dinah's, but we passed their house and kept going. I asked Carl where we were going, he responded, "Silver City."

Carl continued to inform us that he had taken on a new job as a truck driver and the job was in Silver City.

This was someplace new.

We continued in conversation, as he drove. I asked about school and he said he had already contacted them to know of our transfers. I was sad that I didn't get to tell my friends goodbye.

MOTEL LIFE

I WANTED TO TELL CARL ABOUT ALL THE THINGS THAT HAPPENED while we were staying at Edith's home, but I just kept it to myself. I didn't want to pour salt into his wounds.

The drive was long. I kept the radio tuned when the static would start to come across the airwaves. We drove on into the night. I could see the terrain changing into small mountain ranges. The mesquite bushes were turning into actual trees. Even the air was changing into a crisp breeze.

I rolled the window down and stuck my hand out to wave it in the fresh air. The feel of it running up my arm and through my hair was exhilarating and stirred excitement in my mind for our new start in Silver City.

I was so glad we would be away from Edith. I forgot all about her as soon as we pulled into the Motel. I asked Carl if this is where we would be staying the night and he said, "Yes, maybe more than a night, until I can find a house."

Carl told us to stay in the car, as he went inside the office. After a few minutes passed, he got back in the car and drove us all the way to the back room. It was considered a suite. The suite had a small living room that opened into the kitchenette, a bathroom with a shower, and toilet. There was one bedroom with a large closet. I help Carl unload, as the boys went inside and made a bunch of racket.

Carl was quick to quiet the boys and sat us at the small dining table to explain our new living arrangements. We would be attending school, starting Monday. Carl would be off from work that day and would take us to school and get us set up with the bus route.

Tuesday, Carl would have to return to work. He would be working from 7am to 5pm, except when they called him out on overtime, which would keep him out till 10pm.

I was in charge of watching the boys…of course.

Carl looked at me to explain this was the way it would have to be, while we got settled. It was the only way we would be able to stay together. He went on to inform us that this suite would be our home temporarily, until he found something more permanent. Carl made arrangements with the lady in the office to pay weekly, at a reduced rate.

The boys and I shared the bedroom. I slept on the twin bed and they slept on the full-size bed. Carl slept on the couch in the front room. We still had the weekend left before school started back up, so the boys and I went outside during the days to explore our new surroundings.

The motel was set up on a hill that was at the foot of a small mountain side. The highway ran in front of the motel. When I stood at the front door, I could see out in the distance, the town that sat at the foot of the hill. Behind the motel, there was a ravine where water would run, when it rained.

The ravine was at least 5ft deep, because I could stand straight up in it and not see over it. The boys and I would climb down in it and walk the length of it, digging as we would go, pretending to be Archeologists.

It was beautiful and scenic on that mountain side. Everything was a lush green. I thought this must be what paradise would look like. I loved being outside. The air was fresh and inviting. The sun didn't feel as sweltering as it did in Tatum.

Everything was so different and so peaceful.

I wanted that feeling to last forever.

Monday came around sooner than I had expected. I was nervous walking into class, but the people were different. They were friendly and welcoming. Everyone wanted to know my name and where I had lived before this. This was a bit mind-boggling for me to encounter.

Making new acquaintances came easily for me this time. They were all amazed that we were living in a motel. I didn't mind. I thought living in a motel was marvelous. Besides, who can say they live in a motel, if they didn't own it?

Hormones had begun taking charge of my brain and I was starting to notice boys. It was a strange sensation to look at a person of the opposite sex and feel squishing in my guts. My skin would tingle, my hands would get sweaty, and I would feel a rush come over me.

I didn't know how to react when a boy would talk to me. I would just clam up and stutter if I tried to talk. It was a good thing this didn't happen with every boy. Some boys were just like being around my brothers and I was okay with hanging around them.

I wanted to call Dinah and talk to her about it, but we didn't have a phone. We couldn't afford long-distance calling anyway. I missed my friend and hated that we lived so far apart.

I was getting taller and my body was changing more. I was a late bloomer when it came to filling out, especially in the bra area. Unfortunately, I was built like a stick. I was muscular from working on the farm, but I did not have a figure eight like a lot of the girls at school. I was envious of the girls who had curves and were already wearing graded bra sizes.

I was still wearing a freaking training bra.

I assume Carl started to notice the changes in me. One evening, after my brothers and I had gone off to bed, Carl came in and woke me up from sleep. He asked me sit with him in the living room. I got up and joined him on the couch.

The TV was blaring the song "Hey, Hey, we're the Monkey's" on Nickelodeon Late Night. I asked Carl what was wrong, and he told me he just wanted to talk.

It was the "Sex Talk" conversation.

I was initially wary of the conversation and afraid of where it might lead. Carl began the conversation very nervously, which didn't help me. He was able to compose himself and the topic became easier to discuss. Carl explained how boys and girls go through changes and what those changes mean.

> (I was trying to maintain interest, but I was way past those stages, except having the boobs.)

I had already attended sex education at school, so everything he was talking about was a repeat. I would just nod my head in agreement and pretend like it was the first time I was hearing about it. The whole time, I was remembering every sexual experience I had already encountered and the one he had drunkenly forced me to do.

I couldn't believe that he was so good at pretending it never happened.

The only lesson I took away from that conversation was when Carl summed up the topic, "Mandy, what I am trying to tell you is this…"

"Women have it all."

He extended on his thought, "What women don't have, they can get. This is because women have the pussy, and with pussy, they can have everything they want."

Had I been a different person of character, I might have used that advice to my advantage.

I can say that I have no regrets by avoiding his advice. Well, maybe a little bit… I could have had a Sugar Daddy to take care of me…okay, okay, just kidding! It was just a side thought. I am still floored by his words.

FELLOWSHIP IN DEMING

I BELIEVE CARL WAS IN SEARCH OF CHANGE FOR HIMSELF when he happened upon a small Baptist Church on the hill. He was invited in by the reverend and his wife to join in on the services.

Reverend Lindsey was a small and kindly gentleman with a manly, yet kind, woman for a wife. They welcomed us to join them on Sundays at the church for fellowship. This was a new venture for us, as we had never attended a church for anything other than Easter Sunday.

My brothers and I were delighted to attend church and mingle with the other children. Even better was finding out that the fellowship would carry over to a Sunday brunch at Arby's, where I discovered a love for the curly fry and the beef and cheddar on onion bun.

That makes my mouth water just thinking about it.

We were welcomed in by the church with open arms and became regulars every Sunday. We would sing along with the hymnals, but Will found it entertaining to distract me during the songs. Carl would scold us with his eyes when he would catch us bickering under our breaths.

Will enjoyed making faces at me, while I tried to sing. I would try to ignore him, but he would become more creative and distracting.

I had endured Williams antagonizing long enough and warned him, "The next time you stick your tongue out at me, I am going to pull it out of your mouth!"

Will didn't believe me and tested me one more time. He stuck his tongue out at me! To the shock of both of us, my cat-like reflexes were faster than a Ninja! I grabbed onto his tongue and held it for the duration of the song! Will squirmed to get free, but my grip was strong and there was no way loose for him.

From that moment on, Will decided it was best for him to sing along, instead of picking on me.

Our attendance gave us privileges in the Sunday school. Sometimes we got to choose what lessons we wanted to hear. We quickly made friends with the families there. We began spending time with them, when Carl would have to be on the road for extended periods.

A girl by the name of Tiana took me in as a friend and we loved spending time together. We were just a year, or so, apart in age. I was older. They lived in Deming, but attended the church in Silver City. She lived in the middle of a desert plain, about a country block away from Reverend Lindsey and his wife.

Tiana's house was unique, as it was built underground, apart from the roof, windows and entry ways. The layout was quite extravagant. Front double doors opened to a small foyer, with a coat and shoe nook.

An opening from the foyer overlooked the expanse of the open concept living area. On the left, there was a large living room that was lit by long rectangle windows that overlooked the desert plain. An opening of a hallway led down to the three large bedrooms, two bathrooms, a laundry room, and hall closet.

Cascading down two flights of stairs, at the base, was a small area adequate to be used as an office space. It all tied into the receiving area. To the center, there was a large open island kitchen. The music/den room was to the right, through double doors.

When I would spend time with her, we would walk onto the roof and lay there, looking up at the sky. When I say walk on the roof, I literally mean take a step up from the ground, onto the roof. It was absolutely the coolest house I had ever been in, ever.

Tiana had an older and a younger sister. Her mother was a single mom and I believe Carl had a thing for her. They would occasionally go to dinner together. I didn't mind, because we would get to spend more time with the girls.

Tiana's older sister, Lisa would entertain us with music and show us her amazing acrobatic abilities. We did a lot of dancing and tumbling in the den and living area. Phil stayed occupied, while playing with Tiana's baby sister, Jenny, as they played with every toy imaginable. Will had a crush on Tiana, so we couldn't shake him. He followed us everywhere.

Tiana would take us out to cross the desert plain and we would pretend to be Indiana Jones, as we ventured across to go visit Reverend Lindsey. They would often be outside, piddling in their desert garden.

Mrs. Lindsey would hang out in her cross your heart bra and shorts, which was a sight to behold, considering she was a big lady.

The first time I laid my eyes on her, without her shirt, I gasped. But, she was quick to dismiss it by telling me, "This material covers more area than today's bathing suits, so it is completely acceptable attire to wear in my garden."

I couldn't argue with her. So, I didn't mind her hanging around like that in her garden.

The church planned an outing for everyone to spend a weekend camping on the Gila River. Everyone anticipated the fun as we drove up to our area. A handful of the kids went down and found a prime swimming spot far enough away from the fishermen of the group.

After we set up camp, we all headed down to our swimming hole. The water was cool and refreshing. I was the first one to jump in and swim across to the other side, and then sit on the large rocks, waiting for the others to join me. (You are probably asking what happened to my fear of sharks? Really?? We were in a river! There are no sharks in a river! Gosh...)

Our spot was about eight or nine feet deep and about twenty feet wide to cross. Most of us could swim without a floating device. There were a couple of kids who needed floats to make it across. One of the kids, Stanley, had a floating tube that he used to cross over to us. He was scared to swim without it. We tried to convince him to learn how to swim, but he preferred the floatie.

We played until lunch and then we headed back to camp to eat. The day was perfect. All my cares had floated down the river and I never wanted the moment to end. Some of the families decided to leave after lunch. I was glad to see Tiana's and Stanley's family decided to stay.

We couldn't wait to get back out to our swimming hole. When we got down to it, Stanley realized he had forgotten his swimming float. We found a place, just a few feet from our rocks, where Stanley could touch the ground and still play in the water. We all helped make him more comfortable, learning to float and swim.

Before long, Stanley started swimming around on his own. We discovered that the shallow area could be followed around to the rock area near the bank, so he was able to get across and get on the rocks with us.

We all took turns jumping into the water from the rocks. We played until our bodies were wore out and hungry. The sun was going down, so we decided to head back to camp. Everyone was crossing over, and Stanley decided he was going to try, as well. He tried to cross over to the bank. He was feeling confident in his swimming abilities, since he was able to learn how to float.

I was still on the rocks, waiting for Stanley to go across, when he started losing his momentum. He became frightened and started to panic in the middle of the deepest part. Everyone was encouraging him to calm down and keep swimming. He went underwater and fought to get back to the surface.

I realized that he was going to drown.

I jumped in to help him. I was able to get him above water; however, the fear had already taken hold of him and he was fighting in confusion.

Stanley was gasping and struggling when I grabbed him. He pushed me under the water. My feet hit the bottom of the riverbed. I pushed with all my might to get him up and I came up for air.

Stanley began climbing on top of me, pushing me back under the water one more time. I could hear the muffled screams, and kids yelling, as I fought to get my head back above water. I was able to take another breath, just before he pushed me under again.

This time, I knew if I didn't get us across, we were both going to drown, right there in that cove. I mustered up all my strength, and what was left of my stamina, just as I felt the bottom of the riverbed touch my foot. I used the solid ground to push us up and out one more time.

We breached the surface and Tiana reached out in the nick of time to pull Stanley out of the water. I struggled to get to the side, as I coughed out the water that had gone up my nose.

After a brief recovery, Stanley began crying and then gave me a big hug for saving his life. We all gathered in a big group hug. We did not expect the day to end with that kind of drama. We were all grateful that we were safe. I made him promise not to ever do that again! Stanley said, "I promise! That was too scary for me!"

If he only knew how scared I was!

We walked back to the camp, wore out like an old pair of shredded jeans, just in time to partake in the dinner festivities. It was fresh fish and fried taters, yummy!

Saving lives will make you famished!

After being out of the water for a bit, Will began complaining that his skin was hot, and he wasn't feeling well. He had a terrible sunburn. We didn't realize it, because the water kept him cool and we were having too much fun to notice. That night was not a pleasant night for Will, so we ended up leaving early the next morning.

The next week was hell for him, with blisters all over his body. He probably should have gone to the doctor, but Carl put me in charge of taking care of him. I would apply cool soft cloths on his skin to keep the heat off him.

How did I know to do that? I had watched a movie on TV where cold compresses were used for a burn, so I figured that should help Will.

It was heartbreaking to see Will in so much pain. His tender skin was covered in festering blisters. He couldn't lay down to sleep. I had to prop him up and help him move. He couldn't move his arms, so I had to feed him. I was his makeshift nurse.

When Will's blisters would burst, I would have to clean them and place more cloth to capture the ooze. I wanted to take his pain away, but nothing helped. He cried and moaned constantly, while he was awake. Carl finally came home with some Tylenol to help ease his discomfort. It helped enough to get him to sleep.

Around the fourth day, Will's blisters started drying up and it was causing his skin to wither and stretch. His face started wrinkling like an old man. It was hideous, but funny. I took him to the bathroom and helped him up to the mirror, so he could see what the sunburn was doing to him. He laughed and then moaned through the pain.

By the end of the week, my brother's skin was peeling, so he was finally feeling better aside from the itching. I would put anti-itch cream on him a couple times a day to help soothe him. I was just ready for him to get better. He was getting too used to calling my name, keeping me at his beck and call. I was also ready to get back to spending time with our friends.

Reverend Lindsey offered Carl to move onto their property, so we could get out of that cramped Motel. The reverend was a man of means and had a full-size trailer on his property.

Initially, they moved into the trailer and let us live in their home. I thought this was very strange, as their home was a beautiful terrarium that was built by the reverend's own hands out of the rocks and wood located around the property. The living room had a wall built out of flat rock that pictured Moses receiving the Ten Commandments. That wall was mesmerizing.

I loved sitting in that room to read near the black iron fireplace. There were plants and ivy everywhere. Mrs. Lindsey tasked me with making sure the UV lights were on at night and the plants got watered on their rotations.

Our stay in the house was a brief two weeks, then we moved into the trailer. Reverend Lindsey had to work on the bathroom, in the trailer, before he could let us stay there. It was nice to be out of the motel, and in a place, that was more suitable. It was also a plus that we were closer to Tiana.

The move also caused a change in schools. We were now attending school in Deming. It wasn't too hard to leave Silver City schools, since I hadn't been there long enough to form any lasting friendships. I finished my sixth-grade year attending school in Deming. We ended up staying with them for a few weeks.

I spent a lot more time with Tiana during the summer. I thought we would be staying longer, but things fizzled between Carl and Tiana's mom. I believe he became disenchanted with living in Deming, after things didn't work out between the two of them. He made it known that we would be heading back to Lovington soon.

The news of moving back to Lovington was not welcomed, as far as I was concerned. I plotted with Tiana on a way to run away and come stay with her and her family in Deming.

We were so sure our plan would work.

We were clueless children and our plan never came to fruition.

A couple days before we headed back to Lovington, Jon called Carl and told him Dinah had been in car accident and died.

I was devastated.

Dinah was the only reason I looked forward to going back to Lovington. I never got to tell her goodbye, or how much I loved her. We left in such a rush to go to Silver City that I didn't get to tell her goodbye. I never called her the whole time we were gone. She had no real idea of what she meant to me.

Carl told me how it happened. Dinah was driving home from an overnight double shift at Allsups, when she fell asleep behind the wheel. Her car veered off the road and flipped going 60 miles an hour. According to the coroner, her death was sudden.

This did not console me.

The news only made my heart break more, because she was all alone on that long stretch of dirt road, just a couple miles further down from where we had crashed the Camaro.

I ran outside and screamed through tears. My mind went back to all our conversations. Her confession of how she was broken hearted that Jon would not marry her, because of her age, took the breath out of my lungs. I realized she had never married the man she loved. Her dream of becoming a nurse would never be accomplished. The children that she had longed for would never be born.

Dinah was too young to die…I would never be able to share another secret with my friend.

She was a true friend to the very end. She took my secrets to her grave.

Through tear swollen eyes, I looked up to heaven and told her how much I regretted not telling her what she meant to me, and how much I loved her, as a friend. I made a promise to her, and myself, at that moment, to always let the people I love know it. I would never leave anyone guessing where they stand in my life, because that was a regret that is too heavy to carry.

Before we left, I hugged Tiana and, as I had promised to the heavens and Dinah, I told her I loved her and that spending time with her was some of the best times I had experienced. Tiana squeezed me tighter and promised we would keep in touch. I had been down this road already and new that time would separate our best intentions.

I let her lie to me, because she believed it.

RETURN TO LOVINGTON

THE DRIVE BACK TO LOVINGTON WAS LONG AND BLEAK. Our first order of business coming back into Lovington was attending a funeral. Dinah's funeral was nice with all the Members of Desert Iron attending in her honor.

I didn't go back to the club after Dinah's death for a couple of years. I couldn't… It felt different without Dinah.

Carl got in touch with our old landlord from the trailer park on Artesia Hwy and rented the front house, on the left side of the entry, into the area. It was a strange house by design.

It was a one-story house, with a storage room connected at the front of the house and a bedroom located above the storage room, making the front portion a two-story column. The only entry into the bedroom upstairs was a wooden staircase that spanned the outside of the house. The shed could only be entered from the outside as well.

When we lived in the trailer park previously, Stef and her family had lived in the house. Stef had permission to paint the room black, with white sprinkles all over it. We used the room as a club house. So, I continued the tradition and kept the outside upstairs room as a club house. The stairs had deteriorated a bit since I last saw the house, and someone had broken the door off the hinges.

It didn't hold a candle to Tiana's house, but then again, no house I have entered since has compared to that house underground.

I already had many memories in the house, as I had spent several nights there with Stef. On the front porch, Stef's mom, Sheila, pierced my ears with a raw potato and hot needle. The needle got stuck in my left ear and we had to pierce it a second time. I was already deathly afraid of needles, so the entire experience was traumatizing.

While Stef had lived there, Sheila decorated the doorways with beads, instead of doors, and she would often burn incents. I would spend the night over there on an occasion. The last night I stayed there with Stef, we stayed up later than usual in the living room. We were talking and fantasizing about our futures, when we heard an unusual buzzing sound.

We looked at each other with concern. Stef said, "Follow me..."

We began crawling on the floor, to follow the sound. We were supposed to be asleep already. The house was only lit by the television, so we had to strain to see in the dark.

I accidently bumped the door frame, as I passed through the first room.

"OOPS!" I whispered.

"SHHHH!!!" Stef looked back, scolding me.

We continued our journey, seeking the source of the sound. Buzz, buzz, Buzz... The sound would be loud, then muffled. This made us even more curious.

As we crossed through the beads of Stef's doorway, the buzz paused. We paused… The buzz started back up. We could hear the buzz more clearly now. We were close to the source of the muffled, and then loud again, buzz.

With a look of confusion, I asked, "What on earth is that sound?"

Stef's eyes widened. I could see her eyes reflect what little light seeped through the beads. Then she hurried me back into the living room.

"WHAT?"

"What is going on?"

"Do you know what the sound is?" I asked confused.

Stef broke out into a stifled laughter, "It's my moms' VIBRATOR!"

I was clueless…

"What the hell is a vibrator?"

Stef broke out in a hushed laughter again and explained it to me… She got a good kick out of the whole scenario. I was a little disgusted, but realized how funny it was to be following the sound.

(Like I said, I had many memories in that house already.)

I chose Stef's old room to be mine. I missed the beads and wished I could get some to add to our personal décor of the house. I decorated my room with candles and hung some old chiffon from the ceiling around my bed, in order to make my room feel magical. I spent many hours alone in the room, writing in my journal, and drawing in my sketchbook.

Back to my old routines. I was the house maid and haphazard mom to my brothers. While Carl was working, or playing, I was at home taking care of things around the house, and keeping my brothers out of trouble the best way I knew how. I cooked and cleaned to the best of my abilities to help relieve Carl of any added stress.

As usual, I made a cup of coffee to take to Carl in the morning, after I made a quick breakfast for everyone. When I quietly opened the door, I was taken back at what my eyes were seeing. Instead of seeing Carl snoozing away, I saw a large Hispanic woman, half naked against the headboard, with her knees bent under the covers. Her eyes were rolling into the back of her head, as she moaned.

(I don't think she heard me enter the room.)

My reaction was impossible to contain, "Who the hell are you? Where is Carl?"

Carl popped his head up out of the sheets with his hair in disarray, and his face glistening. "Leave the room, Mandy Shawn!" I didn't know what to think. What did I just walk into? A moment passed when I finally realized what was going on…Eww! I quickly left the room with coffee in hand and tried to erase what I just saw from my mind.

Thankfully, that episode was short lived, as it was only a one-night stand.

Going back to school in Lovington was a bittersweet return. It was nice going back to familiar faces. Middle school brought on some challenges with teachers and jealous petty classmates. I guess, at that age, kids are starting to find themselves in the world, while discovering life's little games and dramas to play their part. I was still introverted, keeping mostly to myself.

THE DEVIL MADE ME DO IT

AT THAT TIME, THE WHOLE CITY WAS A BUZZ ABOUT DEMONIC POSSESSION and Satanic worship, among the youth. Dungeons and Dragons had brought about the fear mongering. Small town and closed minds are what I summed it up to be.

I had no fear of the unknown concerning the spiritual things. I mean, I lived in a haunted house and nothing bad ever happened, except for my things moving or disappearing. I didn't believe for one minute that a board game was going to possess those who played it. It was complete nonsense, as far as I was concerned.

I was at the age where I was noticing a familiar pattern with the adults, in regards to their beliefs. Everyone was afraid of sinning, yet they all sinned when no one was looking.

Adults were horrified to go to hell, but still committed unspeakable acts. They then prayed for forgiveness, when they went to church. Adults were hypocrites, but we had to mind what they said. Utter frustration for me…

Teachers were just as bad as everyone else, if not worse. I believe they were worse, because most of them never left their narrow-minded childhood mentality behind, when they became adults. With that being said, many teachers were prone to gossip and stirring the perpetual pot of dissention.

Kids in middle school go through many changes which cause a gangly awkwardness to most. My change was my feet. For some strange reason, my feet outgrew my body first. It was my P.E. teacher that pointed it out to some other classmates, as she watched me run to class one afternoon.

I was devastated to hear the rumor spread that I had Bozo the Clown feet, according to the teachers' reference. Like I could help that my feet were outgrowing my body...

The real blow came when she also called my feet banana boats. That term of endearment came about, due to the pastel yellow high-tops I so proudly sported, because I bought them with my own money. When I heard about that name, I wanted to burn my shoes, but I had to endure the humiliation, until I could afford another pair.

Yeah, her judgement was unkind. I was never able to confront her about it, because she was pregnant and left on maternity leave, shortly after I found out what she had cruelly remarked about me.

I felt like all the teachers in that school had a twisted way of getting their kicks, from making fun of kids going through the changes of adolescence. It is a time when hormones are out of control, acne explodes on the unfortunate, and the feeling of being all alone causes one to hyper focus on the small things.

I was one of the unfortunate ones. For the most part, I had clear skin, but I happened to have a zit pop up on the end of my nose. It was small at first, just barely noticeable... However, I couldn't keep my hands off the zit, because I was trying to hide it, which made the zit worse.

The zit began to form a head on it, so I decided to try and pop it... WRONG DECISION!!

The aggravation from the pressure of my poor attempt at popping the zit only caused it to become inflamed and red. Now my nose was swollen and red and my feet were as big as Bozo's. As I stared at the reflection in the girls' bathroom mirror, I realized that my P.E. Teacher was right. I looked like a clown.

I sulked my way to my Social Studies class, hoping beyond hope, that no one would notice...But, alas, my Social Studies teacher was quick to point out that I should be chosen for the Christmas play, as Rudolph, because I was already in costume. I just wanted to melt away into oblivion.

> (Too bad I didn't have some ties to the Satanist or a Witch Coven, because I probably would have conjured up a way to make him melt into oblivion for his statement!)

I don't know what it was about me that encouraged teachers at that school to be so mean. I was quiet, did my work, and never interrupted during class.

I took everything they threw my way with a smile, and moved through it as though it didn't have any effect on me. Truthfully, it ate away at my self-esteem like hot acid poured on fresh baby skin.

I continued to absorb their unrelenting blows, until a moment came that would change the remainder of my attendance in that school. Pop quizzes were the teachers' favorite ways to keep all the students on eggshells. No one knew when, or where, one would hit in any class.

Upon entering my Science class with Coach Domzowskie, I realized that he was about to pop a quiz on the class. I sat in my desk, as usual, and began preparing my pens and pencils. Coach Domzowskie began talking through the chatter and bustle of the class, as he passed out the quiz. I couldn't hear everything he said, because his back was turned.

I raised my hand to get his attention, to be able to ask my question. He turned and looked at me with a scowl... "What is it, Woods?" Before I could utter my question, he interrupted me, saying, "If you didn't hear me the first time, then it's too damn bad for you."

Coach Domzowskie turned his back to me, to continue walking down the aisle. My hand was still in the air, and with a swift graceful motion, I promptly shot him the bird...he turned abruptly and caught it, as I was bringing my hand down to my desk.

In fact, the whole class witnessed my out of character hand gesture...

The look of surprise on his face was expected, but he didn't say a word, until he made his way back to his desk. When he sat down, he cued the class to begin the pop quiz. I sat through the remainder of the class, wondering what he was planning to do to me for flipping him off.

The class bell rang and Coach Domzowskie released everyone, but required me to stay behind for a talk. I could hear the "ouu's" and the rumor mills brewing, as everyone left out of class.

I sat in my chair, waiting, unsure of what was about to happen. Coach sat in his chair, staring me down, as he patiently waited for the last student to leave the classroom. After what seemed like an eternity of Coach staring me down, he finally asked, "What in the hell possessed you to flip me off?"

His words ignited my reply, "THE DEVIL DID!"

The color left his face, as his arrogant aggressive demeanor was replaced with sudden panic and fear. Stuttering, he managed to utter, "You are dismissed, Miss Woods."

To my astonishment, I had toppled an angry 6'3" giant with three words…the devil did…

I felt empowered!

I left his room without another word. After that day, teachers were nice to me and some avoided me like the plague. I know he went back and told all the teachers in the lounge about what I said. They were all small minded and were easily brainwashed into believing I was possibly possessed, or part of a Satanic Cult.

Nothing could be further from the truth. I was just a girl wanting a little respect and had nothing but three words to lean on to achieve that respect.

Any damage to my dignity, after that, was of my own doing or carelessness. To which, I am reminded of one last embarrassing moment…

I was running late to a class one afternoon, when I ventured around the corner in a sprint. I accidentally ran, shoulder to shoulder, into another girl going the opposite direction. Our Aqua-Net saturated side wings of hair caught and locked together, tighter than clamped joints.

The hairspray glued our hair together and we shared a moment of pain and humiliation, as we attempted to pry ourselves loose from one another.

Needless to say, our perfectly shaped hairstyles were decimated, when we were through pulling apart.

AUNT DEB

ONE AFTERNOON, WHILE I WAS HIDING AWAY IN MY THOUGHTS and working on my drawings, I was interrupted by Will busting into my room screaming, "Mandy! There is a snake outside!"

Without hesitation, I ran outside with him to see the snake he was talking about. We mused at the tiny snake for a bit, wondering if it was safe to touch. I found a stick that I used to pick it up and remove it from our area.

After careful observation I decided to touch the snake.

Will screamed, "NO! It's going to bite you!"

I wasn't afraid and nothing in my body was telling me to be afraid.

(A talent that I suppose I learned from the "voice" of my infancy.) I was able to feel if an animal would harm me and I could tell this snake would not.

As I held the tiny creature in my hand, it slithered around, smelling me with its tongue flickering in and out of its body. Will wanted to touch the snake, so I let him. I did not let him hold it, as he was a bit rough and I was afraid he would hurt or kill it. We decided to keep it and not tell Carl about the snake.

We affectionately named the snake "Jack". Now to find a place for safe keeping.

Where else but under my pillow on my bed…

We figured it was a good spot, since it was a dark place to keep it warm. We couldn't wait to show all our friends.

Carl came home that evening with a woman that I thought was to be another one-nighter, until she began to speak. The inflection in her voice was familiar to me, and something about her face gave me a warm feeling in my stomach.

Carl introduced us after they finished their conversation, when they entered the house. She was my Aunt Deb. She was the middle sister to my mother Anne and Aunt Brenna.

Aunt Deb stood there silently when our eyes met, then ran over to me and grabbed me tightly. She was shocked at how much I had grown. She hadn't seen me since I was a toddler. The moment caught me up in emotion and I began to cry with happiness to see her. Carl interrupted the introductions with the news that Aunt Deb would be staying with us for a while.

This news was great news to me.

I was looking forward to having her there, so we could catch up and get to know each other.

I dragged her around the house to show her everything. I even showed her Jack, but made her promise to keep him a secret and she agreed. She was so overjoyed to be spending time with me, that she would grab and hug me tightly over and over again. It was welcomed at first, then I began to find it a little weird. Thank goodness she calmed down and stopped.

There is such a thing as too many hugs!

Aunt Deb, staying at the house, offered me many benefits. I was at the age when I started paying closer detail to my hygiene and looks. I definitely needed some assistance in the area!

Aunt Deb offered her skills and we would take turns dressing each other. We were like besties, dressing up and telling each other secrets. She spent all her time at the house with me and I enjoyed every minute of it.

One afternoon, while we were in front of the mirror putting on makeup, she told me that she would be leaving for the day. She had recently separated from her husband and that is why she was staying with us.

Aunt Deb's husband had contacted her about spending some time with her son. She was elated to get to spend some time with her one and only son, Jason. After she finished her makeup, she headed out the door. I didn't know if she would be coming back.

Sheila showed up about an hour later to get me, so we could spend the day with her and Stef. We went into town to do some shopping. I used the money I had collected from babysitting some kids at the trailer park to buy a new curling iron, hair dryer and makeup. I couldn't wait to show Aunt Deb.

When I arrived back home that evening, Aunt Deb had not returned. I figured she had probably decided to stay with her husband. I was disappointed, but I knew she had another life and that I couldn't expect her to stay with us.

I went to my room, in my grief, and decided to set Jack free. He was curled up under my pillow, all snug and cute. I stroked his smooth skin, before picking him up and carrying him outside to. I laid him gently in the grass and he slithered away, without a moment of hesitation.

Typical, just like everyone else in my life…

I woke the next morning to the surprise of Aunt Deb shaking me. She had returned! I was so happy to see her, that I didn't even mind the hug! In her excitement, she told me to hurry and get up, because she had something to show me.

I sprang from the bed and ran into the living room with her, to see my cousin Jason sitting on the floor, playing with my brothers. Aunt Deb was able to work out some time with her husband to keep Jason for a couple of days.

Carl entered the room and told us he had made plans for us to go spend some time at Ranger Lake. We were all anticipating the fun and began to gather our things. What an exciting day ahead of us!

Jason and I had an immediate bond. I found myself spending more time with him than Aunt Deb. She seemed to be okay with it, as she was keeping Carl occupied, while we prepared for our trip.

After a short hot drive, we arrived at the lake. All the kids exited the car, as soon as Carl put it in park. We couldn't even wait for the car to be turned off, before leaving. Carl yelled out the window, "Wait before you jump in the water!"

We stopped in our tracks and waited for his permission.

Carl and Aunt Deb walked over to the bank to assess the area. There was an odor that was coming up from the area that made them feel uneasy. It smelled like rotten eggs.

The smell was coming from the lake itself.

"Looks like our plans for the day have been cancelled." Carl informed. "Awe, man!" we voiced in frustration.

Aunt Deb was quick to the rescue, "The whole day isn't ruined."

"We can still enjoy a picnic, since the weather is cooling off and we have shade under the clouds."

We all agreed in disappointment. We set up for the picnic and played chase, while we spent time by the stinky lake.

The day began to wane, as we played. I overheard some tense conversation, between Carl and Aunt Deb, which I believe they were trying to keep to themselves. Carl had hopes that Aunt Deb would consider him as more than a friend, but Aunt Deb was not about moving in that direction with him.

Aunt Deb didn't have affectionate feelings for Carl, so that frustrated him. To avoid a scene in front of Jason, Aunt Deb told Carl to give her some time. He agreed to her terms, and decided it was time for all of us to go home.

Jason's visit was over, and it was time for him to go home. Before leaving, he gave me a picture that he had in his wallet. It was a picture of him, for me to remember our time together.

I ran inside and placed the picture in my record box for safe keeping. I hurried to go back and join him, before he left, but I was too late. I was just in time to see the car leave the driveway.

My sadness was interrupted by the phone ringing. I went over to answer it and heard a woman's voice on the other end of the line.

"Hello?"

"Mandy?"

"Yes, this is Mandy…" I responded hesitantly.

"Do you know who this is?" asked the woman.

A familiar feeling in my gut worked its way up into my chest. Yes, I knew who I was speaking to, but the tone of her voice.

"Yes, I know who this is…"

"You do?"

"How do you know?" the woman inquired curiously.

"I am speaking to Anne, my mother. I know because I recognize your voice."

Anne was beside herself, and so happy to be talking to me after all this time. I hadn't seen, or heard from her, since pre-school. It had been such a long time. I was surprised that I still remembered her voice.

A mother's voice is one that you don't forget…My ears were highly tuned to the sound of her voice coming across the phone.

Anne was able to get in touch with Carl, thanks to Aunt Deb. Anne went on to explain that she tried many times to get in touch with us, but was always cut off by Edith or Carl.

Then I recalled a conversation that I had with Carl a few years earlier.

Carl and I were in the car heading to Hobbs, when we were having a conversation about Kathleen. I managed to ask him about Anne and if he had heard anything from her. Carl told me that Anne was dead for all he knew. I divulged this conversation to Anne, and she assured me that she was not dead.

I realized Carl had told me this to put a stop to the questioning. He wanted me to forget her. So, I put all hope to ever see Anne again in the back of my mind to forget her.

Our conversation continued, Anne asked me how I would like to come visit her for a couple of weeks. Of course, I wanted to visit her. After all, she was my biological mother and I wanted to get to know her. She asked to speak with Carl, and they made an agreement for our visit. Anne was coming to pick me up that following weekend.

I am not sure how Edith found out about Anne coming to get us, but she did.

MONTH OF MOMS

ANNE DROVE UP OUR DRIVEWAY IN A WHITE CUTLASS CIERA. She had kids in the car with her. A sister and two brothers. I was surprised. Will didn't seem to mind either. After a brief introduction, Anne embraced us. The moment was fleeting, as we were ushered to quickly gather our things. Carl was trying to get us off on our travels, before Edith arrived. He was too late.

Edith pulled up in the driveway, just as we were packing our bags in the car. She had driven all the way from Tatum to stop Anne. Carl stood his ground and wouldn't allow her to take control of the moment. Edith was visibly angry, as she shouted slurs and hateful things to Anne. We got in the car and drove away.

Anne shook off the harassment and focused back on us being together. She told us that there were other siblings waiting at her house to meet us. Four, count them, she had four more children besides me and Will. Not to mention that she was pregnant with another child. My mind was blown!

The air-conditioner in the vehicle wasn't working properly, so we had to keep the windows down, as we drove to Coleman, Texas. The drive took us all day. The trip was a lot further than I had expected it to be. I relished the time visiting with Anne and my younger siblings, but the trip was not easy.

Our sister had terrible car sickness and vomited many times along the journey. She puked so much that she ended up vomiting a green liquid I found out later was called stomach bile. I felt sorry for her. I know she was in anguish.

Day turned into night, as the road lagged on into the distance. I had briefly fallen asleep, when Anne reached over to wake me.

"Mandy, look ahead. That is Coleman. We are almost home."

I rose to see light glimmering at the base of a long hill. It was a sight to behold. Everyone was awakened to the news. Excitement filled the car. The final few miles were jolly. We finally drove up to a rock house on a corner lot, on what looked like a small grove. Trees and plants were everywhere. It was beautiful.

Walking inside the house was surreal. It was dreamlike. I was in my biological mothers' home... The reality of the whole situation was almost too much for me to comprehend. We were greeted by Nate and the youngest sibling, another sister.

Anne and Nate had married and started another family.

They seemed to be a happy family. The children were wild and free. I was happy for Anne. We stayed up late that evening, even though we were exhausted. We were trying to catch up with everything we could possibly catch up on, in as quick of a time, as possible.

The next morning, I woke up to the smell of bacon. Anne was in the kitchen cooking everyone breakfast. I went in to help her. During our stay, I made sure to be helpful with everything around the house. We were only allowed to stay two weeks and I wanted to make a good impression, so she would want us to visit again.

Seeing Anne made me feel a pain of guilt. I thought of Kathleen, and I didn't understand the feelings I had being around Anne. I was conflicted, because of my love for Kathleen.

Even with the conflicting emotions, I would never forsake Kathleen. She had been my momma and she would always be my momma. I felt greedy. However, if I was going to have two moms, I was going to enjoy having two moms.

Anne had the whole two weeks planned for us. We helped rearrange her living room to welcome the new baby, once he arrived on the second day there. It was my idea. Then we spent the rest of our days swimming in what Anne referred to as Memory Lake in Coleman. It was a small lake, just a few miles from her house.

Each morning, we would have breakfast, pack up the coolers and towels then head to the lake. The lake was clear and cool. I was glad, because I still had an issue of swimming in water that I couldn't see in.

The kids made it easier for me to get in the lake, because they all plowed into the water without a care in the world. I figured if they could do it, so could I. We would spend the day playing and swimming.

Nate was like a kid. He would climb up a set of telephone poles that were standing in the lake and he would jump off the top like an acrobat.

Nate got an idea and decided to place a board across the top of the telephone poles to join them. The board would be a place to sit or stand at the top to jump off. I was amazed at his climbing abilities, as he scurried up the pole and began hammering away with his tools. He had his youngest brother, Johnny, help him put up the board.

Nate realized that climbing the poles would be difficult for the kids, so he added some step boards ascending the length. That was the best idea he had yet. I had tried to scale the pole previously, but had to jump off halfway up it. I was strong, but not strong enough to get all the way to the top.

It took Nate and Johnny two days to complete their mission.

It was worth the wait. Once everything was completed, we all climbed to the top of the poles. What I didn't realize was how incredibly high the poles were, when standing from up there. Once I got to the top, I felt a bit dizzy from the height. Looking down into the water made me woozy, as the poles seemed to sway in the wind.

One by one, my siblings jumped from the top, just like it was right next to the water. They were bold. I envied them for their lack of fear. It was my turn, but at the moment of my attempt, I froze; I was stuck up at the top of the poles! I couldn't admit that I was scared. I just told everyone I wasn't ready to jump yet.

I could hear everyone chanting below, "JUMP!"

I literally had to talk myself into jumping into the lake from the heights of those poles. I was up there for a good 30 minutes before I could muster up the courage.

3...2...1.... jump! The heat was the final deciding factor.

The leap caused more anxiety as I didn't hit the water when I thought I would. I thought I was going to pass out from holding my breath. SPLASH!!

I hit the water and it knocked what little breath I did have out of my lungs. I struggled to get above the surface.

That's it! I needed a break. I swam to the shore, just in time to have lunch. Nate had grilled some hotdogs and burgers on a small grill for everyone to enjoy. Man, I was starving and thirsty!

After we settled down from our lunch, some of the better swimmers decided we would all go across the lake to a tower.

It probably wasn't the best idea, since it was a good long swim across the lake. But we were all on board and took off swimming.

Once we made it across, we still had to climb the tower. At least it wasn't as high as the poles. I stayed at the bottom for a bit, hanging onto a metal rod that was sticking out of the concrete. It was cool and gave shade to my spot. I was enjoying the water, when I felt something brush up against my ankle. I got spooked and let out a shriek.

"SOMETHING JUST TOUCHED ME!!!"

Everyone laughed. "It's just a fish!"

One of my brothers told me that the fish liked shiny things and I was wearing an anklet. The fish were trying to get the medallions from my anklet. I looked down at my ankle and sure enough, a fish had stolen the yin from my yang! I was mad. So, I placed my foot against the tower and watched the fish as they were swimming around.

Then, just as quick as lightning, another fish darted towards my anklet to steal my yang!

Just like that…gone! I was so mad at this point; I took my anklet off and threw it as far as I could out in the lake, telling the fish to have at it! Those were my favorite medallions! UGH!

To calm down, I decided to climb the tower and jump off with everyone else. We played on the tower for a good hour, or so, and decided we better swim back across, before it got too late.

Thinking about it now, it was quite the endeavor to swim across that lake. I don't think I would have the trust in my children to swim across it without a life jacket, or a float of some kind. It is amazing that none of us drowned from exhaustion on that swim!

The days all seemed to melt together, as our time with Anne was coming to an end. On our last day together, we all hugged that morning and said our goodbyes. I was sad that I wasn't going to get to see all my siblings for a while, but I was grateful for the time with them.

I knew that I would be seeing Kathleen soon. Even though I was looking forward to seeing her this time, the trip would be bittersweet, because I didn't want to leave Anne. I didn't want to leave my siblings…

At least this time, I would get to see Manda and my Grandparents too. Anne met with Kathleen to drop us off at their house. We went to stay with her for two weeks, before returning to New Mexico.

One Friday evening, Manda and I went to hang out on Main St. This was a common custom for teenagers around that time. Teens and young adults would do what was referred to as "drag Main" or "park" on Main Street.

I felt like a grown up, when hanging out with Manda and her friends on Main St. We listened to music, chased each other and danced. I did not want fun to end.

On Saturday, Manda and I went to stay the night with her friend Amy. Now about Amy…

Amy was wild and devious! She came from money, which spoiled her. She was used to getting what she wanted. The night started out innocent enough, however, things would take a dramatic turn before the night ended.

We were in Amy's room listening to music and playing with her clothes and makeup. Amy was biding her time, until her dad fell asleep. Manda and I had no idea of the plans she had in mind. Amy had been seeing an older man who lived in Odessa.

(Now mind you, Amy and Manda were 17 years old and I was a "mature" 14-year-old.)

Amy was itching to go see this older man. But, she was grounded; this did not stop her. She had been on and off the phone all evening, talking with this man, trying to entice him into coming to Monahans. Her attempts to get him to travel to Monahans were futile. Amy was visibly irritated, this tempted her to a challenge.

Amy stepped out of the room for a moment, then came back in and rushed us along to get our shoes. I looked at Manda insecurely, but Manda assured us that everything would be okay.

I went along, what else was I gonna do?

We stealthfully snuck out to her father's car. She opened the front door and put the car in neutral. She instructed us to help her push the car out of the driveway. She didn't want to wake her father from his slumber.

I felt incredibly uncomfortable with everything Amy was doing, but I was in it for the ride.

I didn't want to seem like a yellow belly.

As I climbed into the back seat, I noticed a phone receiver sitting on a large bag. I asked Amy, "What is that?"

She replied, "It's a Motorola bag phone".

I was curious, "What's a Motorola bag phone?"

Amy giggled at my question and explained what the bag phone was, and how to use it, as we pulled quietly away from her driveway.

I was feeling anxious in the backseat, because I knew we just stole her father's car. Manda seemed to be a little more comfortable with everything going happening. I guess she knew what to expect when being around Amy.

Now we were driving down the road and I had no idea where we were going. I was just praying to whomever would listen that Momma didn't find out!

I didn't want her to be disappointed in our unforgivable act of theft. Even though I didn't steal the car, per say, I knew I was guilty by association. (I did help her push it out of the driveway...)

Amy and Manda were talking in the front seat, when Amy divulged the information of where we were heading.

Odessa, Texas... We took off in the middle of the night to go to Odessa from Monahans.

THIS GIRL WAS CRAZY!! Even crazier was me taking the back seat for the ride!

Oh my God!

Oh my God!

Oh my God!

My mind was racing with all the possible scenarios that could play out from this. All of them ended with my ass whooped or me in jail!

I asked Amy to turn around and take me back home. Manda looked at me and said, "Everything will be okay."

"Don't worry!"

Easy for her to say… This was the first time I had ever been involved in a situation like this and I was a captive audience to the whole scene.

After the lengthy drive, we arrived in the mouth of a driveway, leading up to a trailer house. Amy looked at Manda, then Manda looked at me. I breathed a sigh of relief that we had made it safely to our destination.

Amy picked up the bag phone and checked for the signal. This piqued my curiosity… I watched her closely as she dialed up a number and waited for an answer.

Nothing… No answer….

Amy hung up the phone and discussed her options with Manda.

"Just go knock on the door." Suggested Manda

"I don't want to just go bang on his door!"

"What if he gets mad?" Amy considered.

"Oh my God! Amy! You drove all the way over here in the middle of the night!"

"DO SOMETHING!"

"Or, let's just turn the car around and go back home!" I blurted out.

Amy pondered her options and decided she would call one more time.

Ring, ring… "Hello?" a confused sleepy voice came over the line.

I sat back in the seat, wishing that no one answered the phone.

Amy began conversing with the fella. He was tired and didn't want any company. This did not sit well with Amy. She slammed the phone down, got out of the car, and walked straight up to the trailer. Manda and I sat in the car, wondering what we should do, as we watched Amy bang on the trailer door, until it opened.

Amy disappeared inside. Manda and I waited. After a couple of minutes, Amy reappeared and waved for us to join them.

I walked hesitantly up to the trailer and entered. The fella, Ryan, asked if we would like anything to drink and gave me a soda. Manda sat me on the couch and told me to wait there, while the three of them disappeared into the back room.

I waited…

I heard a noise coming from the cupboard. I sat still and listened silently… Another noise… This time I had to get up and investigate what was making the sounds coming from there.

I turned on the kitchen light and carefully opened the cupboard door.

"HOLY SHIT!! A SNAKE!!!!"

It wasn't just any snake, it was a 7ft Albino Burmese Python! My screaming outburst caused the others to come running down the hall towards the kitchen. Ryan started laughing.

"Oh, I see you met Marvin," he said, "I forgot to introduce you when you came in. I was still half asleep and didn't really think about it."

"Can I touch him?" I asked.

"Yes, you can touch him. You can even hold him, if you want."

"He doesn't bite...people." Ryan deviously grinned from ear to ear.

As I mused over the snake, I reflected to myself, this trip wasn't as bad as I thought it would be after all. Who would believe that I am sitting here, in a trailer house in the middle of godforsaken Odessa, Texas, holding an Albino Burmese Python?

After Ryan was sure I was comfortable with Marvin, he and the girls returned to the back room. I was content for the remainder of the night, with Marvin keeping me company.

I had passed out on the couch and was awakened by Manda hurrying me to come around and get to the car. They had overslept and now we were going to be in BIG TROUBLE. We had to get back to Monahans in a hurry.

Along the drive back, Amy did the admirable thing and decided she would take us home, and drop us off, before going back to the house. She didn't want us to see her dad lose his cool on her. Plus, she would be able to use taking us home as an excuse for why the car wasn't there, when he woke up.

Amy's ability to manipulate her situation was impressive. If only I could be so clever!

Momma never knew of our escapades that night. At least, she never admitted to knowing and I never divulged the information either.

Until now...oh, well.

Sunday was our last day in Monahans. It was time to pack up and head back to Lovington...

HELL HOUND

TO GET MORE INVOLVED WITH THE COMMUNITY, Sheila had decided to try her skills at leading a Girl Scout troop with another friend, and they were quick to gather up all the girls they knew to be a part of the troop.

Surprisingly, I was able to join. The only hitch was, I had to find my own way back and forth. I decided I would ride my bike to the meetings. I was fortunate that I didn't have to ride my bike for long. Victoria was a member of our troop and her mother was sweet on Carl, so she offered to pick me up and drop me off.

The Girl Scouts was just the distraction I needed to get me focused and take my mind off everything else. Sheila and Pat were the perfect troop leaders. I knew both of them, which made me comfortable.

Immediately, all the girls in the troop went to work on earning badges. I enjoyed the challenges and the arts & crafts the most. Pat was a by the book teacher and Sheila was more of a hands-on leader.

Sheila would take us out into the field to build and work. Pat preferred staying in the meeting hall and going over our minutes. During one of our meetings, Pat and Sheila told us we would begin earning money towards a spring trip. We got three places to choose from, Colorado Springs, Santa Fe or Carlsbad Caverns. Everyone unanimously chose Colorado Springs, Colorado.

The trip gave us something to look forward to enjoying. For some of the girls, it would be the first time they ever left New Mexico.

We made it our mission to sell as many cookies as possible. I took to selling around the trailer park and the surrounding houses in the area. I was doing well with my sales, so I decided to expand my area and head further into town. I met up with an acquaintance from school. She told me her father would be back later that afternoon and bid me to return at that time.

I patiently waited for the time of his return, hoping for a good order. When the clock struck 2pm, I began my trek back down the road, towards her home. The walk was longer than I liked, but I didn't mind with the prospect of a decent sale to come at the end.

As I entered the covered carport, the house seemed quiet. I hesitantly walked up and knocked on the door. Knock, knock, knock... A loud jarring bark penetrated through the walls and I heard the sound of dog paws pounding through the house.

The sounds were that of a large dog. I was immediately on guard and began walking back away from the door, with a sinking uneasiness in my gut. The bark was now at the wooden gate. The sound was so startling, that I began briskly walking away from the house.

A continuous bark at the gate and then silence. A rattling and a thud came next, causing me to turn in curiosity to see what caused the racket. To my surprise, the large hound had scaled the fence and was now in a guarding stance, with his head lowered and his teeth bared at me, as he growled.

I tried to back away and get distance between us. The hound lunged forward which terrified me. In a state of panic, I began to sprint in the opposite direction, as I heard the hound barreling down on me, closing the gap between us.

In an instant, the hound was on top of me, knocking me to the ground and tearing at my back. I screamed in pain and cowered toward the ground with my face planted, as the hound rendered a final blow to my leg, piercing my calf and tearing into my flesh.

I laid still in shock, as the thought that I was going to die trying to sell Girl Scout cookies crossed my mind. I was right by the highway, yet not a single car stopped to render aid.

The hound eventually gave up the fight and turned away. I laid in the dirt mauled, defeated, and alone in pain. I pulled myself together after some time to make sure the hound was no longer in my presence.

I examined my body with reluctance for the damage I had sustained. My back was scratched up and bruises were setting in everywhere. My pants were torn, with blood saturating the opening. I pulled the jeans back to see a deep mangled gouge. The wound was so deep, that I could see my tendons and muscles.

I managed to move my leg through the pain to make sure I could walk back home. I tore off the bottom of my jeans off, and fashioned a makeshift bandage to get home. I was more worried about Carl finding out, than I was worried about the damage.

I knew if he found out, I would have gotten in trouble for going that far down the highway. Plus, if I had to get stitches, he would be angry for the cost.

The walk back was longer than the walk to sell the cookies. I hobbled the best that I could, still in wonder why no one stopped to assist me. I finally made it home and quickly slipped into the bathroom to nurse my wounds and my ego.

I should have told Carl and gotten stitched. The wound was so deep that it took several weeks to heal. I continued to doctor it and clean it each day, as I watched it slowly form a scar that remains with me today.

Once again, I faced death and lived to tell about it!

I did get to show it off to my brothers and the kids around the trailer park. Everyone thought it was gross and cool to see my tendons move. Eww…

That day ended my cookie selling career.

I told the other scouts what happened, and they were willing to pick up the orders on their end. This gave me a lot of relief. I ran into the girl acquaintance several days later and she asked me why I didn't sell any cookies to them.

After I explained what happened, she was quick to understand my reasoning for never going to her house again. She thanked me for not telling her dad, because he would have had to put the dog to sleep.

Secretly, I had wanted that dog to die for hurting me… But I didn't tell her, and we went on our separate ways.

COLORADO BOUND

On a hot afternoon, Stef and I were in my front yard working on one of our baking badges, by baking brownies in an aluminum foil oven that was heated by the sun. The trip was getting close, so we were fantasizing about it, wondering if it would be snowy and cold. I wondered what the people and the food were like.

"You know, we will be staying in a campground." Stef said.

"I imagine there will be lots of other kids hanging out." I answered.

Stef replied, "I hope there is some cute boys!"

We both giggled.

"Wouldn't it be amazing if we met our soul mates?" I daydreamed...

"I am too young to worry about those kinds of things, Mandy."

"Yeah, I guess I am too..." I said in agreeance. But secretly, I hoped to meet someone I could be happy with and share my life.

The conversation dwindled as we checked on the brownies; my mind continued the thought of meeting my one and only. I imagined what my life would be like to love someone and be loved by him too. I was lonely and longed for a real connection.

The day of the journey had finally arrived!

I took quick stock of all my belongings for the trip as I waited for the van to arrive. We were all anxious to get on the road. Sheila was well prepared to keep us entertained with games and songs, while Pat drove. The trip would be just at eight hours with gas and potty breaks.

We didn't care! It was getting us out of Lovington.

The drive was liberating. We started out by talking about all the things we would do, while we were in Colorado. We sifted through the travel brochures and planned the events of the days. So much to do, in so little time! We would be there a full week and we were going to try to do everything we could possible do.

The closer we got to Colorado Springs, the prettier the scenery became. Sheila rolled down the windows for us to enjoy the cool breeze. The air was crisp and easy to breathe. The road winded along the side of a mountain and all the girls found a window to peer out in amazement.

Eventually we made it…The Garden of the Gods… I thought that was a beautiful name and fitting for such a lovely place.

We pulled into our camp site and everyone got out for a good leg stretch. Our first mission was to find the bathrooms! That was a long ride and we tried to keep the stops short and sweet, so we could get to our destination as fast as possible.

I looked around and saw that we were not the only people just arriving. Many people had the same idea that we had to stay there for the weekend.

Sheila and Pat began unpacking the van. I lent a helping hand, as the other girls walked the campground.

As I was helping set up the tent, I heard a commotion of laughter and looked up to see what was happening. Some of the girls had been bombarded by a couple of curious boys. After finishing the tent set up, I went over to join the fun.

The girls were laughing, because the two boys, Ryan and Brad, had a different accent than what we were used to hearing. We asked the boys where they were from, and Ryan told us he was from Louisiana. We were fascinated by their voices. Ryan was about our ages and Brad was a few years younger. At least the girls would have some company.

A few minutes go by and I felt someone staring at me. I looked up and saw another boy peering around the corner at us. Our eyes met and I felt an immediate electrical jolt through my body. I quickly looked away with embarrassment. Curiosity got the best of me and I look over his way again, only to find he was still looking at me.

What was this?

Again, I felt the same jolt course through my body. My hands started sweating and I began feeling extremely nervous. He was still looking at me!!

Our attraction to each other was palpable, so much so that the air was thick with it!

A voice came booming out from behind a car, "Boy, you better get over there and introduce yourself!"

The voice belonged to Ryan and Brad's stepdad, Billy. Apparently, I wasn't the only one feeling the intensity of the situation.

The boy who had been staring at me was the older brother to Ryan and Brad. He made his way over to our circle. We kept staring at each other. I tried to look away and pretend to be interested in all the other conversations.

It was no use… He had my attention.

"Hi."

"Hi, my name is Mandy."

"Mah naam es Steven Dorrrree." Said the boy.

"Huh?" I couldn't understand a word he was saying. His Cajun accent was so thick!

"What did you say your name was?" I asked, trying to pay closer attention to his words.

"Mah nam is Steven Doré."

"Oh, I think I got it now, Steven Doreee…"

"No, meh… Steven Doré, like Steven Door Ray but toogetta."

I giggled and thought to myself, why am I so nervous? How is he making me feel like this? How am I gonna be able to talk to him, if I can't understand him? I wonder… can he understand me? How old is he? Does he have a girlfriend? So, many thoughts running through my head all at once.

Steven said my name, "Mandy."

The breath came out of my lungs. The sound of his voice saying my name made me lightheaded. Then we both giggled nervously.

We continued small talk in the circle, as his brothers picked and pandered to the other girls.

MANIFESTED LOVE

STEVEN TRIED TO SEEM INTERESTED IN THE OTHER CONVERSATIONS, but eventually looked directly as me and asked, "Would you like to take a walk with me?"

"Yes, I would." I replied, as I realized that my ear was getting more in tune with his accent.

After asking for permission to walk around, I met up with Steven. Our conversation was engaging and fluid. He was interesting and from a land far from my home. He spoke of Louisiana and made me fall in love with a place that I had never hoped to see, before that moment. I paid attention to every detail.

Steven and his family had arrived in Colorado to celebrate his 17th birthday. He had some other family living in Colorado Springs that they would be visiting during their stay.

I wanted to know all about Steven. He was beautiful to me, the most beautiful boy I had ever laid my eyes on, or seen. His eyes were deep dark brown, his brown hair, full and past his shoulders in length. His skin was caramel kissed from the sun. He had braces, which made his lips purse when he closed his mouth.

251

Steven was courteous and considerate. He took time to ask questions about me and where I was from. He listened just as intently as I did to his conversation. He was patient, as I rattled on about things. His eyes never left mine. I wondered how such a beautiful creature would take such an interest in my life. How is it that he never looked away from me? He made me feel important. This was a new feeling to me.

The hours had passed when we were abruptly interrupted by Stef, Ryan and Brad. The boys picked on Steven singing "Steven and Mandy sittin in the tree, K…I…S…S…I…N…G…" Steven scolded them to be quiet. Stef told me that I was needed back at the camp.

I didn't want the day to end. I was having a wonderful time with Steven. We got up and started to make our way back to the campsites, when I felt Steven tug on my hand and turn me to him.

"Can I see you tomorrow?"

"Yes, I would like that very much."

I went on to say, "The troop has some activities scheduled, but when we get back, I will have time to visit."

"I really enjoyed today, thank you."

"So did I." he said in a whisper. We began to walk further; he pulled my hand again. This time he pulled me close, "Will you be my girlfriend?"

My heart soared! Without hesitation, "Yes, I would very much like to be your girlfriend." He pulled me close and hugged me.

I couldn't believe it! I was someone's girlfriend! Not just any someone, but I belonged to a handsome Cajun boy from Louisiana and he belonged to me. I was on cloud nine. We held hands all the way back to camp.

For the rest of the evening, all I could do was think about Steven. All the girls were dying to know what happened. We sat in a circle in the tent, as I reminisced about the day.

The next morning couldn't come soon enough. I woke up several times in the night hoping it was time to get up. I wanted to see Steven before the day started if I could squeeze a quick minute in with him. I guess he had the same idea because when I opened the tent, he was outside waiting. It was almost as though we were thinking with the same mind.

My heart swelled and I could feel a pull towards him, as I walked over to greet him a good morning. Steven was smiling from ear to ear. He was just as happy to see me. He hugged me tight and kissed me on my forehead, telling me good morning. I couldn't think of a better way to start the day.

Sheila and Pat were meddling around, getting prepped for the day's activities. Sheila called over to me to make sure all the girls were waking up and getting ready. I told Steven that I would be right back, he asked if he could help. We woke the girls and then snuck off to have a few minutes to ourselves before breakfast.

Our private time was quickly interrupted by his brothers. They were stalking us. Steven tried to brush them off, but was only successful once girls started peeking their heads out of the tent. Ryan and Brad were more interested in the Girl Scouts, than they were in Steven and me. We were glad for the distraction!

Sheila called out for all of us to round up, so I said a goodbye to Steven and told him about what time we were supposed to return to camp. I didn't want to leave him. I really wanted him to come with us, but I knew I couldn't ask such a thing.

As we gathered around Sheila, when Pat announced that we would be doing something special for the morning breakfast. We would start our day at a nearby facility that was a game room carousel, with treats and eats. Everyone was thrilled with the news! Steven and his family were camping next to us and heard all the excitement.

As we loaded up to head over to the Carousel House, I saw Steven and his brothers riding around on their bikes. I didn't realize they had plans to follow us as far as they could go. We had left the park, when one of the girls noticed the boys were following us on their bikes. I moved over to look and there they were peddling as fast as their legs could move them.

I fell back in the seat, laughing with the other girls. Those boys were being silly. There was no way they can follow us all the way.

We were wrong! They followed us all the way to the Carousel House.

This place was amazing! It was an actual restaurant and game room, on a carousel! After eating a delicious and hearty breakfast, we all gathered in the game room to play our tokens. We thought we had lost the boys, but Stef tapped me on the back and said, "He's here!"

I turned around to see Steven holding on to a bar that supported the ceiling and riding his bike beside the carousel. He was grinning at me, with sweat on his brow. I giggled.

"What are you doing here?"

"I had to see you." He confessed.

"I can't believe you followed us all the way?" I asked, "What are your parents gonna think?"" I asked concerned.

"It's no big deal, my Uncle lives around the corner and we are going to visit after this."

I shook my head in disbelief on how smitten we were with each other. This boy followed me all the way on his bike, just to spend more time with me. I gave my game tokens to the other girls for the video games. Then I sat on the side of the floor, with my legs dangling off the edge, next to Steven, as he continued to hang on to the pole and bike around and talk with me.

We spent the better part of the day at the Carousel House, eventually eating lunch there too. The weather called for rain, so our leaders gathered us up to head back to camp.

Sheila had taken notice that I just met this boy and we were spending a lot of time together. "I see you have been spending a lot of time with that boy. Y'all must really like each other," she stated.

"I do like him very much. I feel like I can't breathe right when I am not around him…is that normal?" I inquired.

"Ahh…young love…I remember being young and in love once. It's a special feeling." She recalled

"You do realize that you only have a week with him…" Her words were like a hot knife searing through my soul.

Only a week…

I hadn't thought that far into the future. I had been living in the moment relishing the thought of just being Steven's girlfriend and hadn't considered our time together. Anxiety began to creep up in my mind and now every moment with him became more precious to me than before.

When Steven and his family returned to camp, I ran over to see him immediately. The look on my face must have spooked him, because he immediately asked me, "What's wrong?"

"Can we go somewhere to talk?" I asked

"Sure, give me a minute and I will be right there."

Steven quickly joined me for a walk to the pool. He could tell that I was bothered, and he showed his concern. We held hands tightly, as we walked. "We can talk now. What's bothering you?"

"I didn't think all of this through...I just realized that we only have a week together..." I said. "It's not fair! I want more time with you."

A look of concern crossed his face and the reality of our situation hit him like a brick wall. After he gathered his thoughts, he turned me to him and held my face, as he spoke heartfelt words, "I promise you, we will find a way to be together."

I believed him.

Steven meant every word he said. His words gave me comfort. I couldn't fathom how we were going to do it. We lived two states away from each other... We had no money and no car... But I trusted that we would figure out a way.

I'm hungry, let's go to the vending machine, so I can grab a soda and something to snack on." I followed him to the vending machine and watched him as he purchased a Root Beer and a package of Bugles. We sat down on a log to continue our conversation, while sharing the tasty snack.

A few bites into the bugles and we were both thirsty. Steven popped open the can of Root Beer and took a big sip. I asked if I could have a sip and he looked at me, shaking his head no.

"NO?!?" I questioned, as I realized he was being coy. He held the soda away to entice me, in order for me to wrestle for it. Back and forth he teased, as we both laughed. I reached across his body, and I could feel his warmth, as he pulled me in close. He looked at me deeply, took a big drink of the soda then leaned in and placed his lips on mine to share the soda from his mouth. My initial reaction was to try and pull away, however he held me gently, so I drank from his lips.

The drink led to our first kiss and then many kisses after… I was in love with Steven. My heart and mind were his captive audience. His kisses caused my body to quicken and made me want him.

Steven asked if I would like to join him in the pool. The evening was a bit warm, especially with all the kissing and hugging. I could use a cool down. We went back to our campsites. After I changed, I met him outside and we headed to the pool.

We had the pool all to ourselves. The water was perfect as I dipped down into it gingerly. Steven joined me after he made sure the water wasn't too cold. We splashed and played around for a few minutes before he came in close to me again.

"I want to tell you something," he said, as he looked deeply into my eyes.

"Okay, what is it?" I asked curiously

"I'm in love with you. I was from the moment I saw you," he confessed.

I melted in his arms.

We kissed deeply and lovingly. He held me close, as we kissed. I could feel his body react to mine, as I wrapped my legs around his waist in the pool. We had ignited each other in our passionate embrace.

I wanted him, and he wanted me. We continued to kiss, as a gentle rain started falling on us. The steam from the pool wisped up around our bodies, intensifying our emotions. I was so in love with this boy that I was helpless. I was willing to give myself to him, and I didn't feel ashamed about it.

Unfortunately, our romantic moment was rudely interrupted by a couple of the girls and his brothers, before we could take it to the next level. We had to return to the camps, because it was raining...

Damn...damn...damn...

Fortunately, Steven was able to join us in the tent for some card games. His brothers were entertaining the other Girl Scouts. Everyone was having a pleasant evening.

The time passed into the midnight hours, when Sheila told everyone lights out. I didn't want Steven to leave, and he didn't want to leave, so I asked Stef and Victoria if it would be okay if he came back to sleep in the tent. They were perfectly okay with it, and even assisted in sneaking him back over, after everyone fell asleep.

We knew we couldn't get caught with Steven in our tent. I was nervous when he entered back into the tent; we planned to be quiet so there was no kissing or necking. Steven laid down and I put my head on his chest. The sound of his heart beating in his chest was soothing. We were both at ease and nervous, but soon fell asleep in the comfort of each other's arms.

I woke early the next morning to make sure Steven could sneak back to his camp, without detection. Victoria and Stef worked their magic once again, by keeping the leaders preoccupied, so Steven would have safe passage. We couldn't have managed it without them.

Even with morning breath, Steven stole a kiss from me, before heading to his tent. He reappeared after a few minutes, pretending to have just emerged from his own space. We were surprised we pulled off the night, without detection.

The group sat around and ate breakfast, as the day's plans were discussed. We still had so much to do. For the remainder of the week we had to visit The Royal Gorge, Pikes Peak, Ripley's Believe It or Not and some old castles. My time with Steven would be stifled.

Billy showed up, just before we finished up for the morning with a Colorado Springs Gazette to show Steven. The headline read, "STEVEN DORE TO HAVE SHOTGUN WEDDING!" Everyone got a good laugh. Billy enjoyed picking on Steven for being so taken with me, and he wanted to commemorate the moment with the gag gift. Steven didn't think it was as funny as Billy had intended it to be.

We left for the day's adventures, however, my mind stayed on Steven. Every breath I took was for him. I couldn't get into the activities, because I wanted to get back to see him. I had never experienced this overwhelming feeling before this point. It was intoxicating, I felt so weak away from him. All I could do was watch the other girls take in the sights and enjoy the moments, as I counted down the minutes to return to Steven.

Each evening, we would return just before dinner time and I would head straight to see Steven, if he weren't already waiting for me. My engagement with the troop had waned. Sheila spoke to me of her concerns. I defended myself with the knowledge that our time was limited, and my interaction with the troop would pick back up after the trip.

Surprisingly, she understood and allowed me time to spend with Steven.

The evenings in Colorado Springs were sprinkled with 15 to 30 minutes of soft rain, just around 7pm every night. Steven and I would run from the campsite to the laundromat near the pool, and sit outside dreaming of our lives together, while cuddling and kissing as much as possible. Our bond grew stronger with each passing moment, as did the intensity of our passions.

I wanted to give myself to him, but I was scared… I had a secret that I was too ashamed to tell him. How could I give myself to him when my grandfather already took what I had to give? I could never tell Steven the truth… I was embarrassed. I didn't want our love to be threatened.

Steven was a gentleman, even though he wanted me, he never pressed the issue. He just loved everything we shared. He didn't want to spoil things by rushing too fast.

We knew we had already rushed up to that point, in our defense, we were up against time.

The day before heading home was somber for the both of us. We would spend the last day at the camp. I was glad we only had plans to pack up for the trip back home. This meant I had more time to spend with Steven, but reality hung over us like a heavy cloud. Stef came and met us at the laundromat. She brought my disposable camera to take some pictures of us together.

Steven was a little camera shy, but didn't mind taking a couple of pictures with me. Steven and I hugged as Stef took a couple of pictures.

"Make sure you send me copies," Steven insisted.

"Of course, I will send you a copy. I don't want you to forget me." I confessed.

He grabbed my face, looked me deep in my eyes and said, "I will never forget you."

Our evening turned late into the night. I didn't want to go to bed. We both wanted the final moments to last for as long as we could manage them. We managed to have one more night embracing each other. I didn't sleep a wink; with every sound of his beating heart, I fell deeper in love with him. I just listened to him all night, till the sun started peeking over the horizon.

The morning was heavy, as we packed up the van. Steven and his family were packing up for their return to Louisiana. The weight of the inevitable began to torture us.

We walked out to the laundromat one last time to spend our final moments together. Steven reached into his back pocket and pulled out the rolled-up newspaper. "Here, I want you to have this to remember our time together." I strained to hold back the tears. We embraced each other like it was the last day on earth.

Steven's parents pulled up beside us, along with the Girl Scout van. His parents got out to tell all of us goodbye. Sheila and Pat got out to share goodbyes, as well. We exchanged our phone numbers and addresses, so we could keep in contact. Steven and I began to cry, as we held onto each other tightly. The magnitude of the moment had built up, and we knew we had no choice but to let go.

We fought it with every fiber of our being.

Sheila and Steven's parents began to pull us apart. We held on as tight as we could. As they began to break our hold, I felt as though my soul was being ripped in half. Steven looked down at me with tear-soaked eyes, "We will find a way to each other, I promise."

I believed him, but made him promise again. "I want to hear you say it again!" "Swear to me we will be together!"

"I swear to you Mandy, with all my heart, we will be together again."

As our embrace ended by being pulled apart, I whaled out in a cry from a broken heart that was nearly collapsing. Sheila hugged my face into her neck, and told me it will be okay. Her words did not soothe me.

I broke free from Sheila, and ran up to Steven one last time. I took the necklace off my neck and gave it to him. "Keep this with you, until we meet again."

"I will wear it always." Steven promised.

"I love you, Mandy."

"I love you with all my heart and soul, Steven."

He turned and struggled to force himself into the vehicle. As they drove away, Steven looked out the back window. I could see him crying, as he placed his hand on the glass to tell me goodbye one last time. I watched until their vehicle disappeared into the crowd of vehicles on the highway.

The first portion of the return home was numbing for me. I was completely devastated without Steven near me. I sat quietly for many hours, as I watched out the window, while my mind thought of ways to get back to him.

Sheila was intent on getting me out of my funk, so she put a tape in the radio and began playing songs to get the girls in a fun mood. Eventually the music took hold of me, after some mild coaxing, and I began to sing along with them.

My sadness eventually turned to acceptance, and then gratitude. I realized I had experienced something incredibly special, and in time we would be able to be together. I just had to be patient.

The song Head to Toe began playing and Stef encouraged me to sing along. That was easy... The song epitomized how we met and how we fell in love. The song made me feel again, it made my feelings for Steven awaken from the numbness of our separation, causing me to sing the song loud and with vigor. I sang it with passion so Steven could feel me, even though the miles that were separating us, as the distance became greater.

My mind went back to the moment that Stef and I daydreamed about our trip to Colorado, and the chance happening of meeting the love of a lifetime. I had met my one true love; I had met my love of a lifetime and I couldn't deny it.

Back to reality, as we made it back to Lovington safely. I couldn't pull myself out of the moments I had shared with Steven. I wanted to rewind time and go back to live those precious memories over and over.

UNEXPECTED BETRAYAL

MY RETURN HOME WAS UNEVENTFUL, almost as though I never left. I went straight to my bedroom and began my first letter to Steven. Our passion would be shared through paper and pen now. I hoped, beyond hope, that he was still thinking of me. I began penning all the hopes and dreams I had for us on paper, so to seal it in our reality someday.

Some things had changed while I was gone. Aunt Deb had begun dating a guy by the name of Norman. He worked at the local pizza diner, Pizza Man. He was a creepy dude and he had eyes like a viper. I don't recall ever seeing him blink... He was so creepy, that I labeled him "Norman Bates".

Apparently, the changes had caused some tensions to rise with Carl, because he had intentions of getting Aunt Deb to see him romantically. Because things had become estranged at the house, Aunt Deb spent more time away, than she did being home.

I was glad when she finally made some time for me to share my adventures to Colorado Springs. She was happy for me, and believed that Steven and I would find some way to be together again. Her hope soothed my paining heart.

At least someone believed in us.

I asked Carl if I could call Steven. Of course, he blew his lid when he realized it was a long-distance call. I assured him I would pay him for the call with my babysitting and housecleaning money. I was only allowed to call Steven once per month, if I paid for the call.

But that was not to play out as I had expected… when I returned home one afternoon and found several of my items missing. My curling iron, hairdryer, some of my clothes and some makeup were gone. I ran to tell Carl, and that's when the hammer came down. He informed me that Aunt Deb had skipped town with Norman.

The story wasn't that cut and dry. Norman had broken into the Pizza Man and stolen all the cash out of the register. They then came to our house, and she helped herself to my things and a couple of guns from Carl.

I felt utterly betrayed. I loved her!! I trusted her!! How could she?!?

They were being pursued by the police, when Norman shot at them. He, in turn, was gunned down in the conflict. The police captured Norman and gave Aunt Deb a choice to turn him in, or go down with him.

It was discovered that this creepy dude was wanted on several counts of robbery and other criminal activities. Aunt Deb made the right choice and turned herself in, as well as gave the police the evidence they needed to convict Norman, once he was released from the hospital.

I was angry at Aunt Deb, and didn't talk to her for several years after she stole my things.

Carl ended up sending us back to Edith's after Aunt Deb left. I can't speak as to why he sent us there. I assume it had something to do with Aunt Deb leaving and he became overwhelmed without her help. I came home one day after a meeting at Girl Scouts, and Edith was there to pick us up.

Ugh…Back to the sweltering grind of working in the fields and the garden. I was once again Edith's indentured servant.

PERSONAL INFERNO

I SUPPOSE AT THIS JUNCTURE I SHOULD UPDATE THE READER on my present situation. When I began this writing, I was on furlough through my employer, due to the COVID-19 outbreak. I have since been relieved of my employment, because of the resulting loss of customers in the field.

I knew the moment when I heard the phone ringing, seeing that the call was coming from my employer at 8am in the morning. It was a dreaded moment that I had hoped would pass over me. I had looked forward to going back to work. I did enjoy the position and the people I worked with as a team.

They will surely be missed.

The loss of my job has caused me some depression and anxiety. I manage to work through it by writing. So much is at stake: our home, our stability and what the future holds for us.

I have researched to find ways to continue to bring in income, in order to help with the finances. The social and work culture dynamics have changed so much in the face of the outbreak, that finding gainful employment is difficult, if not impossible at this time.

We have been mandated by the Governor to wear masks in all our comings and goings in public. I have my own ideas about the masks, as they are redundant and useless in culling the virus. The mandate only angered me. I hate seeing our country so compliant, without question to the laws that are now taking over our freedoms.

This feeling of helplessness only encourages me to write more. I am at a point that even with all my experience and knowledge, I am about ready to throw in the towel and go to work for McDonald's or Wal-Mart, if necessary.

Time will tell how things work out for me and my family.

Enough of my ramble… Back to the story…

The remainder of the summer was unforgiving and hot. I missed the climate in Colorado Springs. I longed for it. I know I had only spent a week in God's Country, but I had been spoiled by the beautiful weather. The days were long, dry and windy. I kept my chin up by thinking of Steven when I was working the fields.

As usual, Will was not holding up to his end of work, while we were out in the garden. I had already scolded him once for playing around. I encouraged him to stay focused, so we could get out of the heat, but he continued his merry way and caused me to linger from my row. I had been hoeing the weeds around the tomatoes, and he was working in the peppers. I went over to check his progress, when he began running from me.

I chased after him into the corn, and lost track of him. So, I headed back to my row, when I saw Edith waiting for me. She was livid and didn't want to hear a word out of my mouth. Will had made his way back to his row, before Edith came to the garden. I found him working as though he had been diligent all along.

I had been set up…

Edith grabbed the board and called me to the end of the row.

"Grab your ankles!" Edith condemned.

"But…"

"I SAID GRAB YOUR ANKLES NOW!!

I obeyed and grabbed my ankles. She raised her hand as high as she could and brought that board down on me with a force that nearly knocked away my breath. Again, and again, she flogged me. I was about to fall to my knees from the pain, when the final contact to my tender backside broke the board in two pieces.

Edith was appalled, but I believe at that moment she realized the magnitude of her anger, and it caused her to turn away and leave without a word. Liam and Will were shocked to see the board had broken.

With tear swelled eyes, runny nose, and sore ass, I picked up the gardening hoe and continued to remove the weeds out of the row, until I was finished. Edith didn't look at me, or speak to me, for the remainder of the day. But, Liam was quick to make fun of the fact that the board had broken on my tiny backside.

The board breaking on my ass soon became a running joke in the household, and of course it was at my expense.

I tried to ignore it and I went to my room, deciding to write a letter to Steven to purge my hatred of my situation. I hoped to find some relief and hope for a better tomorrow.

I finished my letter and took a quarter to Edith, requesting a stamp for my letter. She didn't have any available and told me to place the quarter on the letter, in the mailbox. The mailman would get the letter with the quarter and place a stamp on it for me. I was relieved to know I wouldn't have to ask her for a stamp again. She asked too many questions for my comfort. When she found out it was to a boy, whom I had met in Colorado, she had that much more ammunition for her next level attacks.

Edith decided for me to begin sleeping in her room, instead of sharing a room with the boys. Since John was now working nights and out of town through the week, I would sleep on his side of the bed.

On the weekends, I would sleep on the couch, in the living room. She decided I was too old to be sleeping in the same room with the boys. Her comment was "no telling what Mandy would be prone to doing in the night, with boys all around her." That comment made me sick to my stomach and inspired a deep disdain for her.

The off handed remarks didn't stop there. Edith was always commenting on my body, or the way I carried myself, as though I was a whore in heat. If I did my hair and makeup, I was a jezebel. If I didn't do my hair and makeup, I was ugly. I couldn't win with her. She tore up my self-esteem, one criticism at a time. At least I knew that one boy didn't think I was ugly; he made me feel beautiful…Steven Dore. I hung on to his words and hoped they would never fade from my mind.

I would check the mailbox every day for his letters. Edith would make fun of the delay in his letters. She would fill my mind with doubt, but only for a minute, because I knew what we had was real and she couldn't take that away from me. The day final came when my first letter from Steven had arrived. His letter was reassuring and sent me into a state of mind that helped me through the tough times with Edith.

I read over his letter many times, before I placed it in my white and red record keepsake box. I burned every word of his letter into my memory and in my heart. I was able to come out of the dark place, if only for a minute, but he helped me from it. Every word, of every line, spoke to my soul and I knew he was missing me. Steven loved me and that was all that mattered. That was enough to keep me going.

The letters drew a jealousy out of Edith that cause her to become more malicious towards me. I felt attacked in every moment that I was around her. At night, she would kick me in the bed and tell me to scoot over. Her toenails would gouge into my leg. I became conditioned to sleeping on the edge, in order to avoid her attacks.

I looked forward to school starting again, so that I would have at least an 8-hour reprieve from her constant onslaught.

Aside from the abuse, life had taken on a normal routine with school back in session. I was glad to see my old friend Roger, again and make some new friends. I met a girl by the name of Kenny, and we immediately became friends.

Kenny and I had a lot in common, with broken families, and moving around a lot. Our friendship seemed to gain the attention of an older girl, by the name of Sarah. Sarah was in the 9th grade and she was known to be a bully. When I attended Tatum school in the 6th grade, she didn't pay much attention to me, but this time I unexpectedly became her target.

I made the mistake of trying to befriend her when she came over to talk to Kenny. Sarah did not take kindly to girls who made her feel inferior, or caused any discomfort in her routine. I had crossed the line and didn't know it. She was an Alpha and she decided who she would talk to and when.

No one was allowed to talk to her without her permission.

I was ignorant and not aware of her rules. Sarah wanted to be friends with Kenny, and she did not want me to be part of the equation. She bluffed me into thinking she accepted my apology and pretended to be my friend too, but only long enough to get information on me. Sarah was a master manipulator. I really had no idea what she had in store for me.

Back on the farm, I was having a normal day, as we went about doing our normal chores. I was in process of feeding the chickens when Will began pulling his stunt of not carrying his load and playing. I scolded him and tried to get him to continue with the chores, so we could get on with our day. He began throwing rocks at me and it pissed me off.

I bolted after him and Liam jumped in to help. They both began ganging up against me and hitting me. Liam pushed me to the ground and Will kicked at me.

I had all I could stand and something in the pit of my being broke loose and I lost control. I came up off the ground like a wild banshee, with a strength I didn't know I had. I grabbed Will by the shirt and the pants and threw him against a barrel, and he cut his butt on a piece of metal that was sticking out from the barrel.

Liam grabbed onto me and I began waylaying him in his neck and face, screaming the whole time. I busted Liam's lip.

I WAS A BEAST out of control!

Both boys fled away from me, as I dared them to come at me some more. Neither one of them were having it. It was a moment of triumph for me. I was finally able to stand up for myself against them. I set in my mind that I would never take their bullying again.

I figured one of them had told Edith about the scuffle, but they kept it to themselves. I figured they were too ashamed to admit that a girl had kicked their butts. Single handedly, I might add! HA!

Life became more bearable for a spell and I was good with that. Kenny invited me over to spend the night with her. It was so much fun, we stayed up all night talking and sharing stories. I was so happy to have someone I could talk to again.

Volleyball season was in session and I was all about being part of the team. This was a reason to stay after school and go on trips. I was not going to miss out on the opportunity, so I tried out and was picked for the team along with Kenny. We were thrilled!

I can't say I was the best on the team, far from it. However, I was good at setting the ball for the spike. So, I played to my strength.

Everything seemed to be running smoothly and the season was coming to an end, therefore, Kenny asked me to stay the night at her house in celebration. Only this time, Kenny had invited Sarah to stay to make it a sleep over.

To say I was delighted to hear the news would be an utter lie... I had a gnawing feeling in my gut that this was not going to be as much fun as Kenny had anticipated.

Despite my reservations, I accepted the invite and stayed the night with

Kenny and Sarah. It seemed all was going well, and we had a decent evening. Sarah even seemed to be cool with me, so I let down my guard.

Sarah had managed to glean information from Kenny about me and my life. She used it as a tool to get me to open up, as though she cared for my well-being.

Sarah was flawless in her execution of using information against me. The following Monday, I went to school expecting to hang out with Kenny. Only Kenny wouldn't even acknowledge my existence. She avoided me like the plague.

I couldn't wrap my head around why she wouldn't talk to me. We had just had the best weekend together and we had never even had a fight.

What was happening?

I didn't know what to do, so I wrote her a letter and stuck it in her locker, with an apology for whatever I may have done to offend her, in hopes that she would come around. Sarah met me in the hall, just before last period with the letter. She laughed in my face, as a crowd gathered around us. She ridiculed me as pathetic, because I "lost my only friend". I ran to the bathroom and remained there until the end of school.

I rode the bus home in sheer defeat. I knew Sarah had turned Kenny against me and it hurt. It hurt, mostly because I didn't even know why Sarah hated me so much. It couldn't get much worse than this, or so I thought…

When I got home, Edith was on the phone. I brought her the mail with a smile on my face, but Edith did not smile back. In fact, she snapped at me with her lips narrowly pursed and her eyes glaring at me. Her voice was distinctively hostile, as she continued listening and agreeing with whomever was on the other end of the line.

"Oh? What else went on? Oh, is this true? Go on, yes, I want to know…" Edith said inquisitively.

My mind began to race, wondering what this call was possibly about. It couldn't be about me… I hadn't done anything wrong.

The truth was, I hadn't done anything wrong. I had been in mixed company, with a person who had a vengeance for my annihilation.

Sarah was on the end of the line. She had called Edith in an attempt to humiliate and decimate me further. There was no end to her torment. She had told Edith that I was talking crap about her at school and to all my friends. Sarah knew that wasn't the truth.

When Sarah had asked me about Edith, when we stayed at Kenny's home, I told her that I didn't want to talk about her, because I was afraid Edith would find out.

That was all the ammo Sarah needed. She used that conversation to perpetrate a fabricated lie, in order to get me in trouble.

Like I said, Sarah was a master manipulator.

When the conversation ended, Edith hung up the phone and stood up like a General. She grabbed the belt and began interrogating and accusing me about the night I had stayed with Kenny.

"So, you think you are a smart ass, huh?"

"You are going around calling me a Bitch to your friends?"

"You think you can talk shit about me and get away with it?"

"Tell me the truth, WHAT DID YOU SAY ABOUT ME?"

"I wanna know…You think you are so grown up?"

"I am about to show you what being grown up is all about little girl!"

"TELL ME THE TRUTH!! DID YOU CALL ME A BITCH?" She demanded.

"Grandma, I promise, I would never say anything about you." I admitted.

Sincerely, I was absolutely terrified of Edith and I hadn't said anything about her, for fear of her wrath.

"TELL ME THE TRUTH, GODDAMNIT!! TELL ME NOW!!" Edith said in her fury.

I knew no matter what I told her, she wasn't going to believe me. I continued to plead my case, but nothing I said convinced her otherwise.

"Grandma, please, I am telling you the truth. Sarah is lying to get me in trouble, because she hates me. I swear, I would never talk about you! I SWEAR!" I continued to beseech.

"GRAB YOUR GOD DAMN ANKLES IN FRONT OF THE MIRROR!"

"I am gonna beat the truth out of you, even if it kills you!" Edith declared.

Once again, I obediently went over to the loveseat and looked in the antique mirror that stretched across the wall, from one end to the other. I looked at myself and then looked at Edith, before I bent down and grabbed my ankles. My head was bowed in defeat. That wasn't good enough for Edith.

"Look in the mirror! I want you to see every lashing you take, until you admit the truth!" Edith commanded.

I looked up in fear, as my eyes met her gaze. She began aggressively lashing me across my ass. Her swings were inconsistent. Some lashes would hit my legs. Other lashes would hit my back. Edith was swinging all over my body and with every blow, the pain became excruciating.

Liam came running out of his room, laughing and poking fun that I was getting my ass beat. He continued to prod, as Edith continued to wail on me.

Hit after hit after hit after hit…

What began as pain, turned to numbness. Edith demanded that I admit that Sarah was telling the truth. But, I remained steadfast that I was the one telling the truth, so she continued with the lashing. The constant taunting of Liam began to fuel anger inside of me. Fear had left me and I refused to cry. I just kept my gaze with Edith's eyes. She swore she would not stop beating me, until I cried and admitted the truth.

I continued to hold my ground and refused her demands. I decided she could go ahead and beat me to death, but she was gonna hurt for it. I would not admit to something I had not done, no matter the cost. I was not going to be the victim anymore! The more she hit me, the more desensitized I became, both in body and spirit.

What began as derision from Liam, became concern. He realized that Edith had crossed the line and was taking the beating too far. He called out to me to just admit I was wrong, and to apologize, so Edith would stop. I looked at him and refused. He was laughing no longer. He realized that I was telling the truth and he just wanted the lashes to stop. He begged me to admit it, and I continued to hold out in protest.

Edith had hit me so many times that she was getting sore and had to switch arms. She continued to beat me incessantly. I took it and kept my gaze with her. Liam began to beg his mother to stop. She would not...

When Liam realized that we were in a battle of wills, and that the beating had left marks on me that were going to take weeks, maybe even months to heal, he began to cry and plead with Edith. Her response was, "I will stop beating her when she starts crying!"

I absolutely refused. Edith recognized a look in my eye that began to strike a sense of fear in her. I was no longer frightened of Edith. This was going to be the last time she laid her hands, or any weapon on me. Liam jumped up in that instance and got between us, putting an end to Edith's madness.

Edith asked me one more time, before she gave over the belt, if I had called her a bitch. I looked at her in repulsion and walked away without a single word. She didn't come after me. That was a good decision on her part. I was ready to lay my fists into her, if she did. I was taught somewhere along the lines in life to respect my elders, but she had lost all my respect that day, and I refused to give it to her ever again.

Liam followed me into the room to check on me. He was big enough to apologize for his part in the provocation and said he would never mistreat me again. He asked if he could see what Edith had done. He wanted to help me if he could. She had beat me bloody in some areas. He admitted that Edith had gone too far, and it was horrible to witness. I can't say I immediately believed him, but he was true to his word, nonetheless.

Things did change between me and Liam, one could almost say that we became friends. It was a welcome change. It took me several weeks to recover from that event. Thank goodness I wasn't in sports any longer, because some of the bruises went down to the back of my knees.

I returned to school without reservation. Liam had my back and he wasn't going to let Sarah bully me any longer. I am not sure what he said to her, but she wouldn't even walk down the same hall as me. When she would see me, she would find another route.

Kenny and I never recovered from the Sarah fallout. I couldn't forgive her for choosing Sarah over me. I was her true friend and she betrayed me. I chalked it up to her loss.

The dynamics between me and Edith changed. She seemed to be timid around me, and less demanding. She no longer hovered, or said off handed remarks. It was almost as though she avoided me, because there was a certain unknown fear of what I was capable of doing to her.

Edith was no longer in control of my emotions, and she knew it. She did not have power over me anymore. I was wicked and used that knowledge to my advantage, keeping Edith at bay.

Edith ended up getting sick with Hepatitis shortly after the beating, and to be honest with you, I was hoping she would die from it.

I know that is a horrible thing to say, but THAT IS THE TRUTH!

REDEMPTION

AFTER SOME PLANNING, EDITH WENT TO OKLAHOMA to stay with her brother for a week, leaving Liam in charge of the house. John was off working on a rig for a couple of weeks, so Liam and I had the house all to ourselves. Will had gone to stay with a sitter, which gave us full reign!

Of course, Liam and I took full advantage of our situation, and he invited some friends over, after he scored some Mad Dog 2020, Budweiser and Jack Daniels. That weekend, we threw a party the best way we knew how. We turned on the boom box and got out the cards and party favors.

We played quarters for shots. Then played spoons, dice and cards till our eyes crossed. I had never been drunk before, but I was drunk now. Liam was having a great time. I had never seen this side of him before.

Liam treated me like an adult, with no questions asked. I was enjoying this newfound friendship with Liam. We all laughed and drank, until the sun started to come up. Eventually everyone found a place to lay down and passed out.

I woke up a few hours later to a putrid odor that was filling the air. When I stood up, my head was still spinning, but the odor was making my oxygen intake intolerable. The smell was causing me to gag. I found a rag and covered my face, as I followed the odor to its source.

I made my way through the dim light of dawn, down the hall. The smell was emanating from behind a bedroom door. I opened the door against my better judgement, and was hit in the face with an odor so foul that it would wake the dead.

Liam had vomited while he was passed out. He vomited huge amounts of alcohol and food all over his bed and floor. It was utterly disgusting. He was lying face down in the mess. I was surprised that he had not drowned in it.

I called out to Liam, through bated breath. He did not respond. I had to shake him violently to wake him from his alcohol induced slumber. This was not good... This was not good for either of us. The house was mayhem and we were both hung over. We only had a few hours to clean, before John returned from his two-week stint on the job.

I gathered myself, and made us both something to eat to help soak up the alcohol. We both downed a couple of aspirin to kick the headache hangover. I was able to clear the house of the extra bodies, once they realized that John was returning. Plus, no one wanted to help clean up the mess. It took Liam about an hour to come around, but the food did some justice and helped him get his land legs again.

We worked diligently on cleaning up the house and ridding it of the putrid odor. We worked right up to the moment that John drove up the driveway. Liam and I quickly escaped through the back door, out to the chicken pens to tend to the animals, as though everything was normal.

After we made sure we were in the clear, and John was none the wiser, we were relieved and laughed about it. Liam thanked me for pulling through for him. He also thanked me for taking care of him. He knew I didn't have to do it and after everything he had done to me, I should have let him get in trouble.

Liam didn't know it, but I had completely forgiven him from the moment he apologized. I would be loyal to him, so long as he kept his word.

I confessed; I didn't want to hold the past over him. We were kids and I realized that he was only doing what he had been taught. Liam was taken aback by my ability to let it go, and told me that he had a lot of respect for me because of it. His apology, and that weekend party, sealed our friendship. Liam was a different person now. We went on to share many more nights in the sand of the water ditch and muse over music.

At school, Liam had my back and welcomed me into his circle of friends. I was no longer the lonely awkward girl walking down the hall. To some degree, Liam was now, more or less, my bodyguard.

Ironic, isn't it.

The day came that Carl returned to pick us up and take us to our new residence. Liam took me to his room and gave me some old Atari games, and music tapes to take with me. He told me that he was going to miss hanging out with me and keeping the boys at bay.

Unbeknownst to me, several of his friends had asked him about me and he wasn't having it. Plus, he was trying to keep me virtuous for Steven. I was grateful for his consideration.

Liam didn't know it, but the letters from Steven were getting fewer and farther in between. The delay in his letters set doubt in my mind. Early on, we had spoken of running away and getting married. I held on to hope that the day would come where we could escape together, but that was not to be.

I received a letter in November of 1987 which gave me a hint that his life was getting busy. He was preoccupied with what was in front of him, which caused me to be pushed to the back of his mind. My worst fear was realized when his final letter came in May of 1988. This letter was impersonal. I knew he had moved on, even though he didn't rightly admit it.

I knew Steven still had feelings for me, but I felt I needed to cut ties, so that he could be free to live his life. As I wrote my reply to his May letter, my heart broke, but I knew it was best for him and me. It wasn't fair to either of us to keep hanging on to a pipe dream that we would never realize. Too much was against us, both time and distance were not playing in our favor.

I paused, while writing in reflection of our week together. I imagined that if it were meant to be, we would find our way back to each other, like we promised.

Then I had a vision of us.

We were in our late 30's, early 40's, and we were together. With that in my mind, I could see Steven with long curly hair sticking out of a ball cap. His face covered in a salt and pepper colored beard. I thought that if life got between us, at least by that age if we had any children, they would be grown, so we could be happy together without distraction.

The vision gave me hope, as I finished the final words on the paper. I figured I would set him free to sow his oats, so we both would know what we really wanted in life.

I delicately placed the letter in the envelope and sealed it with a kiss. I had made it to the mailbox, just in time for the mailman to get it. As the mailman drove away with the letter, I had a sinking feeling wash over me.

It was the same feeling I had the day we separated in Colorado. I turned around and began running after the mail truck, but it was too late, it disappeared around the corner in the dust from the dirt road.

I continued to look for his letters, even though I knew the odds were that he would not reply. I had hoped that he would fight for what we had once experienced, but there was nothing.

The mailbox never gave me another letter from Steven…

I never told Liam. The breakup was too personal for me and I wanted to absorb the heartbreak in silence, alone. I didn't want anyone to know that I failed in my promise to Steven. I certainly didn't want Edith to know anything about it either.

Liam and I said our final goodbye and he gave me a big hug and wished me well with my high school endeavors. It was a well-received change of circumstance for me, with Liam on my side.

For the first time, I was going to miss him too.

TEEN STEPMOM

OUR NEW HOME WAS ANOTHER TRAILER HOUSE, quaintly located on the North end of Lovington, just a block shy of the tracks. Shortly after moving to the trailer, Carl had a new love by the name of Cissy.

Now a bit of back story on Cissy. She was only 3 years older than me and I knew her and her family. I had been to her house a couple times with her younger sister Tina, of whom I had met while dragging Main Street one night, with Liam.

Liam had his license and would make his way into town on the weekends, picking me up to cruise with him. Cruising was what all the teenagers did at that time. We would drive up and down Main Street antagonizing the other drivers, while yelling out the windows, playing the music to loud, and parking on empty lots.

Usually we would gather in a semi partying fashion, as we danced, flirted and watched the other cars go, by while hanging out on the tailgate. It was a fun passing of the time and kept most of us entertained.

Lovington was once a booming little town that was slowly becoming a retirement community, so most of the activities for the teenagers had been shut down. First the town council closed the movie theater, then they closed the skating rink, and finally the bowling alley.

All that the youth had left was the dance hall for Friday night dances, held by the school, and dragging main. Those who didn't attend the dances hung out on main, only to be joined later by those leaving the dance.

We would gossip and play, while plotting a plan to get someone to buy us beer. Sometimes we would be lucky enough to get some adult beverages. Everyone would meet at a parking spot we affectionately called the hangout to indulge in the drinks and smokes. We felt bold and daring, because we were getting away with something that was against the law.

Stavy was loud and boisterous. I could hear her across the parking lot and she eventually made her way to our tailgate. She had a thing for Liam, but he was hard to tie down. She liked the chase, so Liam's rejections didn't slow her advances. I wasn't sure about her when we first met, because she came off a bit aggressive and that made me uncomfortable. Before the night was over though, we were buddies.

It wasn't long before Stavy was dragging me all around with her. I didn't mind, she was different. Drama always followed her. I knew when she showed up that the night was going to be interesting. I admired her nerve.

Stavy eventually took me to her home, where I met her large family. Her mother had married Cissy's dad. They were a blended family with 8 children combined. I became a staple around the house, for a spell, getting to know everyone, and even going on a family trip to the lake with them. This was a trip which led to Cissy and Carl meeting.

At first their romance was kept in secret. Cissy eventually admitted to the affair and before I knew it, she was going to be my stepmom. I liked

Cissy, but I didn't like the idea that a girl who had just graduated high school was going to be married to my dad.

I swallowed my pride and decided if she made Carl happy, I was happy for them. I even figured this would play in my favor, since we were friends first and she was my age. Boy... I was never so wrong!

Did no one see what I was seeing? I mean seriously?!? This girl was 22 years younger than Carl and only 3 years older than me, his daughter!

Come on!

It was so painfully obvious to me...

Carl was either going through his midlife crisis, or his deepest desires were playing out in his life like a Freudian Slip! She was looking for a sure-fire way to get out of her house and a ride to college. In any case, it was sickening to me. To make matters worse, her parents approved of the relationship!

Their affair was brief. The wedding was planned and held in our trailer by the tracks with Desert Iron Club affiliates in attendance. The wedding was short and sweet, so the festivities could begin. Along with the festivities, the tension between Cissy and I also began.

Cissy immediately took her role as my stepmom as her right to boss me around, and I wasn't having it. If she told me to do something, and I refused or didn't agree with her, she would go to Carl and tattle on me and he would straighten me out quick. She knew how to get me to do anything she wanted, because I didn't want to disappoint Carl. I wasn't afraid of Cissy, if anything I was disgusted with her for marrying Carl.

Just as I thought, Carl put her through college to become a nurse. May

I remind the reader, I was 16 years old and his only daughter. He hadn't even bought me a car, but he was putting this stranger through college!

Yeah, there was definitely some jealousy too. I was jealous of the things my Dad was doing for her, and she was jealous that I still had my freedom.

I tried to keep my focus on other things and stay away from the house as much as possible. I formed a friendship with Laura, the eldest sister to Cissy and Stavy. Laura and I found an instant connection through the love of art and music.

Laura was going to Vogue Cosmetology to become a hair stylist. She began using me as her model and play with my hair and make-up.

For a time, Laura got me involved in modeling for Vogue Shows and I enjoyed the limelight. Secretly, I wanted to become a real model, but knew the cards were stacked against me, because I was short. So, I lived it up while I could, with Laura always doing some crazy thing to my hair. She was incredibly creative. I loved to brainstorm new ideas with her.

Laura and I would go out on the town and hang with people she knew. This became the norm for us, for a time. However, Cissy would put a stop to that at the first opportunity which, came a week before homecoming of my 9th grade year.

I had permission to hang out with Laura until 11pm on the weekend. Out of respect and compliance, I always made my curfew. One odd night came about, and Laura was having car trouble. Laura wanted to stop before dropping me home and pulled into Allsup's, so she could get a soda, when her car died.

After several attempts to start the car, with no success, I used a quarter and called home to inform them I might be a few minutes late, because we were stranded. Cissy answered the phone and adamantly stated to be home by 11pm, no exceptions. She had no give with me. I told Laura we needed to figure something out quick, because Cissy wasn't budging on the curfew.

We were able to flag down a friend who was generous enough to give us a ride to the trailer. I walked in the door at 11:00:15pm. I was met with Carl and Cissy sitting on the couch, with a clock facing them.

Cissy immediately called out to me, "You're late."

"No, I am not! It's 11 o'clock." I refuted.

"To be more accurate, it's 15 seconds past 11pm…you're late!"

"Oh, come on… are you serious? It's 15 seconds."

"It took me 15 seconds to get from the car to the door."

"I was on the property on time." I settled.

"Your dad and I agreed that if you were late, you would be grounded for two weeks." Cissy added.

"You have got to be kidding me! Are you serious? Homecoming is next weekend! You are grounding me for 15 seconds??"

"This is unbelievable!!" I said in disbelief of what was happening.

"Dad, I was with Laura! I even called ahead to let y'all know what happened, so I wouldn't get in trouble!" I pleaded.

It didn't matter, they weren't moved to my plight. I know Cissy reveled in her victory over me. When I looked at her, she smirked and then kissed Carl. I was so pissed. I went outside and told Laura.

On my behalf, Laura went to talk to her sister and try to win some leniency. That just made matters worse. Carl said if another thing were said about it, I would be grounded for a month. At which point, I was almost willing to get a month of grounding, since I was already missing the much-anticipated homecoming. I already had a corsage and a dress that I just wasted money on buying. To top it off, I had to tell the boy that asked me to the dance that I couldn't go.

God, my life was sucking…

I wasn't allowed to hang out with Laura after that night. Cissy had convinced Carl that it wasn't a good idea for me to be around older people. I guess it was good timing, Laura had met a gentleman and she really didn't have the time for me anymore.

I became solitary for a spell, and stayed in my room away from everyone. I didn't mind the solace. I found time to read and draw again. I had plenty of time for reflection.

I began to think on where I wanted my life to go, as I daydreamed over Rick Springfield and Corey Haim hanging on my walls. It was comforting to be alone and away from the drama that people caused in my life.

Will was the only one able to pull me out of my self-made prison. He met several of the kids in the neighborhood and found out that there was a homemade basketball court in the back alley that everyone hung around.

Will busted into my room one day and asked for me to join them. I was apprehensive at first, but I decided that it would be good to get out of the house before I became a permanent hermit.

TEEN STEPMOM | 295

I became a regular at the basketball court for a few weekends and made a few friends too. It was nice to have a distraction away from the house. However, I missed hanging out on the drag with Stavy and Laura.

My body was going through more changes and I began to obsess over my looks and what I wore. It was a little unhealthy, looking back at it now, but I think every girl and boy goes through that stage to some extreme or another.

I would stay up late and play with my clothes and costume jewelry, trying out different looks and styles. Recreating myself was enjoyable. I don't know why, but my hair would always look so on fleek when I was just playing around, but when I tried to fix it the same to go somewhere, it always decided to flop...go figure...

Late one evening, I was playing with some jewelry that Laura had given me. A pair of hot pink lightning bolt earrings were lingering at the bottom of my jewelry box. I decided to see what they would look like with my new style hair.

The first earring went into my right ear with ease. I was surprised, since I hadn't worn earrings in some time. I had developed an unusual allergy to certain metals and quit wearing earrings after my ears got a terrible infection.

I attempted to put the second earring in my left ear, but realized my ear hole had closed. I wasn't going to give up. I applied pressure till the earring pierced through. The pierce was painful, but tolerable. Some blood dropped from the pierce, so I decided to go get some alcohol and peroxide to doctor it.

At that moment, I realized I would have to go into Carl and Cissy's bathroom to get the meds. The kids' bathroom med cabinet only held Q-tips and toothpaste.

It was past midnight, so I should be able to slip in there undetected. Everyone had been in bed for a few hours so surely, they would be asleep. I crept down the hall, through the living room and then into the kitchen with ease.

As I got to the second hall that entered Carl and Cissy's bedroom, I got nervous. I stopped to listen for any sounds, but couldn't hear anything through the door. Taking a deep breath, I cautiously opened the door. I began to tiptoe through,, when I was alarmed by Cissy screaming "GET OUT!"

The startle from Cissy's scream caused me to look in their direction, when I witnessed something that made me want to burn my own eyes out! Carl had Cissy hanging naked off the bed, as he was hammering away on her, their bedding was in shambles...Oh my god... The sight was so distressing that it froze me for a second, before I was able to move.

"GET OUT! GET OUT!!" Cissy continued in a high-pitched scream. She didn't have to say it again. I ran out as fast as my legs would carry me. I couldn't look her in the face for a time after that night. Cissy avoided me too.

About a week later, I overheard Carl talking to Cissy about some money he was missing out of his wallet. Cissy assured Carl that she had no idea what had happened to it, when the phone rang and interrupted them.

The Manager from the Kentucky Fried Chicken down the road called to speak to Carl. I was carefully listening in, when Carl blew his top.

"He did what?!?"

"How come you didn't call me sooner? Yes, I am missing some money!"

"Stop him…what do you mean it's too late?"

"So, you let him spend the money and then call me? This is unbelievable!!"

"Thanks for nothing!" Carl slammed the phone down and began cursing Will to Cissy.

Will had stolen the hundred dollars from Carl's wallet. He took several of the kids we played basketball with to Kentucky Fried Chicken and bought them parfaits to impress them.

The Manager of the restaurant had allowed Will to make the purchase, and then realized whose kid he was after Will had left the restaurant. I was so glad I wasn't a part of that situation, because I would have been grounded for the rest of my life. Carl took that hundred dollars out of Will's ass all the way home, when he found him eating the parfait at the basketball court.

Will was prone to sticky fingers and would help himself to anything he desired. Carl didn't realize he had that problem, until the money disappeared. I tried to warn him when Will would come to my room and take my things without permission, but no one listened to me.

Harvest season came upon us quickly and Edith was soon banging on the front door to pick us up to help. I saw her pull into the driveway when I was in the bathroom and had already made my mind up that I was not going with her. I had talked to Kathleen and was planning to go spend time with her.

Edith came into the door like she owned the place and she was already placing judgement on Cissy. That marriage did not make Edith happy at all. For the first time I was in agreeance with her, but I wasn't going to sit back and watch her bully Cissy either… That was my job!!

The look on Edith's face was priceless when I told her to leave Cissy alone. I had never back talked her, or spoke to her in that tone. I told Edith, Cissy was doing the best she could and what she did in her own house was none of Edith's business. Edith tried to save face and ordered me to get my things and to get in the car. I told her with a straight face, "I am not going anywhere with you."

"I have already made plans to go spend some time with Kathleen."

Edith's face grimaced, as it turned red with anger and jealous, before she began cussing about Kathleen and calling her every name in the book. I had all I could stand and stopped her in her tracks, "I will not sit here and listen to you talk shit about my Mom, when you were part of the problem in her marriage!"

"You are a miserable old lady and misery loves company!"

"If you continue to talk shit old lady, you can just walk your happy ass back out that door and don't come back!!" I continued.

"How dare you!" Edith said in disbelief.

"How dare me? How dare you!!" I retorted

"You need to leave now, before I push you out the door!" I sternly insisted.

Cissy watched in complete surprise. She walked over and gave me a high five, when Edith bowed out of the fight, because she knew she had bitten off more than she could chew. Edith turned around in a huff and left.

I felt amazing to be able to face her like a woman and not be scared any more. Cissy and I celebrated the moment briefly. I was concerned that Edith would say something to Carl about it, but as far as I know, she never mentioned it to anyone.

Mom showed up that weekend. I told her about what happened with Edith. Mom was pleased to hear that I stood up for her and put Edith in her place.

Someone had to do it, sooner or later.

I felt like I had put that demon behind me, and made my mind up that I would never go back out there to help her.

No one was going to tell me otherwise either!

MEEMAW'S WISDOM

I HAD BEEN LOOKING FORWARD TO SPENDING TIME WITH MOMMA AGAIN. This time I spent a couple weeks drooling over Dirty Dancing with Manda and running around like a kid again.

I was blessed with a visit from my MeeMaw and Papaw coming to see us during my stay. I hadn't seen them in quite some time. In fact, the last I could recall seeing them was when I lived in Monahans and Mom was married to Carl.

MeeMaw and Papaw were my Grandpa's mom and dad. I loved them dearly. Papaw had taught me how to lasso with a rope. That skill was short lived, when I lassoed Papaw around the neck and almost choked him to death in my excitement of his capture. Carl grounded me from ever using a lasso again.

MeeMaw treated me with favor. I don't know what I ever did to make her love me so much, however, I wasn't going to question her affections towards me. She had come bearing gifts during this visit.

The gifts were specifically for me. MeeMaw grabbed my hand and took me to the car to get two boxes. One box was filled with blue and white plastic plates and bowls with oriental designs. The other box was filled with authentic Silver wares.

"What is this for MeeMaw?" I asked curiously

"This is for you my dear…" she answered

"But why? I don't understand." I questioned

"My dear, every daughter or granddaughter is bequeathed something of value and importance from their parents or grandparents, when they come of age."

"Soon, you will find yourself getting married to someone special and this is my gift to you."

"I wanted to give you these things now, just in case I was unable to see you later." She continued.

"I don't know if I will ever be worthy of someone to marry me…" I admitted remorseful.

"Why would you say such a thing?" She looked at me with concern in her eyes.

"Because I am damaged goods and I have nothing to offer a man." My words stung me, as I realized the weight of their truth.

MeeMaw had heard enough and sat me on the porch to share a bit of wisdom.

"My child, this world can be cruel. I know that at your tender age you bear many scars already. If I could change the world for you, I would. The truth is, I do not have the power in me to change it for you. This is your lot in life, and you will have to rise above it. What happens to you in life can either make you or break you. You and only you can decide what it does to you."

"No one else can do it for you." MeeMaw paused in reflection then continued.

"I can share many stories of life's wisdoms with you, but our time is limited so I will tell you this… Some people have life easy and everything is given to them. Those people grow up and do not appreciate life or its bounty. Some people must work for everything they have, only to appreciate and care for everything around them.

You my child are the latter. You will grow up and appreciate everything; that is why I have chosen to give you some of my most precious possessions.

Think of a sword, you have a love for them, don't you? I have seen them in your collection of things. In order for the sword to become perfect in its design, it must first be beaten and heated by fire. This is known as tempering steel.

Right now, you are the raw metal that has been beaten and placed into fires, until you become your perfect self. Your hilt will be your past. Your future will be fashioned by your blade. You will become stronger than metal. You will become the tempered steel with sharp edges that will cut through anything holding you back.

Understand, women are often taken advantage of and underestimated. I see a strength in you that people will underestimate. I hope that someday, you too will see your own strength, as well. So, I want you to stop thinking that you are not worthy of love and that you are damaged goods. Nothing could be further from the truth. I love you and I want you to be all that you can be and more."

MeeMaw finished with a strong hug.

MeeMaw's passionate words burned in my heart. I believed every word that came from her in that moment. I had to wipe away the tears from my eyes, as she kissed me on the forehead and bid me back inside with the others.

That was the last time I saw MeeMaw. She died a few months later from cancer. She knew she had it, when we were sitting on the porch. She didn't tell anyone, as she was being brave in the face of her own fires.

HIGH SCHOOL BOYS

AFTER RETURNING HOME FROM TEXAS, I WAS OUT PLAYING BASKETBALL with Will, when we were called back to the house. Cissy and Carl informed us that we would be moving. They had decided to move back to the trailer park on Artesia Highway.

We would be living in the same house that we lived in with Carolyn and Eva. I didn't mind. I knew the house and it was better than living in a trailer by the tracks.

I couldn't believe that 10th grade was upon me. School seemed to drag on, until then and now, all the sudden, graduation was within reach. School shopping was stressful, with them.

My problem was that I was too tomboyish to be hip with my style.

Oh well, my hair always looked great! I was down with the Aqua Net hairspray and had the high tower with wings hairstyle down to a science!

I started my days at 5am with a shower and then an hour on my hair and makeup before going to the bus. The first day of school was frantic, but I was looking forward to being a sophomore, no longer a peon freshman. Being a sophomore held some clout around the school. We didn't have to put up with the juniors and seniors picking on us.

I was still a bit shy, but I did have a couple of friends and I was happy with them. I had made a new friend by the name of Cecelia. She suffered from seizures, but didn't tell me right away.

It wasn't until a month into the school year when I found out about it. We were sitting in the gym when she asked me to escort her to the office. I wasn't sure why, but I was happy to oblige.

As we walked, she grabbed my arm and asked if it was okay to hold me, because she wasn't feeling well. I asked her what was wrong, and she told me she was feeling dizzy.

As we approached the doorway to the hall of the office, Cecelia became heavy as she began falling and I quickly tried to brace her. I was able to keep her head from hitting the concrete, but didn't know what was happening.

Cecelia's body began seizing and shaking, as her eyes rolled into the back of her head. I screamed for help as I held her, but it didn't seem like anyone was listening. I was desperate to help her, unfortunately, I wasn't prepared and had never seen someone experience a seizure

After yelling several times for help, the school nurse came running down the hall. By the time she reached us, Cecelia was beginning to calm down. The nurse took over to assist Cecelia. I was relieved, but concerned. I didn't see her again for about a week.

Upon Cecelia's return, she finally confessed her condition. She said she was afraid to tell me, because she didn't want me to make fun of her. I assured her that I would never make fun of someone for any reason, especially with a condition that they couldn't control. Cecelia ended up moving away, not to long after that incident. I have always wondered where life took her and if she was happy.

In the meantime, I was getting noticed by a senior boy by the name of Mike. He was handsome and manly. I was approached one day, while I was at my locker, by a couple of his friends. They asked me if I would be willing to go on a date with Mike. I responded that I wouldn't date anyone who didn't have the guts to ask me himself. His friend gave me a smug look and a chuckle as he left my presence.

When I turned around, Mike was standing there behind me. God he was good looking. Tall, dark, and handsome.

He smiled down at me and asked, "Would you like to go out with me this Friday to the football game?"

How could I tell him no? I mean, he did muster up the guts to ask me. We exchanged numbers and he grabbed my hand and kissed the back of it like a gentleman. OH, he was good, this player knew the game and he was good at it.

That Friday, Mike showed up at my house to introduce himself to Carl. That was a plus in his book. He walked me to the door of the vehicle then opened it for me. Add another star to his portfolio! This guy was the full package, handsome, charming, and chivalrous. Any girl in her right mind would fall for him... right?

The night went without a hitch, he took me to the game, then out to eat. I had forgotten what it was like to be treated so well. We ended the night with a kiss. Just one and then he walked me to the door. I was pleasantly surprised to get a call from him the next day.

Mike thanked me for a wonderful evening and hoped that we could see each other again. Yes, I was crushing on him and was hoping he would ask to see me again. When I said yes, he went on to ask if I would be his girlfriend. Once again, he got another yes out of me.

Monday morning, Mike was waiting at my locker. He grabbed my hand when I walked up and placed his class ring in my hand. "Would you do me the honor and wear my class ring?"

I was astonished, "I would love to wear it!"

Mike place the ring on my finger and said, "There, now it's official."

The ring was a little big, no matter, I could manage it with some yarn. Mike kissed me on my forehead and walked me to class.

To get a class ring from a senior was a momentous occasion. It was an honor most girls thirsted for in school. I walked into the class tall and proud. I made sure that my hand was visible for all the students to see. I could hear whispers and murmurs, as I made my way to my desk.

Becky sat behind me and she smiled as I approached, "Congratulations! Who is the lucky Gent?"

"Mike…" I admitted with a grin from ear to ear.

Becky was also dating a senior by the name of Gene. I had always thought their relationship was a bit odd, but never said anything about it. Becky was what some would refer to as Amazonian in build. She was all country and all about the rodeo and the school band. Gene on the other hand was more of an uptown boy who also played in the band. I had supposed, but never asked, if they met in band.

Becky went on to welcome me to the "club" of dating a senior. She admitted that she was only dating Gene for the perks of dating a senior. She got into all the cool activities and was invited to parties that the lesser classes were never invited too.

Knowing that Becky was shallow made me sad for Gene, however, that was none of my business. So, I kept that information to myself. I guess I was quite naïve in the constructs of social behavior in high school. I never thought of dating someone for social status or to climb the ladder. I was in it for the connection. I learned a lot from Becky after I started dating Mike.

Each day we would sit in class and muse over our relationships with the senior boys and share our adventures in dating them. Mike and I were taking things slow, because I was not ready. I let myself go with Steven and fell into him quickly and I can't say that I had recovered from him yet, so I wanted to take my time and get it right.

Homecoming was approaching and my friend Griselda was there to bail me out with a nice dress to wear. She had fashion sense and was willing to help me out. She asked me to get ready at her house. I met up with her early that Friday and we did some shopping before heading to her house.

While we were getting ready, I saw a cockroach cross the floor. "Griz! There is a roach on the floor!"

"Kill it." She said nonchalantly, as she was applying mascara to her eyes.

"Gross! You kill it!" I said repulsed.

"Fine…" as she stomped it into the carpet.

I assume she saw the look of disgust on my face when she laughed and said, "If you think that was gross, check this out!"

She went over and hit the wall with her fist. To my surprise, the walls oozed thousands of roaches all over the ceiling and the panels.

"YUCK!!! How can you live with that many?"

Griselda laughed and said, "You get used to it."

I had planned on returning to her house after homecoming to spend the night, but seeing all those roaches scatter, quickly changed my mind. Griselda got a good laugh about it and picked on me while we continued getting ready.

That girl was a clown.

After we finished getting ready, Griselda's brother took us to meet with Mike and her date. Of course, Mike was looking handsome as ever and he was waiting patiently for me with a bodacious corsage. It was almost too big for me to wear. He pinned it tenderly on my dress jacket and we entered the dance.

The night was magical, as it marked our three-month anniversary since our first date. I felt fairly good about the direction we were heading and thought I would go a little further with Mike the next time we made out. After the dance, Mike took me home. I was surprised that Cissy and Carl were not at home, when I remembered they went out to the Club house and would be gone probably till the next morning.

I invited Mike to come inside and stay for a bit. We started making out. We made our way to my bedroom and continued kissing and rubbing on each other. I pulled back and I took my shirt off. Mike was surprised, but didn't say a word, as he continued to kiss on my neck down to my chest.

He took his shirt off and pressed against me as he kissed me longingly. I went with it and began to melt into the moment. Our hearts raced as he was emboldened to remove my skirt. I now stood in front of him with my bra and zebra striped French cut panties on. Just a thin veil of cloth keeping him from knowing me completely.

The moment was heated as he laid me down on the bed and crawled on top of me slowly kissing as he placed himself on top of me. He began to grind his member between my legs, as we continued to kiss and stroke each other. I was at his mercy, when we heard a car door slam. The moment was interrupted abruptly, as we jumped up and got dressed as fast as we could.

We ran to the living room as though we just got there. I looked out the door to see who it was and was soothed to see it was only the neighbor. Whew, that was a close one! I turned to Mike and he encouraged me to return to him in the bedroom. I felt horrible, when I told him we better not. That scare was too close for my comfort and I didn't feel like we should carry on at that time.

I could tell he was not happy about the disappointment. We were both so close to a dry hump climax and to cool that heat was painful. I kissed him and asked him to forgive me. Mike assured me it would be okay and then decided it was time for him to go home.

I didn't hear from Mike for the remainder of the weekend and he didn't return my calls. I was beside myself in confusion and hurt. Why wouldn't he return my calls? I almost had sex with him. I bared my body to him, well almost my whole body. We shared so much passion and he promised me everything was okay.

What was going on with him? I was so perplexed.

Monday morning arrived... I rode the bus to school with dread. When I walked into the hall, Mike was not standing at my locker like he did every day before that for three whole months. As I was getting my things out of my locker, a boy ran up to me and called me a slut. Another boy ran up behind him and accused me of going all the way with Mike.

I was appalled. My world was spinning. How could he? Mike played me! It was all a game to him to get in my pants. He didn't really care about me and he wasn't the gentleman I thought he was in the beginning. I was a dare and he played it through.

However, Mike didn't get the prize. Mike got close, but he was no winner. In a moment of spontaneous anger, I walked over to him in front of his friends and handed him back his ring. I then assured everyone that I did not sleep with Mike and he lied to save face. Mike was a slimeball and I was breaking up with him!

Mike was shocked and tried to talk to me. I wasn't having it; I was over him! I pulled away from him in disgust and walked to class.

Becky noticed right away that I wasn't wearing my ring anymore. Of course, she had to know all the details. Some of the other students were already gossiping about the drama that just played out in the hall. I didn't care. I laid out all the details for her.

Becky was amazed and told me she was planning to break up with Gene after the semester. She had met another boy at the rodeo that she had been seeing behind Gene's back. Again, I felt sorry for him.

Second semester had started at school. I was glad for it. The new semester meant a change in classes and halls for me. I didn't have to see Mike anymore. I was absolutely repulsed by him now. His friends still talked to me and tried to keep me in their circle.

I wasn't interested in being a part of that crowd anymore. They seemed too shallow and vain for my tastes.

I couldn't trust any of them.

I didn't know who took part in the debacle with Mike and I didn't want to be made a fool again. I remained cordial, but never went out of my way to talk to them after I broke up with Mike.

GENTLEMAN GENE

I ROLLED THINGS BACK TO KEEPING TO MYSELF and spent a lot of time at home. Carl had purchased a Nintendo for us, and I was getting into the gaming world again. Super Mario Brothers took the place of my love life for a spell.

At school, I was getting close to a girl by the name of Patsy. We were friends before, but mostly in passing. During our time in Junior High we had gone on a field trip with the one of our teachers and had to put on an act, just an hour after our arrival. The teacher was severely under prepared, so we only had about 45 minutes to come up with something to bring to the stage.

At the time, Exposé was a popular band. Patsy, I and another girl were chosen to perform a dance and lip sync to the song "Come Go with Me" by the band. We were the most coordinated of the group I suppose.

It was exhilarating to get up on stage and perform as the crowd cheered us on. We brought the magic when Patsy and I placed glitter in our pockets to throw around, as we performed our dance behind the lead singer.

I do not recall exactly why we had glitter with us for the trip, but it worked!

To our dismay, we were beat out by one girl who sang "Girls Just Wanna

Have Fun" by Cyndi Lauper. Her performance rocked the house and caused the stadium of students to leap from their seats and join her on the stage. It was a sight to behold, so I wasn't so burnt about losing to her.

Now Patsy and I had classes together in High School and it gave us an opportunity to really get to know each other better.

As the days passed, Patsy became Pip to me, and I became her Dee. We would hang out with Griz, Trisha and another girl by the name of Stacee in the same grade. For the first time in the history of my childhood, I was part of a group of girls who were on my level. I just wanted to be a girl and have fun! (See what I did there? Haha!) I was a teenage girl after all.

I was standing in our group by the lockers, between class as the girls and I were catching up on some gossip, when Becky and Gene passed by us. Becky reached out and poked me and Gene smiled at me. This became a routine for them, as they passed me each day. Gene even started picking on me, as he walked by, whether he was with Becky or not. I didn't think anything about it at the time.

One solemn morning, as I was going to my locker, I noticed Gene without Becky. His locker was located across the hall from mine, which made it easy to see him coming and going.

Curiosity got the best of me, as I walked over to playfully pick on him about being alone. His face was sad, so I asked what was wrong. He turned to me, with a heartbroken look, and told me that he and Becky had broken up. He found out that she had been cheating on him. Wow, I was surprised that he had finally found out. It was sad to see him in that condition. I could remember him driving up to Kitten's Korner at lunch to meet Becky when we were in Junior High.

Gene was considered a "cool" band geek. He drove a maroon Beretta GT, which helped with his coolness. He was at all the games playing his tuba, so he was active in many things with the school, including photography.

I tried to console his heartbreak and told him that someone else was out there for him. He just needed time. My words seemed to perk up his spirit a moment, so I said goodbye and headed to class.

What was an innocent gesture had opened a door to opportunity…

Gene began paying more attention to me between classes. He continued picking on me on our breaks, which I didn't mind.

Becky had noticed Gene hanging around me more and asked what was going on. At the time, nothing was going on. We were just friends and he was just doing the same thing he always did…pick on me…

Becky's questions caused me to reflect on my own words… Was something going on? Was Gene making advances on me and I was being oblivious?

Those questions would be answered that afternoon, as I was putting my things in my locker to go home. Gene walked over to my locker and asked what I was doing on Friday night. Just so happened, I didn't have any plans.

He was hitting on me and I had been none the wiser.

I had only considered Gene a friend because he had dated Becky. I had never thought of him romantically. But now, that consideration was on the table. Before I could collect my thoughts about the next words to come out of my mouth, Gene asked me to attend the football game with him.

I said I would attend the game without hesitation. As soon as I said yes, I immediately felt guilty and asked Gene, "What about Becky?" Gene responded, "What about her? She isn't my girlfriend or my God, so I can do what I want and it's none of her business." His answer was good enough for me, so I went with it.

"So...are you considering Friday a date or are you just wanting to hang out?" I needed clarification. I knew at some point I was going to have to answer for being seen with him. "I'm good with calling it a date, if you are good with it." Gene answered. "Fine, then a date it is..." I settled.

To say I wasn't skeptical about Gene's intentions would be a lie. I was skeptical, but I was willing to play along. Was he asking me to go on a date with him to get back at Becky? Did someone put him up to dating me, so I could be played like Mike did to me? Whatever his agenda was, I didn't care at this point. I was only glad to have something to do, other than play that damn video game.

On Friday, I had Cissy drop me off at the stadium to meet Gene, before he went to join the band. Gene looked kinda goofy and handsome in his band uniform. I hadn't really taken much stock in his looks before, but I was starting to notice he was cute.

Gene's eyes were brown and expressive, with a sweetly intense gaze. He was taller than me, with an average build and he stood straight. His shoulders were broad, but not too broad. He had a bit of a crooked smile that he tried to hide, because his teeth had been stained from the poor Lovington water supply.

As I looked at him, I realized he had a similar likeness to Tom Cruise, which made me smile awkwardly. Gene caught me in my moment of measuring him up and asked me what I was grinning about. I just shrugged it off with a giggle and said "Nothing. Aren't you going to be late?"

I had to divert his attention to keep him from asking anymore questions. I sat in the seats next to the band, as he sat directly across from me. When the game was over, he asked if I would like to go grab a bite to eat. I was famished and could use something in my stomach, so he drove us to Ole Jax for a burger. I thought that was a good decision since, Ole Jax did have the best burgers in town!

We cruised up and down Main Street for a while, after we ate, and made small talk to get to know each other better.

Gene was easy to be around. He was carelessly funny, with a decent sense of humor. I found as the night lingered on that I was really enjoying his company. We talked about our past relationships. He told me about Becky, the good and the bad.

I briefly spoke about Mike, as I wasn't too interested in sharing all the sorted details of the breakup. It didn't matter... Apparently, Becky had told Gene all the details of our break-up, so my life wasn't as private as I had hoped it would be.

Gene didn't seem to mind that I had a jaded past with another senior and he changed the subject to lighten the mood. He impressed me with his love of music. He was well versed in many genres and was more than willing to share the new sounds with me. Gene introduced me to the underground world of music. I must hand it to him, I would have never known about Depeche Mode, The Cure, Violent Femmes or My Bloody Valentine.

I was born with rock-n-roll in my veins. I loved the roar of guitars and the beat of drums. Gene inspired a new love of music for me and opened my mind to a whole new world of possibilities.

Of course, Monday rolled around, and I had to face a different kind of music... Becky...

When I arrived in class, I expected to get a cold shoulder from her, but she surprised me. She started the conversation with, "So tell me, how did your date go with Gene?"

"Becky, look... I..." I began nervously.

Becky interrupted before I could continue, "Let me stop you there...You don't have to worry. I figured he already had a crush on you when he kept talking to you in between classes."

"Really? It doesn't bother you that he moved that quickly after the break-up?" I asked confoundedly.

"No...I have been over him for a while, before we even broke up. I am completely okay with it," She reassured.

I was grateful that she wasn't angry with me and was taking it so well. She was a big girl by the way, and she could take me out with one stomp. I knew I was no match for her.

One date turned into two dates, and before I knew it, a month had passed by. Gene decided he would take me to Allsup's where his mom worked one evening, so I could meet her. I thought that was odd, but he explained that his mother had weird hours and slept during the day. That made more sense to me, so I was okay with meeting her at her job.

Vivian was her name. She was beautiful. She had the most piercing blue eyes that I had ever seen. Gene definitely had her downturned captivating eye shape, but he must have gotten the brown color from his father's side of the family.

Gene introduced us. Vivian was nice and cordial, but I could tell she was busy and probably not too keen on Gene dating again so soon. We left after a few minutes and headed out to Chaparral Park.

We decided to hang out by the pond, to sit and visit, while watching the wildlife of the park. The night was pleasant, with a crisp breeze. Gene held me close to keep me warm, as we walked around the pond to the bench. Something was shifting in our relationship and a bond was starting to form.

Our spark wasn't instant. It wasn't love at first sight, like I had with Steven. It wasn't an immediate physical attraction like I had with Mike. It was solid and consistent. I had a sense of stability with Gene. Every moment I spent with him brought us closer together. We were beginning to fall in love with each other.

Gene wasn't trying to impress me with anything to get in my pants and I loved that about him. He was as real as they come. He was as committed to trying to make a lasting relationship with me, which earned my respect. I had come to the realization that he was in this relationship for the long haul.

SIBLING JEALOUSY

GENE AND I FINALLY MADE IT AROUND TO MEETING EACH OTHER'S PARENTS in a respectful way. After Gene realized who my stepmother was, he was quick to pull me to the side and inform me he had something to tell me about Cissy.

Cissy had graduated the year before Gene's senior year. At some point they had ended up at the same party and Cissy started talking to Gene. She had been dating another boy that was a year older than her. As the conversation continued, she looked at Gene with concern and asked him if she could get pregnant by swallowing.

I almost fell over myself when he told me that about her. Gene said at first, he thought that Cissy was joking, but he quickly realized she was being serious. She was ignorant to the workings of how a woman got pregnant during sex. This blew my mind, considering she was going to college to become a nurse. I hoped that she would figure it out by the time she graduated.

I never admitted to knowing that information about Cissy, but it did give me a certain sense of satisfaction knowing she wasn't as smart as she led other people to believe. I found her petty and tiresome with her antics of trying to cause tension between me and Carl. She had no idea of our history and I wasn't too concerned with him walking away from me anymore.

Finding out that Cissy was my stepmother opened a whole can of worms. Gene couldn't believe that Carl was married to a girl that was only 3 years older than me and that he was paying for her college expenses too. Gene felt the same way I felt about it and it did not settle with him well.

It wasn't long before Gene started a job at Pizza Hut to have money for our weekend ventures. To spend more time with me, he began picking me up for school and bringing me home after. Cissy was jealous and always trying to find ways to hang me and get me grounded, so I couldn't spend time with Gene. I stayed one step in front of her, by making sure I did all my chores and did as I was told, without a fuss.

Little did I know, Will was jealous too of the time that I was spending with Gene. I had to put a stop to Will picking on Gene a couple of times, but I thought nothing of it until on afternoon, Will pushed Gene too far and they began to scuffle outside, by the trailer next door.

Gene had Will pinned up against the trailer telling him to calm down. Will was yelling at Gene, "You can't have my sister! You will never be good enough for her!"

I was taken aback at Will's comment. I didn't even know that he felt that way about me. We fought all the time. Gene yelled back at him, "I love her and someday I hope to marry her and there is nothing you can do about it!! Our relationship is none of your business!"

I managed to break the two of them apart and sent Will on his way, as Gene looked at me, still fuming from the incident. I was in shock, but flattered at Gene's statement to Will.

"Did you mean what you just said?" I asked timidly.

"What? That I love you and hope we will be married someday? What if I did mean it? What does that mean to you?" He said, as he stood tall, waiting for my reply.

"It would mean the world to me, because I love you too," I admitted, as I pulled him in for an embrace.

We kissed and hugged each other tightly. It felt good to hear him say those words and felt even better for me to admit my feelings. I asked him if he would like to join me inside for a game of Super Mario Brothers, to which he obliged.

Gene and I had been preoccupied in the game for a good while, when I noticed an orange glow penetrate the curtains, just outside the window and behind the television. I got up to peer out the curtains. As soon as I pulled them back, the window was wrapped with flames from a huge fire. I screamed, which caused Gene to jump up and grab me.

We quickly ran outside to see the trailer that Gene and Will had just fought against was now on fire. I ran back inside to tell Carl and Cissy, who had been lying in bed. Cissy called the Fire Department as all the occupants of the trailer park gathered around in disbelief. Some of the men grabbed water hoses to try and put out the fire, while others were filling up buckets.

All their efforts were for not. The trailer burned to the ground, within a matter of minutes. By the time the Fire Department made it to the scene, all they could do was smother the rubble with water.

Everyone was questioned on what happened to the trailer. No one had any idea what happened, or how the fire started. Finally, Phil spoke up about what happened. He was afraid that if he didn't tell the truth, he would be taken away from our family. Will had taken Phil inside the trailer to play. Then, Will had set fire to the trailer.

Carl was livid. He beat Will all the way back to the house. Will admitted he set the trailer on fire, because he was mad at me for being with Gene. That was no reason to burn down the trailer. Carl was even more concerned that Will took Phil in there with him.

Carl's concern was more than understandable. Our landlord made his way to our house and told Carl that we had to move, or he would sue us for the damages. He was doing Carl a kindness, since we had lived there so many times.

The mandatory move caused tensions to be high in the house. Gene was forced to go home, and we were forced to start packing. Luckily, Carl was able to find a house in a better neighborhood, located in the middle of town, just minutes from shopping and six blocks away from Gene.

Will may have caused us a loss of a home, but his actions placed us in a better circumstance.

EVOLVING LOVE

WHAT WAS INITIALLY A DREADED MOVE BROUGHT ON EXCITEMENT for everyone, as we drove up to the new home. It was a Lima bean green, colored home located quaintly on the corner of 6th and Adams.

The back had a privacy fence encompassing the whole yard. On the side of the house was a storage shed that we were not allowed access to, because the landlord used it to store his repair material for the home.

As we walked up to the house, Will and I began peering into the windows, while we waited for Carl to unlock the door. I knew right away which room I was going to pick; I could see it through the windows.

We entered the house into a large living room, separated from the kitchen by a large arched opening. The living room was complete with a shoe and coat closet upon entry. On through the archway to the right was the kitchen, separated by the hall space by a bar.

To the left of the archway was a small hall that lead to what would be my room, located directly across the hall from the community bathroom. At the end of the hall was a bedroom that the boys would share.

Walking straight through the archway and to the back of the house, was the master bedroom that had a large walk-in closet and a half-bath for private use. On the right side of the room was a large sliding glass door, providing a scenic view of the neighbor's house and garden.

There was a door on the right, located just upon entry into the master bedroom. The door led downstairs to a room that harbored space for an additional room and the laundry area.

This home was roomy. It was nice, though I admit, it wasn't as nice as the house out near the Tatum highway. But, it was better than what we had been living in. Its location made up the difference to me. Now I was just down the road from Gene. We would get to spend more time together.

October came around, which is my favorite month, because of Halloween. This year I had my costumed planned and I was going to wear it in a contest. I had scored a Jester costume at a cut rate and it was made of quality material. I couldn't wait to show it off to everyone. Gene was going as a skeleton soldier. Our pairing was mismatched for the festivities, but it didn't matter to us; we were in it for the fun.

Gene and I met up with some other friends and we made our way down to a Halloween Party that was held near the dance hall. I was in awe of all the spectacular costumes, as we entered the door. Costumes had become more extravagant since I was younger. People took more interest in leaving an impression with their choices of costumes, and it worked. I was impressed.

We walked through and saw Dorothy with her cast of the Wizard of Oz and another team of Star Wars characters, among many others. After drinking from the spiked punch bowl, I was feeling more social and started participating in the games. Gene worked his way around the room making small talk with everyone.

I attempted bobbing for apples, but alas, I was not the winner. Pin the Tail on the Black Cat was my strength. I won that game fairly easy, because I was short, and the tail end of the cat was about boob high for me. Easy target, if you ask me, haha!

On to the costume contests… They held three separate contests, one for best group, one for most original and one for best costume. I won second place in best costume, beat out only by the Lion from the Wizard of Oz. My prize was a bottle of Crown Royal in a purple and gold bag. I guess they didn't care that I was underage. I wasn't going to tell them either!

Gene and I left with Sean and Lisa, friends of Gene, to head over and partake in taking care of the Crown Royal. We were lightweights. One drink had my head spinning and I was concerned about making it through the front door undetected. Gene decided we would save the rest for later and took me to get something to eat to calm my head. I was grateful he had a plan, because I sure didn't know what to do.

While we were at the restaurant, I ran into Laura. I hadn't seen her in a long time. I missed her. She asked if I could go visit her at her new place and we made plans for the following day. I made it through the door and to my room undetected, with onions masking the alcohol on my breath. However, I didn't escape the glares darting from Cissy's eyes, as I worked my way through the living room.

Tension was mounting between Cissy and me, even though I avoided her at all costs. I began to become suspicious of her, because I noticed that makeup and perfume were missing from their containers. My clothes would be moved around in my dresser and closet too. She denied using my things when I confronted her about it.

The relationship between Cissy and Carl was starting to show strains too. I didn't say anything about it, as I figured it was none of my business.

The following morning, I woke up refreshed. I went to Carl and asked him if I could go spend the night with Laura. I guess she had beat me to the punch and had already talked to Carl with our plans as he quickly told me yes. I was shocked, but happy. Plus, Gene would get to come visit over at her house.

Gene and I arrived at South View Apartments. It was a new apartment complex that had just been built. I was happy for Laura; she now had a place to keep both of her kids. Yeah, it had been awhile since we saw each other. She was a struggling single mother and she gave up her dream to become a hair stylist, shortly after we stopped hanging out with each other.

I admired Laura for her fortitude in making a life for her and her children. We spent the day catching up. As the night began to get late, Laura fell asleep on the couch, leaving Gene and myself to our vices. We had been alone before, but never in this capacity. We had kissed before, but our kisses never led to anything other than more kisses and some mild groping.

We were watching a movie down on the floor, when he began kissing me. The kissing led to rubbing on top of clothes. I don't know what came over me when I grabbed his hand and placed it under my blouse. He went with it, not questioning the momentum. We began to get heated, when he gently placed himself on top of me. A small motion with his hips led me to spreading my legs, so he could place himself on me comfortably.

I was becoming increasingly aroused as I could feel his hardness between my legs. We began to grind together as our kisses became deepened with a longing passion. I was quickening at his touch. My skin was sensitive to his embrace.

His gentle nudging became more of a thrust, as we both began to climax in the heat of dry humping. I went with the feeling, leaving all inhibitions behind. He knew what he was doing. He knew how to get me there.

Grinding and kissing, until we couldn't contain ourselves anymore, I let out a moan in satisfaction, as he covered my mouth to prevent Laura from waking up. He let out a stifled moan, as he finished up.

Gene continued to lay there kissing and caressing me. I looked lovingly into his eyes and told him thank you. He asked if I was okay with what we did. I was perfectly okay with it. Clearly, we both needed the release.

One session in dry humping led to several sessions in dry humping. We had found a way to release without taking things all the way. I had made up my mind that I was not going to have sex with Gene until I was able to get on birth control, because I didn't want to find myself in Laura's shoes. I needed to protect myself the best way I knew how, and condoms were not of interest to me.

Gene and I discussed it and he agreed that it would be a good idea for me to get on birth control too. Our love continued to grow, as did my trust in Gene.

We became a known couple in school and Becky no longer talked to me. I believe after she realized our relationship was going to last, she was no longer in favor of it. I was spending more time with Gene than I was my friends, but I guess that was to be expected.

CONSUMMATE LOVE

GENE WOULD INVITE ME TO JOIN HIM IN THE DARK ROOM to help develop film for his photography class during my free time. I learned so much that I decided I would take photography the next year.

Art and Communications became the focus of my time at school. My art teacher, Mr. Phillips recognized my raw talent and allowed me to explore it without any binds to hold me back. I was proud to commission an exhibit on the art wall of what I referred to as "Woman of the Universe."

The painting was of a woman holding the world in her hand, as she spanned the universe with her wisdom and grace. Secretly, I wanted to be that kind of woman, graceful and powerful. I guess to some extent she was my subconscious expressed through painting.

I found I had a knack with molding clay to my imagination and made the perfect harlequin clown. Unfortunately, it was destroyed during the glazing phase in the kiln, due to some idiot turning up the heat. I managed to salvage the clown with glue, however, it was never really the same.

The school year was moving along, when my communications teacher, Ms. Pearce came to us during class to inform us of the Waste Isolation Pilot Plant aka WIPP that was going to start construction in Carlsbad. We had no idea what she was talking about in the beginning, but soon discovered it was going to become a repository for chemical waste.

Ms. Pearce's concern rallied our consideration, as no one was in favor of the idea of the chemical waste being stored that close to our own lands. The class formed a petition to stop the construction of the facility. Our petition picked up momentum that caused concern for the CEO's of the company. We were making waves that they did not want, or need, so the company arranged to come to our school with information on WIPP. They wanted to educate us on the positives it would hold for the environment.

We were so naïve... The Executives railroaded us with lies and fodder to quiet our involvement.

On the romantic front, time had passed between Gene and me within a blink of an eye. Our love had grown, as did our trust in each other. Gene had a tender romantic side to him that kept me swept off my feet.

I decided I was ready to move our relationship to the next level. I had taken all the precautions, making sure I was taking the pill regularly, so we wouldn't have any unexpected surprises. Gene and I planned an arrangement with an acquaintance of mine, Rene, at school to use her home.

Rene and her family were going to be going out of town for a few days and she offered for us to stay at her place to house sit. I was happy to oblige. On the day of their departure, I met with her for the key.

I couldn't have planned the night better. The air had a chill in it, so cuddling was going to be a definite. I was at Rene's house for about forty-five minutes, waiting for Gene to get off work and meet me.

I tidied up the house a little better and sprayed my perfume around. I took time to dolly up my makeup and hair a bit, then placed some music on the record player. I heard a knock at the door and a spring of excitement coursed through my body. When I opened the door, I could smell the aroma of pizza emitting from Gene's clothes.

Gene apologized for not being dressed up for the occasion. It didn't matter to me. If everything went according to plan, he and I would be naked in each other's arms within the hour. He walked in the door and we began kissing but my excitement soon faded, as I realized I had been keeping a long-held secret from him. A secret I had put behind me, but now it was coming back to haunt me.

I knew as soon as Gene started to make love to me, he would realize that I wasn't a virgin and he would probably be mad at me, or worse…leave me.

Gene was sensitive to my emotions and a look of concern covered his face, as he asked me what was wrong. I stopped him and turned my face from him.

"I have something to tell you. I haven't been completely honest with you." I shakily spoke.

Gene assured me that it didn't matter, I could tell him the truth now and all would be forgiven. "You don't understand… I don't know if I can even tell you." I continued to stumble.

Tears began to swell in my eyes, as the gravity of the moment came into view. I couldn't move forward without telling him the truth, one way or the other. The decision was his, if he wanted to stay. This moment would test our future together and I knew it with every fiber of my being.

"What is it? You can trust me, just tell me." He confirmed with a tender voice and a warm embrace, as he wiped away my tears.

In a trembling voice, I spoke the words I didn't want to admit to myself, "I am not as pure as you deserve. My virginity was taken from me, before I was 10 years old, by a person in my family. I have been molested since then, and I feel dirty because of it. You deserve some one better than me…" Tears of shame streamed down my face, as my heart began to utterly break at my own words of truth.

"If you don't want to be with me anymore, I understand…" I continued as grief poured out of me uncontrollably. Gene grabbed me tightly. I could feel his anger, as his breath became anxious. He confessed, "I don't know who hurt you, Mandy, but if I ever find out who… I am going to kill them! I want you to know, right here and now, that I love you with all my heart and I would never judge you for something you had no control over!! I love you! Do you understand me? I love you!"

Gene looked me in the eyes, as he held my face steady to meet his, "I don't care if you are a virgin. I can't worry about that because I am not a virgin. But, I guess you already knew that, huh?" He giggled, unsure of my reaction to ease the moment.

I was thankful for his ability to relieve the tension with a cheesy question. Of course, I knew he wasn't a virgin. Becky had already laid all the dirt out on Gene to sway me from his affections. It didn't matter if he was a virgin, or not, because his virtue wasn't on the line. My virtue was on the line, but I had lost it years ago…

I guess it's pointless to say my little outburst of truth dampened the romantic evening. Gene decided it was best that we just watch a movie over the pizza and hold each other till we fall asleep. I was satisfied with his proposal.

All was not lost; my honesty opened a dialogue between us that kept us up through the night. We talked until our mouths ran dry and the talked some more. As the morning sun began to rise, our conversation turned to kisses.

One kiss led to another; one caress led to another. I made the first move by taking off his shirt and kissing him across his chest and neck. Our eyes met and he began taking my clothes off with care, kissing my bare skin as it came into his view. Lovingly we embraced, as we let our bodies flow into the moment. We lay both intertwined, with our bodies naked.

Gently, Gene placed himself ready for entry. He gazed deeply into my eyes and asked if I was sure I wanted to go through with the next motion. I nodded my head yes, and sealed it with a deep passionate kiss, anticipating his penetration. He had me worked up to the point that the bed was wet from my juices.

Gradually, he began to press into me. I winced in pain, as his member crossed my threshold. My reaction caused Gene's confusion. "I thought you weren't a virgin."

"I'm not…" I assured him.

"Well, I guess it grew back together, because you feel like a virgin. I am having a hard time getting in there. Do you want me to quit?" Gene replied in a considerate whisper.

"No, don't stop. I want this with you." I said determined to see it through.

Finally, Gene was able to make the moment happen, and he rested for a moment, before moving through the motions to completion, giving me a break from the pain. We kissed and stroked each other, as he lay inside me.

Our passions were reignited, as I could feel him throb inside me. I began to lightly make a thrusting motion with my hips, as we kissed. Gene began to move with me through the motions. It didn't take long for either of us to reach our apex, as we had been stimulated for what seemed like hours. We climaxed together in one final thrust, when Gene quickly pulled out to release on the bedding.

"I didn't realize that sex was so messy." I immediately joked. We laughed it off and got up to spot clean, before laying back in each other's arms once more, passing out from exhaustion.

I woke up to tender kisses on my forehead. Gene refused to kiss me, because he had morning breath. I could still feel his heaviness between my legs, as I turned over to get dressed.

"How are you feeling this morning?"

"I feel great actually, aside from a bit of tenderness down there. How are you feeling?"

"I feel relieved! Duh!" Gene quipped. We both laughed and embraced.

"Will I see you again tonight?" I asked, as I was seeing him out the door.

"You bet your sweet cheeks! I will come over after work. I love you, Mandy." He confirmed, as he got in the Beretta to leave.

I kept myself busy throughout the day, washing the bedding, straightening up our pizza mess from the night before, as I waited for Gene's return. The hour drew near that Gene should be arriving, but no Gene.

I became uneasy that he would not show up. Maybe he decided it was all too much for him. I started to doubt all his sweet words, as my mind began spinning out of control with doubts. Another hour passed, still no Gene. I was beside myself with heartache. I could still feel him inside me, which made my grief all the worse.

I lay on the couch in despair, as tears welled in my eyes. I felt sorry for myself. How could I let myself go that far with him? I thought I knew him, and I thought I could trust him. Suddenly, my self-pity was interrupted by a loud bang on the door.

I hesitantly opened the door, low and behold, it was Gene.

"Were you worried?"

"Damn right, I was worried! What took you so long?"

"I had to go home and shower after work and decided to pick us up something to eat besides pizza!"

I jumped into his arms and kissed him gratefully.

We spent another wonderful night together, but this time by the fire light of the heater. Winter was setting in and the house was unbearably cold.

Gene left for work just minutes before Carl and Cissy arrived at the door. I was surprised to see them, since I had already planned to get a ride home with Rene. Cissy was up to her usual of trying to get me in trouble for something with Carl. She would have succeeded, if they would have shown up just moments earlier. I would have been busted with Gene.

I just wanted her to leave me the hell alone.

MOUNTING SUSPICION

I BEGAN TO QUESTION WHY SHE WAS SO FOCUSED on getting me into trouble all the time. When I arrived home, I went straight to my bedroom and noticed my things had been moved around again. I darted to the living room, accusing Cissy of messing with my things.

Obviously, Cissy denied the accusation, but the look on her face gave it away. I caught her, now she was certainly on my radar. I decided to pay attention to everything she did from that moment on.

Before that moment, I did everything in my power to avoid her and stay out of her way. However, she just wouldn't stop taking advantage of her status in the family and she wouldn't leave me and my things alone. Enough was enough!

I had a suspicion she was up to no good and that is why she was always trying to keep focus on me. Time would play devil's advocate in finding out the truth with her story.

I told Gene about my suspicions and he agreed with me. He thought he had seen her downtown with a guy in her car one afternoon, while he was at work. But, she drove past too quick for him to get a good look and wasn't sure if it may have been Carl.

That was all I needed to hear. Cissy was going to get what was coming to her.

I refused to sit idly by, while being attacked by her anymore.

This time, I was coming prepared! I was coming with ammunition!

She was never going to see what hit her.

Time passed quickly, as we found ourselves at the end of senior year 1989, as I watched Gene walk across the stage to receive his diploma. I was sitting next to his parents, Joe and Vivian to witness his rite of passage into adult hood.

Gene and I had been together long enough that I was now considered part of his family. I spent about as much time with his parents, as he did during the waking hours of the days.

Vivian I would spend time together shopping, and having brunches together, when Joe and Gene were working. I loved being part of their life and was grateful for their attention. I even went on a few day trips with his family to places like Carlsbad Caverns.

Soon, Gene would be attending college and I would be a junior in High School. I followed in his footsteps and decided to add photography to my career path for my junior year. He was certainly proud of my choice and admitted that I had an eye for imagery. I couldn't argue with him.

When fall came around, Gene wasn't thrilled to be going back to school so suddenly, but knew for our future that it was a good choice. I was focused on getting through junior year without him by my side, but I knew I could do it.

Between work and college, Gene was a busy man. I made a new friend by the name of Monica to keep me occupied, while Gene was busy. She was part Navaho Indian and was simply beautiful and amazing! She giggled all the time, which caused me to giggle too. We bonded instantly, after I met her at a party I attended with Laura.

When I wasn't at school, at Gene's home, or imprisoned at my own, I was with Monica goofing off. She had a crush on Laura's younger brother Patrick but was keeping it secret, so we plotted on him all the time to get his attentions turned to her. He was so oblivious to her advances that it was head spinning, but we never gave up.

Life at home was filled with high tensions now. Cissy was gone all the time working on her "LAB" requirements for college. When she was home, she would fight and argue with Carl. She wasn't happy and it was painfully obvious.

One of Carl's biker buddies, Jaime, moved into the room in the basement, shortly after the new school year began. He had gone through a terrible break up and needed a safe space to get his head back in the game.

Jaime and I became buddies and would hang out when I was stuck at home. He was a fun person, with an eccentric personality, but he was kind. He treated me like his little sister, and I enjoyed that status. We would often listen to his new records; he had an unquenchable crush on Paula Abdul, so of course you know that was a main feature in his music. He was my go-to for male advice and I was his go-to for female advice.

Hey, what can I say, it worked for us!

Jaime came to me with a concern he had about Cissy. She had begun wearing scantily clad attire around the house, when Carl wasn't home, and she was making it a point to bend over in front of Jaime, practically showing him her goods.

Was this my smoking gun? No, if I went to confront her on Jaime's accusation, she would just deny it. I needed more. I didn't know how, or when I was going to get it, but I knew something would come around eventually.

Luckily for me, Gene was going to the same college that Cissy was attending, so he could keep an eye on her to let me know if she was up to something. The day came when some real material came into light. Gene had witnessed Cissy parking her car at the college and leaving with a male.

It finally made sense to me why my makeup and clothes were disappearing and moving. She was getting all dolled up for a man, not my dad, but another man! An opportunity to speak to Carl about our concerns presented itself.

Carl was home on the couch one afternoon, during my half day at school. I sat down next to him and we began talking. I hadn't really had a conversation with him in what seemed like years. He was always too busy, and I was always preoccupied. We sat and spoke for about an hour on whatever crossed our plates, when I asked him if he was still happy with Cissy.

Carl admitted that things had become very rocky and he hoped they would be able to work through their problems. I decided to gently nudge and see if he had any suspicions of her seeing someone else.

That's when the conversation went south.

I assume I hit a sore spot with him. He was resolute in his denial that Cissy was capable of doing something like that to him.

I dropped the conversation and diverted to another topic. I assessed Carl had his suspicions, but didn't want to admit it to himself. He was 22 years her senior; at some point he had to realize that the age difference was going to catch up to him.

I spoke to Jaime about the conversation and he advised that it was best to let it go. He didn't want to hurt Carl, because he had been a good friend to him. Jaime decided it was probably best swept under the rug to avoid any ill feelings, I agreed with Jaime, after seeing the hurt it caused Carl.

CAUGHT RED-HANDED

AFTER I STARTED TAKING THE PILL, MY MENSES BECAME UNBEARABLE at times. Having sex seemed to exacerbate the cramps and flow to the point that I would become bedridden during that time of the month.

I had gone to school one Friday morning in hopes that I could manage through the pain to complete my day. Unfortunately, the pain became so intolerable that I had Gene take me home so I could down some medicine and rest. Carl and Jaime were out of town on a job and Cissy was supposed to be at college working on a lab till seven that evening.

I thought myself lucky to have the house to myself until 3:30pm, at which time Will and Phil would return home from school. I took some aspirin and laid on the couch, watching television to rest.

I was near the point of taking a nap, when I heard a car pull up in front of my house. I quickly sprang to the window to see who could possibly be outside. To my astonishment, it was Cissy...she had a guy in the passenger seat of her car...

I immediately ran to my room to hide.

My heart was pounding, and my head was racing. I didn't want her to know I was home. I wanted to see what she was up to, so I hid in my closet and waited patiently.

The silence surrounding me, combined with the sound of my heart pounding was deafening. My breath was rapid and shallow, as I tried to contain my anxiety of the situation and keep my presence concealed.

I heard the front door open as Cissy entered the house. I listened intently, as I peered through the crack in the door of my closet. She had left the car running outside, so I knew she didn't plan to stay long.

I heard some rustling around and then her footsteps heading back toward the front of the house. I sat back in my closet, waiting for when she opened my door and entered my room. I watched as she walked over to my vanity table and spritzed herself with my perfume. I was infuriated!! I now knew, for certain, that she had been using my stuff!

Cissy continued over to my dresser and scavenged through my delicates. I couldn't believe she was helping herself to my personal undies. That was just crossing the line for me. Then she turned to the closet.

I had to stealthfully place myself in the center of the closet, against the bookshelf that divided the two-door closet to conceal myself, when she rummaged through one side and then the other side, taking one of my favorite slinky blouses.

My blood was boiling!

It took every ounce of my being to contain the rage inside of me, as I waited for her to leave. I wanted to bust out of the closet and beat her ass. However, I needed to see who was in the car and have evidence to prove what just happened.

Cissy finally left my room. I heard the front door open and close, so I hastily ran to the window to watch her leave. It was a man. I had never seen him before. As I watched her enter the car, she leaned over and kissed that man on the lips before driving away.

Cissy was having an affair! I had just caught her red handed.

I called Pizza Hut to talk to Gene. He described the man he saw with Cissy and it was the exact same man she had seen in the car. I explained in detail everything that happened. Gene wanted to know what I was going to do. I said I was going to tell Carl!

That evening when Cissy came home, I was still enraged. Of course, she immediately went after me on some petty agenda of hers. I was rigid and not moved by her gas-lighting.

I walked away from her without hesitation, ignoring her demands, as I went into my room. Cissy followed after me. I continued to ignore her, as she continued to rant. Once she was inside my room, I turned to her and demanded she get the hell out of my room.

Cissy looked stunned at the tone of confidence in my voice. "How dare you talk to me like that!" She declared, angrily.

"I will talk to you how ever the hell I want to talk to you. You are not my mother!" I insisted.

"I am your step-mother and you will address me as such!" Cissy demanded.

I laughed and retaliated, "You don't deserve that kind of respect! You are only three years older than me!"

"I don't have to do a damn thing you say anymore!" I added.

"Oh, we will see when your daddy gets home, and I tell him how you are acting!" She threatened.

"Go ahead!" I insisted.

"Go ahead and tell Carl how I am acting, and I will tell him how you are acting too!" I said spitefully.

"Like that is supposed to scare me, what is your daddy gonna do to me…his wife?" she asked unsure of my next words.

"Hmm, let me think…What do you suppose my daddy would do to his wife when he found out that she is a liar and a cheat?"

That question shook her foundation. "What are you talking about?"

"You are just saying that to make me nervous!" her constitution now showing retreat.

"I saw you! I saw you with that man, and I am not the only one who saw you! Gene saw you too and I am telling Carl when he gets home!"

"Say goodbye to your free ride, bitch!" I sneered through my teeth.

Cissy lunged at me and we began wrestling around my room. I wasn't backing down, if anything she had lit my dynamite and I was about to explode on her. I maintained my stamina as I was getting the better of her.

I had Cissy pinned with a hand wrapped around her neck, beating her with my other hand. She was fighting, trying to break free, but I was fuel with anger which made her no match. Will managed to break us apart and Cissy ran to her room in desperation.

Cissy packed all the things she could carry and left out the door. GOOD RIDDANCE, as far as I was concerned. That is until I realized she was gone and now I would have to deal with telling Carl. I didn't anticipate Cissy leaving right away.

I thought at least she would put up a fight to save face, or at least right her wrong, but she didn't. She simply left.

BROKEN HOME

CARL RETURNED FROM THE JOB WITH NO CONCEPT of what had transpired during his absence. Before he could ask about Cissy not being home, I went to him.

"Dad, we need to talk…"

"What is it?" he asked as he was bringing his bags through the door barely paying mind to me.

"Cissy left and I don't think she is coming back."

My words paused him in his tracks, "What do you mean she left?"

"I caught her with another man." I confessed sincerely.

"You're lying! Where is she?" He asked with desperation in his voice.

"Dad, I have no reason to lie to you. She is gone and was cheating on you."

"I saw her, and Gene saw her. I confronted her, so she left. I tried to tell you before, but you didn't want to talk about it."

I watched as his face was overcome with the realization that I was telling the truth. He immediate became embittered towards me. Blaming the whole situation on me.

"That's not fair. I am coming to you, as your daughter to tell you the truth, and you are blaming me for your wife cheating on you? How is that my fault? You are not being rational!" I turned away from him and quickly left the room.

Carl left, searching for Cissy. Jaime stayed behind and I told him about everything that happened. He had a genuine concern for Carl, now that Cissy was gone. Jaime was glad that Carl now knew the truth, nonetheless, he had hoped things would turn out different for them.

The search for Cissy was in vain. She had left with the mysterious man and they were hiding out for a period. Carl became disconnected with everything to the point of severe depression. He would lay on the couch for days at a time, only moving to use the bathroom or grab a bite to eat.

I would sit at the end of the couch to keep him company, getting barely any response from him. Jaime attempted to keep him occupied with the Club and managed to get him to go to a couple of meetings.

Several months passed. Cissy had filed for divorce and I was starting my senior year of school. Carl had started drinking again and would stay gone for days at a time. Jaime was getting back on his feet and started looking for his own place to live. I didn't want him to leave, but he told me he couldn't watch Carl drink himself to death anymore.

Gene was struggling in college and decided to have a heart to heart with me, one evening after our date. "I have been thinking... I might join the Army." "What? Join the army...Why?" I asked feeling extremely insecure.

"I am not doing well with college and work. I feel overwhelmed with it and I just need to take a different path." He acknowledged.

I turned to him with apprehension, "I don't feel comfortable with you joining the military. What if you have to go to war?"

"I don't think it's a good idea and I don't want you to go."

"You will be gone for months…what does that mean for me?"

"I will be left behind, waiting."

"I don't want that kind of life!" My words were selfish.

I couldn't help the way I felt. I became angry at just the thought of him leaving.

Gene could sense the struggle with me and decided it would be better left alone. "Fine, I will try to do better in college. I only have another couple of years."

Gene's statement gave me relief, but I wasn't satisfied. I made him promise me that he wouldn't join the Army. Once the promise was made, we kissed each other good night and I headed inside the house.

As I entered the front door, I caught the backside of Jaime crossing the archway into the dark kitchen. I called out to him to talk about what just occurred with Gene, but he didn't acknowledge hearing me.

I thought it strange, but followed him into the kitchen, when I realized no one was there. I turned on the kitchen light and saw that the kitchen door was still locked from the inside. I looked around, in disbelief, of what I just witnessed.

I know I saw the backside of a shirtless man wearing red shorts, while walking into the kitchen.

There was no one… I was in the house all by myself.

Will and Phil were staying with Edith, Carl was out drinking, and Jaime was no wear to be found. An uneasiness washed over me. I grabbed the cordless phone and ran to my bed. I hopped in and covered my head, as I frantically dialed Gene. He must be home by now, I thought. After a couple of rings, Gene answered.

I told Gene what I had seen, as I walked into the house and he assured me that it was my mind playing tricks on me. He summed it up to the stress of our conversation and told me not to worry.

I heard clicks and then the front door open. I became hysterical. Gene shushed me on the phone and told me to calm down. I took a deep breath and realized it was Jaime walking in. I was relieved, but confused. Gene laughed and told me not to worry about it and he would see me tomorrow.

After hanging up the phone, I went to speak to Jaime. I told him about what I just experienced, and a look of worry crossed his face. Jaime disclosed that he had been seeing something familiar on an occasion. We both sat in silence for several minutes looking around the house, wondering what in the world was going on.

"That's it! I am definitely getting my own place, before I get possessed!" Jamie joked. We both laughed nervously. I regaled him with the memories from the Monahans and all the strange happenings I encountered, while living there. We continued to carry on conversation, until we were too tired to talk any more. We finally called it a night and I retired to my room to sleep.

Jaime got a call the next morning. I took the phone to him and lingered to listen to the call. Jaime had been informed that the house he was interested in renting had been made available, so he could move in right away.

I was happy for Jaime; however, I was sad that he was leaving. He had been a source of comfort and a good friend. He was going to be missed. Jaime assured me that he wasn't leaving across the country. I could always go visit him in his new home.

Over the next couple of days, Jaime moved completely out, leaving me at the house by myself for the most part. My brothers were staying with Edith and Carl stayed gone mostly for work, or on a drinking binge.

Monica started staying over more often, as she and her father had a falling out. I enjoyed her company and was glad to spend time with her. She eventually moved in with me. It was almost like the house belonged to us, because we were usually there alone.

Carl gave Monica his room. He no longer had a need for it, since he would only sleep on the couch after Cissy left.

MISS TEEN NEW MEXICO PAGEANT

I RECEIVED A PACKAGE IN THE MAIL REQUESTING MY PARTICIPATION in the Miss New Mexico Teen Pageant. I was profoundly surprised to receive such a request. I ran to Monica and asked her if she received a package too.

She had not.

I was perplexed as to why I would receive the request and Monica did not. I found out later that week, during communications class, that Ms. Pearce had elected me as a candidate for the prestigious event. I was honored to know that Ms. Pearce thought so highly of me and I wanted to make her proud.

Gene was proud when I told him the news. A lot was required of the candidates. We had to prove our worthiness and what value we gave to our community. Monica helped me out by setting me up with community service at the local retirement home. She figured since I was taking vocational technical studies at New Mexico Junior College for Nurses Aid, I would be able to handle the workload.

I had a job down working for Burger Builders at the time and my boss was a part time photographer, so he offered his services to help me. Vivian was willing to take me to the event and show her support. I was moved by everyone willing to help me in this endeavor.

For the next several weeks, I worked tirelessly to meet the deadlines. My boss took me to Chaparral Park for a photo session. Ms. Pearce set aside time to help me choreograph a dance to perform. An elderly lady bit me and I got flashed by an elderly man at the retirement center. Then I wrote an essay on why I was a good candidate to be chosen and finished up all my requirements, just in time, as the day quickly arrived.

I met with Vivian and we set out on our journey to the pageant. I didn't have my hopes up to win, but I knew I had just as much of a chance as any other girl. That knowledge gave me the confidence to go through with the competition.

We arrived for my check-in. I looked around at all the other girls that were there to compete. Some of the girls were so beautiful and confident that it made me feel small and not worthy of taking part of the competition. Vivian could tell I was having doubts, reassuring me to push through the feelings.

Unknowingly, I had overlooked one of the items on the agenda. We had to be interviewed before entering the hall to be orientated. The interview consisted of one question...

If you could be a tree, what kind of tree would you be and why?

'What kind of question was that?' I thought to myself. I had no idea how to answer the question, much less any actual knowledge of tree types. Trees were just towing shade providers, as far as I was concerned.

Answer the question Mandy, my mind said, breaking through the shock. I had been side swiped by the question and my emotions were at an all-time high. Before I could think about it, the lady across the table informed me that we only had a couple of minutes to answer, before they moved to the next candidate.

This question was a test of our reactions under pressure. I failed miserably...

I blurted out, "Weeping Willow!" Oh god...why did I say that? I said it because that was the only tree I could think of on the spot. Chaparral Park was lined with Weeping Willows, so naturally, that is what came out of my mouth.

"Tell me why you chose a Weeping Willow..." The Interviewer encouraged, with a curious look on her face.

My reason for being a Weeping Willow was even more pathetic than the tree itself and I began to choke, as big tears started streaming down my face.

I lost it...

I could tell the Interviewer was ready to get me out of there. She pretended that everything would be okay and reassured me that many girls are overwhelmed and cry during the interview.

Great...now I was a statistic...

I wanted to throw in the towel and quit. I went to Vivian, devastated, but she wouldn't allow me to be defeated. "The competition isn't over Mandy. You didn't do all that work to give up now. Pull yourself together and show them what you are made of!"

The first interview set the tone for the rest of the competition for me. The DJ cut my music short for my dance, so I was still dancing when the music stopped suddenly. I dropped makeup on my white coveralls that I had for the dance competition. My gown had loosened, due to me losing a few pounds from the exercise, while preparing for the competition. So, it kept slipping down.

Anything that could go wrong, did…

I was so glad when the competition ended, and we could go back home. NEVER AGAIN, would I partake in such a nightmare!

Vivian did her best to keep me in good spirits and explained that at least I had a story to share some day, that most people would never have a chance to take part in.

I guess she was right after all.

Back home, I had to face the humiliation of defeat. Most people didn't care that I didn't win, they were glad that I got to be a part of the pageant and represent Lovington.

BETRAYED INTENTIONS

I WAS SURPRISED TO SEE CARL AT HOME, WHEN I ARRIVED. I didn't expect him to be. He didn't take an interest in my personal life enough to be concerned of my coming and going. He stayed drunk, or passed out, when he was home.

I walked past him, to take my things to my room, when he called out for me to come back and talk to him. I was curious what he had to speak to me about, since we really didn't interact much anymore.

Carl had alcohol on his breath, as usual. He wanted me to sit next to him on the couch, as he boohooed over his life. I sat with him, obediently, not really interested in his confessions. Not once did he ask about the competition, or how I had placed.

I guess we were both being selfish in our pity.

He dragged on and on, up to the point of admitting he had fathered a boy in Vietnam. That caught my attention. He had been in love with a Vietnamese woman, before meeting my mother, Anne, but his Sergeant separated them and returned Carl back to the states, when they discovered the woman was with child.

Carl swore me to never tell my brothers or the family, so up until now...I never told a soul.

Carl cried uncontrollably over the heartbreak, as he laid his head on my chest. I didn't know what to do, so I just held him, until his storm calmed. He asked me to stay with him in the living room, until he fell asleep, so I stayed.

Monica had been staying with another friend, while I was attending the Pageant. During her stay, she finally got Patrick's attention and went on a date with him. She returned the day after I arrived back home, only to tell me about Patrick and that she was moving out. I tried to convince her to stay but she was ready to move forward.

I didn't blame her. It was boring at the house and who wants to hang out with a belligerent drunk all the time.

Carl became needier of my attention and it was beginning to make me uncomfortable. When he was home, he wanted me to sit on the couch with him and rub his back. He would lay his head in my lap and hold me like a hostage, until he fell asleep.

On a phone call, I voiced my concerns about Carl to Monica, and she confessed one of the reasons she decided to move out so abruptly, was because she had caught Carl sniffing her dirty panties.

The news was unnerving! Of course, I couldn't blame her for leaving!

I immediately called Gene to come get me, so we could talk. I told him what Carl had done to Monica's unmentionables. Gene was disgusted, but expected nothing less from Carl, since Monica was of age and he liked young girls.

I told Gene if I ever called for him to come pick me up, no matter what time it was, I needed him to promise me that he would drop everything and come get me, no questions asked.

He agreed to my request.

The following day, Gene had to leave and visit his grandmother in Truth or Consequences, New Mexico. He was going to be gone a few days. I wanted to go with him, but he had a reason for me staying behind.

I didn't think much about it, until I got an unexpected phone call. It was Gene on the other end of the phone. Gene had something to tell me and he knew I wasn't going to be happy.

"Babe, I have something to tell you." His voice sounded unsure.

Curious, I had to ask, "What is it? Why are you acting so weird?"

"I want you to know I love you and I am only thinking about our future." Gene assured.

"What are you talking about Gene, spit it out!" I demanded, with anxiety welling up inside of me.

"I lied to you…I am not in T or C… I am in Dallas, Texas."

"Why on earth are you in Dallas? That is the opposite direction of T or C…Did you get lost?" I said teasingly, trying to lighten the conversation.

"No, Mandy… I am here to speak with a Recruiter."

His words cut through my heart, as I fell to my knees, "You said you weren't going to join the Army, you promised!"

"Yes, I know I did, but I changed my mind and I knew you were going to be mad, so I didn't tell you." Gene defended.

"Why are you telling me this now?" I asked in dismay.

Gene conceded, "Because I leave for Basic Training in a month. You needed to know before I got back to town; this is just something I have to do."

I hung up the phone, devastated over the conversation. This is not what I had planned for my future. I didn't want to be an Army wife! How could he take my future into his hands and make plans, without even considering what I wanted?

For the first time, I felt betrayed by Gene. The hurt cut me deep and I had a lot to consider over the next month.

The end of my first senior semester was closing in, as finals week tormented me, along with the dread of Gene leaving for Basic Training. I had been taking extra shifts at Burger Builders to save up for a car of my own. I finally found some time to spend with Gene and I needed his distraction to get me out of the house.

I decided I would make a go of this new endeavor he chose, the best that I could, and spend as much time with him before he left. Carl didn't like that I was too busy for him, but that was not my concern.

I came home late one evening and Carl was sitting on the couch waiting for me. When I walked in the door, I knew he had something on his mind. "You have been spending inordinate amounts of time with Gene."

"Yes, I have. I told you he was about to leave for basic and I wanted to spend time with him." I defended.

"I have a question…" He began.

Before he had the chance to ask, I spoke up and said, "You want to know if we are having sex…"

Carl looked stunned that I was so intuitive, "Well?"

"Yes, I have had sex with Gene. We have been together nearly two years, what did you expect?" I admitted without hesitation.

Carl was stunned that I just told him the truth, without a second thought. I had already made up my mind if he ever asked, I was going to tell him the truth, so it was easy.

"Has it been that long already?" He realized.

"Well, are you at least using protection?" He continued with concern.

"Yes, Dad… I am using protection. Is that all you wanted?" I asked in frustration that he didn't realize I was a responsible person.

"Yes, that's all." He released me to continue about my way.

UNFORGIVEABLE OFFENSE

FINALS WEEK AND I WAS BURNING THE CANDLE AT BOTH ENDS. I hated finals week. It always fell on my birthday and made everything suck in school.

By Wednesday of that week, I wasn't feeling good and doing my best to keep my head in the game. My head hurt and my throat was feeling sore. That's all I needed now, being sick during finals.

I called into work and decided to go home early, so I could get some rest, before hitting the books again. When I got home, Carl was on the couch passed out from drinking. I tiptoed into my room and crashed on my bed. I fell asleep and didn't wake up until my alarm went off the following morning.

Thursday morning, Dec 20th, I got up in a rush, completely disregarding the fact that it was my 17th birthday. All I had on my mind was getting to school on time to have a few minutes of prep before class. The day was stifling, and I was feeling worse than I had felt the day before this. I was having a hard time swallowing and recognized the pain. I had tonsillitis taking hold of me.

FREAKING GREAT! I thought to myself, as I went to the nurse's office for some meds. Luckily, the nurse had some Tylenol to ease my pain. I had one more day of tests and then I could rest during Christmas break.

Just one more day…

That afternoon, I called in to work again. I informed my boss that I had a sore throat and he thought it was best for me to stay home, until I recovered. He didn't want me serving his customers with my sickness.

I went to the medicine cabinet and found some more Tylenol to deaden the pain in my throat, and my head. I dragged myself back to my room and began pouring over the materials for Friday's test.

Evening came, before I looked up and noticed the time. It was close to 11pm. I figured I could stop where I was and try to get some sleep. I took some more Tylenol, then curled up under my blankets.

I was woken by Carl stumbling into the house, around 2am. He yelled out in a drunken stupor, "MANDY SHAWN! Come in here and keep me company." I rolled over, trying to ignore him and go back to sleep.

I dozed off, only to be interrupted again. "Mandy Shawn! I told you to get in here and keep me company! I am lonely!" Carl rambled. I prayed he would just pass out and leave me in peace.

Carl yelled out a third time. Only this time, I was furious! "Dad, I am trying to sleep! I am not coming in there! I have tests in the morning!!"

Carl was incorrigible upon hearing me deny him. "Young Lady, you will not refuse me when I tell you to do something! You get your ass in here and do what I say!"

"I will not! I am going to back to sleep so I can go to school in the morning!" I said with a hoarse voice, still standing my ground.

My refusal enraged Carl, he stomped heavily into my bedroom and stood by the door, demanding that I get my ass up and go lay with him in the living room. I sat up in my bed, insulted that he would expect that of me.

"I will not lie with you! I am your daughter, not your wife!!"

His demeanor became volatile, as he moved toward me in a predator fashion, "You will do as I god damn say!"

"If I want to fuck you, I can! You are my property and I can do whatever I want to you!"

He squared up in my face, "I will not have you fucking that boy and not fucking me! You owe that much to me!!"

I couldn't believe the words that were coming out of his mouth. I wanted to blame it on the liquor, but I knew it was a sickness inside of his mind.

Something swelled up inside me, bursting out in a loud violent defense, "YOU ARE A SICK MOTHERFUCKER AND I WILL NOT FUCK YOU EVER!!! HOW COULD YOU? I AM YOUR MOTHER FUCKING DAUGHTER, YOU SICK BASTARD!!!"

Carl stood up in a threatening pose, "Little girl, you think you are big enough to talk to me that way? I will show you, I brought you into this world… I will take you out of it!"

With a brutal blow, Carl punched me in the jaw that jolted me back, breaking the wall with my face. The punch should have knocked me out, but the adrenaline coursing through my veins gave me strength to pull myself out of the wall and turn to him.

I lunged at him with all my force, knocking him to the ground, "GET THE FUCK OUT OF MY BEDROOM!!!!!" My hit sobered Carl enough to realize I wasn't backing down. I screamed at the top of my lungs, a shriek so loud that I thought the glass would shatter.

The noise had to be heard by the neighbors and I was hoping someone heard.

Carl looked back at me, as he left out of the doorway, "You can just pack your shit and get the fuck out of my house!" I grabbed the nearest item to me and threw it at him with full force, as I said, "I will gladly leave this hell hole!! FUCK YOU!!"

I heard the front door slam behind Carl. He went outside to smoke a cigarette and cool down. The cordless phone was on my dresser, so I called Gene as soon as I knew I had a chance.

"Hello?" Gene asked still asleep.

"Babe, this is Mandy. Can you come get me now?"

"Right now? What time is it?" He asked in confusion.

"It doesn't matter what time it is, just come get me please." I asked as my voice cracked.

Gene woke up to the sound of distress in my voice. "Babe, I will be right over. I just need to grab something."

"Okay, thank you. I will be waiting."

I hastily grabbed everything of importance to me and threw it into some of my overnight bags and backpack. Carl lingered outside for a little longer, as I continued to pack my things.

My mind was racing, what was I going to do? Where was I going to stay? Gene was leaving in a couple of weeks… It didn't matter. I would live on the street for all I cared at that moment. I was getting the hell out of there; my mind was made up.

I heard the front door open, but it didn't shut. I continued packing. Carl walked to my bedroom door and watched me for a few seconds before finally speaking up. "I don't think you know what you are getting yourself into. You can't fathom what life is like out in that cold cruel world."

A knock at the door interrupted Carl's lecture. "Who is that? Is that your little boyfriend?" His voice giving away the fact that he was uncertain of who I called.

I brushed quickly past him to see if it was Gene. A sigh of relief came when I saw Gene's face peering through the screen door.

"Are you alright?" Gene asked, with wide eyes, unsure of what he was walking into. "I'm okay… let me grab my things, then we can go…"

Carl slowly came around the corner to speak to us. Gene stopped him in his tracks. "Look, Carl, I don't want any trouble. I am here to pick Mandy up. I don't know what happened. I don't wanna know what happened… All I know is its 3 am in the morning and I get a call from her in distress. I am taking her now and y'all can talk later."

Remarkably, Carl shook his head in respect of what Gene said and allowed him to help me carry my things to the truck.

I went in one last time to grab my purse. Carl stopped me and said, "You don't have to do this. I'm sorry Mandy, I crossed a line." My mind was made up. I wasn't giving him another chance.

When Carl realized that I wasn't moved by his apology, he spouted in retaliation, "You will never make it out there in that big world alone! Mark my words! You'll be back, begging for me to help you!

I walked out the door and on to the porch, as I heard his words call out to me.

I took a couple more steps, turning around with bold certainty, "That's where you are wrong! You have no idea who I am, or what I have been through!"

"In your neglect, you taught me how to be strong and how to survive!"

"In your abuse, you taught me to withstand the fires which removed my fear!"

"You and those sick fucks like you, tempered me... and YOU are the first man to underestimate me!"

Deliberately, I turned around, took a deep breath and walked out of that life... never looking back...

ACKNOWLEDGMENTS

I would like to thank every person who helped make this book possible. I am so very thankful to all who inspired me to write this first book of my story.

To My loving husband, Steven Doré. You know my story and encouraged me to tell the world, because you believe it will help others find their strength. Thank you for seeing me the way I always wanted to be seen. I love you with my whole heart!

To my children, Hayden, Clifton Jr., Hannah, Evan, Elijah, and Kodie. You are my true strength and the reason I want to become a better version of myself every day.

To my mother, Anne for choosing life and giving me an opportunity to live it.

To my momma, Kathleen for loving me as your very own and always being in the background with support and encouraging words.

To my dear friends, Dawn and Rhiannon. You were patiently supportive, while withholding any judgement. You diplomatically offered feedback with the success of the book foremost in your minds.

I also want to thank my daughter, Hannah for her critical insight on the various iterations of the book.

To my friend Tammy, even though we are miles apart, I feel you sister!

I would like to thank my friends and co-workers, Heather, Jennifer, Lynne, and Jenn. Even though it has been a while since we had our conversations, I remember the encouragement you gave me to write my story. Although this is only the beginning of the story, but not the story we discussed, I want each of you to know, I had to start somewhere, and I will get to the best story soon!

Lastly, I want to thank every person that entered my life. Whether you were the friend or the foe, each of you have made an impression on my life that made me who I am today. Without our chance meetings and inevitable conclusions, I would have no story to tell.

ABOUT THE AUTHOR

Mandy Doré is a New Mexico native, now living in the state of Louisiana which she affectionately calls home. She has a love of travel, art, music, and writing. Her first passions are committed to her husband and six children.

Mandy is a survivor of abuse and an advocate for children and women without a voice. Mandy's life is a testimony of resilience and strength that she hopes will encourage and inspire others to move forward.

CPSIA information can be obtained
at www.ICGtesting.com
Printed in the USA
LVHW091558201020
669303LV00004B/67